Legends In Their Time

Legends In Their Time

YOUNG HEROES AND VICTIMS OF CANADA

GEORGE SHERWOOD

Illustrated by Stewart Sherwood

NATURAL HERITAGE BOOKS

TORONTO

Published by Natural Heritage / Natural History Inc.
P.O. Box 95, Station O, Toronto, Ontario M4A 2M8

www.naturalheritagebooks.com

Library and Archives Canada Cataloguing in Publication

Sherwood, George
    Legends in their time : young heroes and victims of Canada / George Sherwood ; illustrated by Stewart Sherwood.

Includes bibliographical references and index.
ISBN 1-897045-10-7

1. Heroes—Canada—Biography. 2. Youth—Canada—Biography. 3. Canada—History.
4. Canada—Biography. I. Sherwood, Stewart II. Title.

FC25.S53 2006   971'.009'9 C2005-907663-1

The front cover artwork and all black and white original illustrations are by Stewart Sherwood
Back cover: Toy Jin Wong with her sister, *courtesy of Arlene Chan*; Terry Fox, *courtesy of Darrell
    Fox and the Terry Fox Foundation*

Cover and text design by Sari Naworynski
Edited by Jane Gibson
Printed and bound in Canada by Hignell Book Printing of Winnipeg

Natural Heritage / Natural History Inc. acknowledges the financial support of the Canada Council for the Arts and the Ontario Arts Council for our publishing program. We acknowledge the support of the Government of Ontario through the Ontario Media Development Corporation's Ontario Book Initiative. We also acknowledge the financial support of the Government of Canada through the Book Publishing Industry Development Program (BPIDP) and the Association for the Export of Canadian Books.

*To Ellie, to my three "heroes" – Jennifer, Kathryn and Laura –
and to my special heroes – Liam, Connor and Rylan.*

Table of Contents

ACKNOWLEDGEMENTS

I want to thank my wife Ellie for the inspiration, my friend Kelvin for his "prodding" perseverance, my daughter Laura for the final typing, and my brother, Stewart for his generosity and talent involved in producing artwork to enhance these pages. Of course, this book would not have been possible without the resources and support of the archivists associated with the museums and libraries noted in the credits accompanying the text. Of particular help was the generous access to resources provided by the Ontario Archives, the Toronto Reference Library (as well as my home base, the Northern District Library branch of the Toronto Public Library system) and the Library and Archives Canada in Ottawa. Special thanks are also extended to Heather Pantrey for her loan of the West Humber Collegiate Institute yearbook and to Erwin Schild for his fascinating interview and generous donation of photos. I would also like to thank Arlene Chan for her generosity in sharing time, stories of her Mom, and photographs with me. Her assistance, as well as that of her aunt, Dorothy Lu, was invaluable. In the same vein, thanks to Darrell Fox of the Terry Fox Foundation for his interest, his kind words and his contribution of photos for the final chapter.)

I must also express my sincere appreciation to Barry Penhale for his efforts to preserve our Canadian heritage and his full support of Canadian authors. He and his colleagues at Natural Heritage are a pleasure to know and to work with. Thanks also to my friends, students and colleagues who have been so patient in waiting for the final product. I hope it is worthy of your forbearance.

INTRODUCTION

The hackneyed notion that Canadian history is boring and uneventful has been put to rest by a number of excellent social histories. This book is an effort to follow the objectives of these earlier works and demonstrate that we are indeed a nation brimming with a rich pageantry of heroic accomplishments and tragic exploits that make our story a fascinating and entertaining tale to recount.

In the pages that follow, the reader will meet eighteen specific young Canadians – teenagers or younger – who played a prominent role during their brief time on the stage of events from our past. Male or female, people of colour or white, Anglophone, Francophone, Native Canadian or new Canadian – all enhanced the fabric that was to become Canada. Each also represents an opportunity to step back and examine an era, a concern or a theme from Canada's past. The definition of both terms, "hero" and "victim," as used in this book, are to a large extent subjective. Over thirty years of teaching Canadian history to high school and university students and writing resource material for other educators have afforded me the opportunity of developing an understanding of these two words. While there is a more detailed explanation of what constitutes a hero in the final chapter on Terry Fox, it might be useful to establish the perspective taken in this work from the outset.

A "hero" in this book can be defined as a person who has a significant and positive impact on the evolution of our nation. This individual possesses personal qualities or commits herself or himself to such a course of action that history is changed for the better. That person is not a spectator, but a forceful participant in events. A "victim" in this book is someone whose mistreatment or exploitation is worth noting because of the results that impacted on the history of our nation as well as on the victim. The individual represents a theme, a concern or an episode that is important to a better understanding of Canada. Perhaps there are some things we would prefer to bury in the past, but each story is a part of our heritage.

Sixteen of the eighteen chapters deal with individuals who were teenagers or younger at the time of their story. Chapter 13, dealing with the Baby Derby, deals with not one but a number of babies and their families. It is a chapter that examines the time period of the Great Depression and the public fascination with the "birth race" that captured the attention of a nation in need of an escape. The final chapter on Terry Fox is also a bit different in that it deals with a slightly older person. Terry was twenty-one when he ran his "Marathon of Hope" but as explained in the beginning of that chapter, no examination of young Canadian heroes could exclude this remarkable individual.

The opportunity to research a time period can be as interesting as taking a trip to an exotic locale. I was fortunate enough to have several "destinations" during the research process. Writing about the individuals was both daunting and humbling; telling another person's story is a serious responsibility. I hope that I spoke as they would speak in the same circumstances. For me, this has been a fascinating experience. I hope the reader's pleasure matches mine.

CHAPTER ONE

Domagaya and Taignoagny: Iroquois Heroes and Victims

omagaya and Taignoagny were sons of a man who was the leader of their community and the most important political figure in the surrounding area before the influx of European explorers. One of them became the first recorded person ever to administer medicine in North America and one of them gave our nation its name. The young boys were the first European-trained translators in Canada. Together they would become victims of not one, but two, of the most famous kidnappings of their day. Yet very few people in Canada have heard of either Domagaya or Taignoagny. Indeed, not many have heard of their father, Donnacona, the leader of thousands of Iroquois living in the region that today is Quebec City. Yet this is not surprising – distressing and shameful yes, but surprising no – given the sordid treatment of the Native Peoples by the white population that came to the "New World" in the years following Columbus's fateful voyage in 1492. It seems appropriate that Domagaya and Taignoagny, two teenagers, would come to represent children in Canadian history both as heroes and as victims – a foreshadowing of a fascinating theme in our nation's evolution.

Their exact age in 1534 will never be known. Donnacona, a member of the Bear Clan,[1] had married and moved into his wife's longhouse, as was the practice among the Iroquois.[2] As a result, the two boys were members of the Turtle Clan, from their mother's lineage.[3] Although their father was a chief, neither of his sons would be guaranteed any accession to authority, since the "sachems" (or chiefs) were chosen by the eldest woman in the clan, after consulting with other women elders. Using the criteria of valour, dignity and eloquence, the women chose carefully since it was the 50 sachems (ten from each of the five nations making up the Iroquois Confederacy) who determined all matters and made decisions for their people.

By the beginning of the sixteenth century, the Iroquois had developed one of the most sophisticated political and social structures in all of North America. Consisting of five distinct First Nations (the Mohawk, the Oneida, the Onandaga, the Cayuga and the Seneca) the Confederacy stretched from today's Quebec to Kentucky and from Pennsylvania to Illinois. Moreover, the Iroquois held a strategically important location through their control of the lands surrounding the Great Lakes and the St. Lawrence River, the water route to the heart of the continent. The origins of this confederacy is not certain. It may have started with the great Mohawk chief, Hiawatha, or the legendary Dekhanahwideh, who is said to have planted the "Tree of Peace," the symbol representing the pact of union that brought the five nations[4] together. Whatever its beginnings, by 1500, the Confederacy had representatives from all five nations meeting regularly at the "Great Longhouse" in present-day Upper New York State and making important decisions, always by consensus. All five nations had their "local governments" and chiefs, but on matters of mutual concern it was the League of the Longhouse of Fifty Chiefs that spoke. Some historians suggest that the Iroquois Confederacy was the model for the federal systems of government for both the United States and Canada.

Just as the origins are uncertain, so too is the exact number of Iroquois living in the Five Nations. The most conservative estimate is about 16,000, but this number ranges up to 60,000, including some

Although they were sons of a great chief, Domagaya and Taignoagny lived communally with other clan members in a traditional Iroquois longhouse, similar to this one reconstructed at Midland, Ontario. *Indian Village, Little Lake Park, Midland, 1958. Courtesy of the Archives of Ontario, RG 65-35-3, 11764-X3024.*

10,000 Mohawks under Donnacona's influence, living around Stadacona (Quebec City).

Whatever the origins or numbers, Domagaya and Taignoagny likely led a very happy early life. Like all Iroquois children, they were rarely disciplined or punished and were loved and raised not just by their parents, but also watched over by dozens of other mothers and uncles in their longhouse and their village. Corn fields surrounding the village were tended by the women. Corn, along with the beans and squash grown, represented about half their diet. The men hunted and fished to provide more food. These foodstuffs, combined with nuts, berries, tubers, herbs and maple sugar, meant that the children were rarely hungry. The ample food supply also meant that the Iroquois never abandoned their infirm or elderly. It was an accepted precept that the community cared for all its members.

Donnacona was a chief, but being an Iroquois chief did not mean exerting power. A chief was expected to be generous and giving. He was spokesman for the collective will of the people not the authoritative ruler of the people. Like all Iroquois members, he followed a moral imperative to care for others in the community, to be tolerant of those who were different, to always be eager to share and show respect for others.

This is what the boys were taught from birth. But this was not all that they learned, for the Iroquois were a proud people with a proud heritage. If food was plentiful, life was still a struggle. Every Iroquois boy knew that he was born to be a "warrior" for his people. The Iroquois did not wage "wars"[5] in the days before Columbus, but they did engage in frequent raiding parties – particularly against their cousins and enemies, the Hurons. If an Iroquois village were decimated by disease, the men would attack the enemy – not to kill or enslave, but to adopt replacements for the lost population. Thus, a child born a Huron, an Ottawa or a Cherokee, might become a victim of a raid and be raised as a full-fledged Iroquois citizen. The importance of these raids to the maintenance of their nation's existence, meant that Domagaya and Taignoagny must be well prepared for their future life as Iroquois men.

Life for them revolved around the six major festivals in the Iroquois year and participation in the games that would prepare them as warriors. Wrestling, running, archery and lacrosse were the main physical activities. Playing was preparation for adulthood and the boys learned very early that you never show weakness or acknowledge pain. In all likelihood, they would experience torture at some point in their lives – either as the tortured or the torturer. Consequently, it was imperative that they understand the dignity of the ceremony of torture[6] when it was experienced. There could be no crying out, no acknowledgement of pain no matter how severe. In their culture, the torturer and the tortured had assigned roles, including mutual respect that demanded a specific procedure to be followed. The pain inflicted must be creative, enduring and spread out over as long a period as possible. The victim must taunt his torturers and enthusiastically demand more pain. This was the symbiotic relationship they would experience if their lives evolved as they anticipated.[7]

But their lives were to be changed forever in the summer of 1534. For that was the year that the explorer Jacques Cartier sailed from St.

Malo, France, to the St. Lawrence River. At that time in Europe, it was believed that a shorter route to China, a major trading destination, had to exist in the northern reaches of the New World. The first nation to discover this route would reap the rewards of increased trade. It was this belief that sent Cartier across the Atlantic that summer, and it would be this same belief that sent other explorers later. Cartier had departed from his fishing village in late April with two ships and sixty-one men, searching for the elusive short cut. Reaching the Gulf of St. Lawrence in July, he presented an appealing prospect for Donnacona. The Iroquois were not merely farmers and hunters, they were also active traders. Using furs and crops, they traded for shells from the south and tobacco from the west. Donnacona had heard tales of strange white people who came in giant boats, carrying lightning sticks that made a loud noise like thunder and killed people instantly. But these strange beings also brought magic reflectors and sharp knives that could be traded for furs. Surely the great chief and his sons should greet this visitor and welcome him as a new friend and trading partner. So his people danced and sang him a welcome.

The warm feelings did not last long. Donnacona was outraged when Cartier planted a 30-foot cross on the land belonging to the Iroquois. Was Cartier naïve enough to believe the chief so stupid as to accept his explanation (by sign language) that it was just a marker for future whites? For Donnacona, this was the land of his forefathers, his people, his sons. It was arrogance for this new visitor to claim otherwise. Then, whatever trust may have developed was shattered when Cartier took his two sons back on board the ship and immediately set sail for France! This was not a "meeting of two worlds" as some historians describe it; this was a collision – a collision that would have catastrophic conse-quences for the Native Peoples.

Cartier arrived back in France before winter set in and brought with him his loot and his proof that he had landed in the New World – Domagaya and Taignoagny. Snatched from their homeland, the teenagers were thrust into the Europe of the late Renaissance period. British ships under Henry VIII had humiliated the French fleet and gained dominance

The narrow winding streets and imposing brick buildings of Paris were a sharp contrast to the natural wilderness that the young Iroquois had left behind. *Courtesy of Library and Archives Canada/1981-074 #230.*

of the English Channel. Nevertheless, the French king, Francis I, was a formidable ruler who was respected throughout the continent. Flamboyant, authoritarian and pleasure-loving, he was the first King of France to insist upon being addressed as "Your Majesty."[8] For the two Iroquois boys what a contrast he would have been to their father, who saw not power and glory in his leadership role but responsibility and generosity. But encountering Francis I became but one of many strange and exciting experiences that were to come for Domagaya and Taignoagny.

There was much to impress the involuntary guests of the French expedition to the New World. France reflected the glory of the Humanist and Renaissance spirit[9] for this was the day of the great Italian artists Leonardo da Vinci and Michelangelo. The spires, the stained glass, the beautifully ornate carvings of Notre Dame Cathedral stunned the youngsters into silent awe. So too did the noises, the bustle and the activity of the streets of Paris. Horses and carts, cobblestone walkways, beggars, merchants hawking their wares and homes built on top of each other were all sights that stretched their credulity.

Nor were the people any more understandable. Francis I was tall and handsome and a skilled hunter. But at the same time, there were so many men who did women's work in the fields. And the women were beyond explanation. They wore powder and paint and wore clothes that seemed to cover their bosoms but at the same time pushed their breasts upward and forward for partial viewing. Strange as well, was their bizarre treatment of children. An Iroquois would never punishing or spank a small child as the Europeans did. Everything was so alien. Why would these people want to grow hair on their faces? How could they allow hunger and begging when others had so much? Were they not all people? And why did Francis kill 3,000 of his people at Provence because they wanted to worship their god in a different way?[10] Some would say that Cartier was correct when he drew a line between civilization and savagery. He just placed the wrong people on the wrong side.

Yet Domagaya and Taignoagny had no time for philosophical musings. Cartier had promised their father that he would return the boys by next year, and he needed them to learn enough French to serve as his translators. Their days would be filled with successfully learning the language of a culture that they would never be able to understand. The words would have meaning, but the values and concepts being conveyed would always be a mystery.

So pleased was Francis I with Cartier's bounty that he granted him 3,000 livres, three ships and 110 men to embark on a second journey. The Native captives had talked of a kingdom called Saguenay that was rich with gold and silver and rubies. Both Cartier and Francis wanted wealth and the tantalizing prospect led Cartier to set sail the following year on May 19, 1535, with his ships and his men and his two translators in tow.

Their excitement was palpable as Domagaya and Taignoagny approached their beloved homeland. Enthusiastically, they pointed towards their village and Cartier inquired as to where they were. When one of them responded that they were near a collection of villages (the

Iroquois word for village would be *Kanata*), Cartier carefully noted the name of this new land. Thus, as recorded in Cartier's journal of August 13, 1535, Canada was given a name.

But Cartier was perturbed by his dealings with the Native People. Donnacona was naturally ecstatic to be reunited with his sons, but he still did not trust this stranger. Even worse, Cartier's new translators and guides were betraying him. Instead of acting like grateful and loyal French subjects, they were behaving like Iroquois men. Taignoagny now refused to guide Cartier to the Kingdom of Saguenay. Domagaya agreed to do so, but Cartier did not fully trust either of the boys any longer. Donnacona (perhaps mindful of Cartier's arrogant seizure of his sons last year) suggested both boys would go if Cartier left behind a Frenchman. But, Cartier refused and decided to continue down the river on his own. He was partially successful in his exploration, finding the village of Hochelaga (now Montreal), but returned to Stadacona to encounter even more difficulties. The two Iroquois teens, instead of extolling the virtues of French "allies," had counselled their people to be wary of trusting the French and to demand a fairer return for the furs they were trading. Outraged at this betrayal, Cartier felt his dealings with the Iroquois would be tainted as long as Donnacona and his sons exerted influence. They had to be replaced with a more malleable leader.

Yet for Cartier, there was an even more urgent crisis than an unfriendly ally. Winter had set in and the French crew members were about to encounter bone-chilling coldness unlike anything previously experienced. Even worse was the scurvy[11] that swept through the besieged sailors and threatened to wipe out the entire French expedition. By mid-February, 25 of his men lay dead and another 85 were deathly ill. There were only ten healthy men when, once again, Domagaya come to the rescue. Introducing the foreigners to a Vitamin C-rich brew made from the bark of the cedar tree, Domagaya was responsible for a dramatic intervention that led to a virtually immediate cure for those suffering from scurvy. Cartier and his band were saved by this first recorded occasion of medicine being applied to cure a disease in Canada.

When spring came, Cartier laid preparations for his return to France. Included in his plans was a scheme to replace Donnacona and his sons with a new, and it was hoped, more accommodating, chief. Attempting to lure his adversaries onto his ship, Cartier was met with resistance. Taignoagny, in particular, distrusted Cartier and urged his father to be on guard. Frustrated, Cartier had Donnacona, Domagaya, Taignoagny and seven others (including small children) seized and forcibly held on the sailing ships. Once again, the two boys were taken from their homelands, this time with company, and this time never to return.

When Cartier came back to Canada on his third voyage in August of 1541, he left behind in France nine Iroquois corpses and one surviving female captive. Blithely assuring the new chief, Agona, that his brethren were so enamoured with France they had no desire to return to Canada, Cartier felt smug satisfaction at once again fooling the "ignorant savages."[12] Tragically, he could never acknowledge that the Iroquois would reject such an absurd claim. His comfortable assumption of having "put one over" on the Indians established a pattern of mistrust by our Native population that started with the death of two early Canadian heroes, a pattern that is still prevalent today.

CHAPTER TWO

Étienne Brûlé:
First Coureur de Bois

When Samuel de Champlain arrived at Quebec in the summer of 1608, he brought with him a dream of the first permanent white settlement north of Florida, an empire carved from the trees of the wilderness. Standing beside him, sharing his vision, was a young boy, born of peasant stock just outside the City of Paris sometime between the years 1592 and 1595. Lured by tales of glory, riches and adventure, Étienne Brûlé left his home in Champigny to become the greatest explorer and pathfinder of the pioneer days in early Canada. His list of exploits accomplished during a brief life span remains remarkable to this day. He was the first coureur de bois, the first white diplomat and the first European translator in North America. Forefather of the voyageur, he was the first white man to see Lakes Huron, Ontario, Superior and Erie. He was also the first white man to shoot the Lachine Rapids in a canoe. He was the first white man to enter what is now called Ontario, ascending the Ottawa River, travelling to Georgian Bay, descending the Humber River to present-day Toronto, and viewing images never before seen by a European. He was the first white man to travel across the territory known today as the State of Pennsylvania, all the way from Lake Erie and along the Susquehanna River to the Chesapeake Bay. And tragically, although appropriately, he was the first – and probably only – white man to have been boiled and eaten by the Indians with whom he had hunted, fought and lived for so many years.

Given the life that he was to lead, Brûlé's initiation to Canada was fitting. Under the mighty leader, Hiawatha, the Iroquois Nation had attempted to unite various tribes scattered across the lands of Ontario, Quebec and New York State into a "universal peace." The Huron, however, resisted these efforts and ongoing skirmishes between various Native nations were the result. For a number of reasons, Champlain had committed the strength and the modern weaponry of the French nation to the Huron cause,[1] giving them a temporary advantage in their prolonged struggle with their traditional enemy. For Brûlé, the immediate result was to find himself in battle against the Iroquois upon his arrival in Canada. In June of 1608, he watched in horror as arrows pierced the throats, the eyes, the hearts of his allies. As the incredulous teen (by then believed to be somewhere between the ages of twelve to sixteen) stared in disbelief, the Native warriors pulled the arrows from their wounds and flung them contemptuously to the ground, scarcely pausing in their battle. It is evident that this early dramatic lesson in bravery would remain with the impressionable Brûlé for the rest of his life. Over his lifetime he would be called many things by those who knew him – scoundrel, villain, traitor, savage – but never would anyone use the term "coward."

The first winter at the fledgling French settlement would prove to be a harsher enemy than the Iroquois. As snow and wind bore into the bones and souls of the dispirited inhabitants, scurvy and dysentery attacked the weary community. Every one of the twenty-eight settlers fell ill during the siege, and twenty of them would not see the spring. When the long-awaited supply ships finally arrived from France in 1609, only Champlain, Brûlé and six other desperate men were there to greet them. Brûlé's survival was made possible by his early contact with the Montaignais First Nation, who lived near the settlement of Quebec. He shared their food, accepted their help and discovered that he had a gift for their dialect. Thus, as the promise of spring drove away the cruel winter, Brûlé emerged from the ordeal with two important assets. The first was the reinforced confidence that his mentor directed towards the young charge; Brûlé had now become "my French boy" or "my lad" to Champlain. The other benefit secured was his mastery of the Cree language. Since nations from present-day Quebec to Saskatchewan used a form of this language, he was in a position to begin his journey of discovery and adventure.

Within a year, Brûlé was able to combine his two advantages. After fighting alongside Champlain in another battle against the Iroquois in June of 1610 (during this struggle, Champlain pulled an arrow from his ear and throat while continuing to fight),[2] Brûlé approached his leader with a strange request. Willing to forsake the relative security of the settlement, Brûlé wished to live amongst the Indians for a full year. He wanted to do what no other white man had ever tried – to completely abandon his white heritage and immerse himself in an alien world with no contacts with his past or present. The undeniable initiative, independence and courage that the calm youngster possessed were obvious to Champlain. So too were the unique advantages of such a venture. Champlain's dream of empire would receive an outstanding boost if he could have one of his most trusted followers become a "Native." Brûlé would be vital in the alliance between French and Huron and in the fantastic fur trade that could ensue. And so, a remarkable exchange took place. The Algonquin chief, Iroquet, "adopted" the French teenager for one year. He was to travel down the mighty Ottawa River on a "white water adventure." A thrilling surge of blood flowed through the reckless Brûlé as the canoe shot through the treacherous rocks and swirling rapids. He was entering a secret world, a hidden site denied to any other white man. The rules, the strictures and scriptures of the past could be cast off with his clothes as he pursued the life of the "noble savage." In return for entrusting Brûlé to Iroquet, Champlain was given Savignon, a young brave who returned to France with Champlain.[3]

The freedom from constraints were to become so appealing to Brûlé that he would spend the next twenty-three years living among the Huron. Raised with only a rudimentary religious training, and becoming

Étienne Brûlé's easy comfort with Indian life is readily evident in this sketch by C.W. Jefferys. *Courtesy of Library and Archives Canada/ C-073635.*

a part of a new culture during his formative years, he was enticed by seductive virtues of Native life. Endurance and courage were the qualities most admired among the Huron. Children were rarely disciplined, and a fair-skinned teenager was the special object of female admiration. In an atmosphere of no sexual inhibition, Brûlé soon adapted to a way of life that would be condemned by the moral Champlain and the devout priests of the Catholic Church.

When Brûlé returned to Quebec one year later, Champlain was initially pleased with the treatment accorded to "my French boy" and was excited by all that Brûlé had seen and learned during his habitation. His ease with the Huron language should have proven invaluable to Champlain. Not only could he be his liaison in trade and communication with the Native Peoples, he could also be the key to a great French Empire that would extend into the heart of this new continent, civilizing and Christianizing the "savages" who lay beyond the pale of the settlement.

But it was not to be. Brûlé was in the process of adapting totally to the Huron way of life. During his year in Iroquet's village, he had discovered that he much preferred the carefree excitement of his new people. The restricting European clothes were symbolic of the emptiness of his former life. Dressed in animal skins, Brûlé – with his spirit of independence, adventure and courage – was much more comfortable in the woods and rivers of the vast wilderness.

Yet the transition was a gradual process. For a while, Brûlé would become a man of two worlds and would, from time to time, slip away from the shadows of his Indian life to serve as a guide, translator and ally of Champlain. It was during one of these periods that he accompanied Champlain during his third campaign against the Iroquois during the summer of 1615.

Champlain, Brûlé and a handful of colonists set out to join the Huron warriors in their battle with the hated Iroquois. For Champlain, this was to be the final confrontation. He envisioned a European-style war with thousands of Indians marching orderly under his command. Villages would be razed, towns destroyed and homes torched. The strategy was to destroy the principle town of the Onondaga, near present-day Syracuse, New York. From this victory, the warriors would strike out systematically against the other Iroquois, the Mohawk, Cayuga, Oneida, Onandaga and Seneca. The balance in the struggle would be tipped towards the Huron because of their access to European weapons and support. The enemy would be demoralized and the road to Champlain's mission to the wilderness would be clear. His vision was not to be. For Champlain, the dream would soon lie in ruins. The Iroquois defeated the few hundred Huron who actually showed up for the battle and Champlain was wounded and carried off in hasty retreat. The eventual downfall of the Huron can be traced to this encounter where they shifted from the offensive to the defensive in their long struggle with the Iroquois. When the allies of the French were finally defeated at Ste. Marie (today's Saint Marie-Among-the Hurons) some years later, so too was the dream of a French Empire in North America.

Yet for Brûlé, the campaign was not for empire, but for adventure. Before the actual fighting, Champlain decided to send a delegation of twelve of the bravest Huron warriors to travel through hostile Iroquois country in an effort to persuade the Susquehannah Nation (of today's Pennsylvania area) to join them in the war. To be captured by the Senecas meant certain torture and death for the braves, a risk they were willing to take. Incredibly, Brûlé both sought and secured permission to go on this perilous journey. Leaving Champlain at Lake Simcoe, he travelled down the Humber River to Lake Ontario, went around the western shore of the lake, and landed near the Niagara and Genesee rivers. During the overland trip through the present-day State of New York, Brûlé and his group did encounter a band of Seneca warriors, but they were able to evade them and arrive at the Susquehannah's main town of Carantouan. From there, Brûlé and the chief, Andastes, returned with 500 warriors, but by the time that they arrived at the town of the Onondaga, the siege was over. With Champlain and the other Frenchmen already having fled the scene, Brûlé readily accepted Andastes' offer to spend the winter in his home. It was during this time period that he travelled across the State of Pennsylvania to Chesapeake Bay. It was also during this time period that he became the first white man to be tortured by the Iroquois.

While returning to Huronia, Brûlé was captured by a band of Seneca warriors who were delighted with their prize. Tied to a stake, he had his lessons of courage and endurance sorely tested. The Indians tortured him, but Brûlé stoically refused to acknowledge the pain. In frustration, the Indians then tied him naked to the ground and proceeded to apply more torture to his body. Still, he refused to yield. The only occasion for his crying out came when one of the Seneca attempted to rip a religious medallion from his neck. At this point, Brûlé screamed that if they continued, his God would be angered. Although he was in no way a religious man, he hoped to use the threat to secure his release.

Miraculously, a storm burst out and Brûlé convinced them that his Great Spirit was indeed guarding him. Terrified, they released their hostage and permitted him to return home. In 1618, Brûlé was back in Quebec, reporting to Champlain and showing him his scars. Champlain believed him, but the close bond of earlier years had been weakened. It was evident that he did not share Champlain's vision of a religious mission in the New World. For Brûlé, the empire would rest with furs, not with souls. He was receiving a lucrative income for his role as middleman and was finding increasing satisfaction with his new Native lifestyle. The white settlement would be a place to visit and exploit, but the woods were where he belonged.

For the next decade, Brûlé would offer his services to the Récollet priests[4] who were establishing their missionaries in Huronia. He continued his explorations westward, discovering Lake Superior and Lake Erie, but he also found time to serve as translator for Brothers Sagard and Brébeuf.[5] It was with Brûlé's assistance that the Récollet priest Sagard learned the Native tongue and began to develop the first dictionary of the Huron language, a work that would be completed by the Jesuit priest, Father Brébeuf. Yet neither the Church nor the pious Champlain could be comfortable with this man, now in his early to mid-twenties, who seemed addicted to vices. He mocked their religion, preferring the Native values to what he condemned as civilization's veneer of hypocrisy. They, in turn, decried his womanizing, his debauchery and his failure to observe Catholic rituals. The stage was being set for the complete separation that was to occur in 1629.

For a number of years, British ships had arrived at Quebec under the command of Captain David Kirke[6] of the British Royal Navy. In 1628, he cut off the food supplies to the settlement and demanded its surrender. When Champlain refused, Kirke abandoned the attempt, but was determined to return for revenge.

This revenge would come on July 19, 1629, when Kirke sailed up the St. Lawrence with three ships and again demanded the surrender of Quebec (despite the fact that England and France had signed a peace treaty the previous April). Champlain appeared in a hopeless situation. His colonists were subsisting on acorns, dry roots and Indian charity. In a final effort, he sent Brûlé and three others to guide French supply ships to safety. When Brûlé canoed down the St. Lawrence, he soon discovered that the English were in total control of the river and, subsequently, in control of Quebec. Realizing that the French cause was futile, and, realizing that he cared more for the Indians than the whites, he betrayed his

This plaque honouring Étienne Brûlé can be found mounted on the outside wall by the entrance to the Old Mill Restaurant in Toronto, near the Humber River. It recognizes a small part of Brûlé's legacy. *Photograph by the author.*

leader. For Brûlé, life meant living with the Indians and visiting the European settlement. It mattered little to him whether the settlement was French or English. This coureur de bois was a Canadian; his loyalty was to the new community of Canada. By guiding the English ships to Quebec, Brûlé assured the defeat of Champlain. For Champlain, this betrayal was the one act that could never be forgiven. For Brûlé, it was not a denial but an affirmation – he belonged to the forests.

Ironically, within three years, the destinies of these three men were secured. Champlain returned triumphant as governor of a New France, the colony having been restored to France by Charles I of England. Kirke was knighted and made governor of the British possession, the Colony of Newfoundland. And Brûlé was living in Huronia with the Bear Tribe.

Brûlé's self-imposed exile was destined to be short-lived. The motives for what happened were never discovered, and the events surrounding the circumstances remain a mystery to this day, but for whatever reason, in June of 1633, the Bear Tribe turned on Brûlé, killed him, cooked him and ate him. Even in his death, the Indians acknowledged his bravery, for cannibalism was often associated with acquiring supernatural powers and human qualities of valour and accomplishment from the victim.

Yet even in death, Brûlé would not rest. Shortly after the summer of 1633, a smallpox epidemic swept through the Huron Nation, breathing death on about half of the people. It was said that his avenging sister was stalking the land, seeking revenge for the murder of her brother. At the sacred ceremony of the Feast for the Dead, held every twelve years, the Hurons wanted to bury Brûlé with their own people in an effort to assuage the anger of this Spirit of Death. Indeed, the various clans argued over which one would gain Brûlé's body for burial.

At this juncture, the priests stepped in. For all his corrupt ways, Brûlé was still a baptized Christian. As such, he could not be buried with the people he loved. Many were unbaptized heathens who must be kept separate. Father Brébeuf, in particular, insisted on this treatment of his long-time adversary. A compromise was reached – Brûlé could lie beside a large pit of Indian bones, near but not a part of Indian death. Again, the various clans argued over the honour of being beside this feared individual and Brûlé remained in an unmarked grave.[8] As a result, he was lost to posterity. Somewhere in Ontario in the region known as Huronia today, lie the remains of the most colourful of all the coureur de bois – his exact grave site unknown and unmarked.

CHAPTER THREE

Madeleine Jarret: Heroine of Verchères

anada is a nation whose written story stretches back over 400 years to the initial contact between the French explorers and the Native Peoples who greeted and helped them adapt to a new land. Consequently, there is no surprise that a number of heroes and heroines have emerged from the pages of our history books. There have been countless opportunities and countless examples of sacrifice and courage. Yet in all the pages of Canadian history, there is but one moment when every citizen was a hero, during the one period of hardship and achievement that remains unmatched to this day. This one glorious epoch marking the flowering of the colony of New France was remarkable for its proliferation of both idealism and action. There neither age, sex nor status mattered in these glorious days of the French Empire of the Sun King, Louis XIV,[1] who ruled from 1638 to 1715. During his reign, everyone, no matter how far down the social, political or economic scale, had the opportunity to be inscribed forever in the annals of our nation. In the Canada of the late 1600s, every day of every year had its own story of valour and accomplishment.[2] This was a time when a number of circumstances combined to create a unique period, unparalleled to this day, that saw the first meeting of two worlds – the Native and the European – as residents of the same land. Because the population of New France was so small and so concentrated, the "collision" of these two worlds was felt by all.

Key to this unique era was the primitive pioneer community being carved from the vast forests along the St. Lawrence River. The harsh wilderness was a natural force for democracy, as the seigneur and his family toiled alongside the habitants here in the fields of New France. Privilege had no home in a society where the ethic was work or perish, here the hardships of climate, disease and death affected every subject of the Sun King. Gone was the distinction of class that contributed to the rot of the older society in Europe. Canada was a young society that promised each and every person the opportunity of toil, sacrifice and privation. Blending with this notion of hardship was a missionary zeal that was unique to the people of New France. Convinced that they were sent to the New World by God, these devout subjects of France had but one overriding desire – to fulfil God's will! No one could question the simple sincerity of these children of God who were certain that they had a duty to serve mankind. For them it was not a belief, but a knowledge of a mission for God in the New World. It was the obligation of every French citizen's in New France to civilize and Christianize the indigenous people that they regarded as heathens.

Leading this zealous group were the Jesuit missionaries who were prepared to make every sacrifice necessary in the service of their God. The suffering of Father Isaac Jocques is typical of the courage and endurance displayed by the "Black Robes," as the Jesuits were known. He witnessed a comrade killed, then calmly knelt down to receive his own deathblow. Instead, he served as slave for the Iroquois nation that had captured him, all the while praying daily for the victims and perpetrators alike. He endured torture and finally secured his martyrdom when he died. All this, he accepted calmly as being part of God's will.[3] To serve God was a reward that made all suffering not only acceptable, but desirable!

With hardship and suffering, there was also present the spirit of adventure. The tales of the coureurs de bois were renown throughout

New France. Shooting the rapids, fighting in Indian wars, hunting in the wilds, exploring lands unknown to any white men – this was the lure and the promise for the "runners of the wood." A free life beckoned for any one who wished to leave the confines of civilization. Adventure lay in the forests of the New World.

Adventure lay also in the fledgling community. Louis Hébert would be Canada's first farmer, working the land before the plough had even arrived from the Old World. Marguerite Bourgeoys would found the Congregation of Notre Dame, the first religious order established in Canada and become the first teacher at a time when there was only one school-aged child. The beatific Jeanne Mance would found the first hospital and rescue a settlement from Iroquois attack by her tender care of a wounded Mohawk. Pierre Esprit Radisson would become one of the individuals crucial to the development of the Hudson's Bay Company,[4] which would extend its domain from present-day Ontario and Quebec through Manitoba, Saskatchewan and Alberta all the way to British Columbia. This truly was an age of heroes!

Into this emerging society marched the famed Carignon-Salières Regiment – 100 officers and 1,000 foot soldiers led by the glamorous Marquis de Tracy, whose reputation as a heroic and appealing person was well known in both France and New France. In June of 1665, this military division was sent to the new world by Louis XIV to consolidate his empire. The French Empire was in great peril.

A state of war existed between England and France. For years before, and for years to come, these two European empires would struggle for supremacy in the New World. Using the Natives as allies, the colonists of New England and New France continually meet in skirmishes that failed to resolve the long-standing conflict. The British armed the Iroquois with rifles and encouraged them to harass the people of New France. (The Onondaga were the only one of the five Iroquois Nations not at war with the French settlements). Habitants were ordered not to work in the fields unless it was absolutely necessary. Houses were fortified in every settlement and wells were dug in the courtyards of the seigneuries since it was too dangerous to go to the

riverside. Into this scene came the Carignon-Salières Regiment, ultimately restoring order and earning the gratitude of the people. Their
organization, strategy and prowess secured a twenty-year truce with
the Iroquois Confederacy. It appeared that the fledgling colony of New
France would finally have a chance to grow and thrive.

Ensign François Jarret de Verchères was a member of this regiment
and had been personally involved in two campaigns against the
Iroquois. When most of the soldiers returned to France in 1668, he
remained behind. A grateful colony had provided grants of land to any
member of the Carignon-Salières who wished to make Canada his new
homeland. The young twenty-four-year-old remained in Quebec, fell in
love with the fourteen-year-old Marie Perrot and married her in
September of 1669. By 1673 François Jarret could be considered a young
man with a promising future. His seigneury at Verchères contained two
islands and land that fronted on the St. Lawrence River and, to the
back, stretched almost to the Richelieu River.

Situated about thirty-two kilometres downriver from Montreal, the
seigneury had two notable forts on each side of it – Fort Richelieu and
Fort Chambly. Although both of these were considered strongholds,
François Jarret realized that they were too far removed to be of any
value to Verchères in the event of an Iroquois raid. Ever the military
strategist, Jarret turned his seigneury into a well-fortified community.
The manor house was secured by a strong stockade and protected by
cannons at the bastions. The outlying fields would be under the watchful eyes of armed soldiers during times of trouble. This foresight proved
beneficial as Iroquois raids once again began to stalk the scattered settlements along the St. Lawrence.

Marie-Magdeleine Jarret was born on March 3, 1678. She was the
fourth child of a family that ultimately would become twelve in all. At
the time of her birth, her father's reputation had so grown in stature
that he was one of twenty notables selected by King Louis to advise the
Sovereign Council on the wisdom of trading brandy to the Natives.
Madeleine, as her family called her, grew up in a happy and comfortable environment. The pointed stakes sixteen feet high forming the

stockade that enclosed the seigneury seemed a formidable barrier to dangers from the outside world. The large stone blockhouse and the covered passageway were wonderful places for a young girl to play and hide in with her brothers and sisters. Madeleine ran in the fields, fished in the rivers and hunted in the nearby woods. In fact, her ability with a rifle soon gained her a reputation as an expert marksman. On special days, Madeleine would accompany her mother in the *bateau* as they visited neighbours.

Enriching her carefree existence of childhood were the important values instilled in the Jarret family by both her mother and father. The vast holdings of Verchères represented responsibility and duty as well as privilege. Service to God, service to King, service to family and service to the land; these were the obligations that being a seigneur entailed. Every child was made to realize that duty was the order of life. Madeleine learned at a young age that the family of the seigneur must provide example and leadership for the habitants working on the seigneury. It was at the Jarret manor that justice was dispensed in disputes between habitants. It was at the family mill that wheat was ground and it was on the family estate that Madeleine and her mother led in the husking bees at corn harvest time, as part of their preparation of food for winter.

Just as Madeleine was raised with the spirit of duty, so too was she aware of the increasing dangers that confronted the seigneury. By the late 1680s New France was once again reeling under the ongoing Iroquois attacks. In August of 1689, the entire colony of New France trembled at the news of a massive attack at Lachine[5] on the St. Lawrence River. Horror invoked by the stories of invasion spread across the colony. The nightmare ended with Lachine being set ablaze.

New France was being besieged on all sides. England had escalated its warfare against the French, and, in 1690, Sir William Phips[6] demanded of Governor Louis de Buade, Comte de Frontenac[7] the surrender of Quebec to the British fleet. The fleet, consisting of 2,000 armed men, anchored in the St. Lawrence was not successful on its first siege, but a subdued French colony shuddered at the rumours of a massive assault from New England. These continual struggles heightened the hardships confronting the brave souls in the colony. Soldiers were billeted in the habitants' homes and a starving populace was forced to share their meagre food with the fighting forces. Famine was a very real threat to a people rummaging for roots and acorns to eat.

Meanwhile, the Iroquois grew even more emboldened by the weakened plight of the settlers and stepped up their attacks. The people were paralyzed by fear as every day brought news of more casualties among friends and relatives. On one day, a mother and her fifteen-year-old daughter were working in the fields under the protection of armed soldiers. The fifteen-year-old disappeared forever on that day. On another occasion, two habitants working in the fields just outside of Montreal were surrounded and taken away. When Madeleine was twelve years old, she and her mother successfully fought off an Iroquois attack on the seigneury when François was away on business. By the age of fourteen, Madeleine had already lost a brother-in-law. A number of settlers, including the Jarrets, alarmed by the increasing threats, abandoned the seigneuries for the safer confines of the armed forts at Richelieu and Chambly or the stronghold city of Montreal. This was the background to October 1692, when Canada was provided with one of her earliest episodes of individual valour against overwhelming odds.

As summer was transformed into the vibrant colours of autumn, a hesitant community breathed a tentative sigh of relief. A hopeful group had come back for the harvesting season from the safety of the armed forts. Verchères had been neglected for two years because of Iroquois unrest and the threat of imminent attack by the English from New England. To the Jarrets the seigneury represented home, but it now was a home in decay. Palisades had rotted, providing easy access in the event of an attack. Gaping holes were evident upon closer inspection of the fortifications. There was much work to be done before seigneury would provide a safe haven for the people of Verchères.

A group of temporarily assigned armed soldiers protected all groups and labourers went under escort from the fort to the field; harvesting was a truly community endeavour, involving every man, woman and

Artist C.W. Jefferys (1869-1951) captured the drama of Madeleine Jarret's heroism in this early historical sketch, *The Iroquois attack of Fort Verchères, 1692; Madeleine closes the gate, Courtesy of Library and Archives Canada/C-010687.*

child of the seigneury. This constant vigilance finally seemed to create an impact as the Iroquois attacks abated. By mid-October, with winter approaching, there no longer seemed to be a serious threat and the seigneury grew more confident.

Unfortunately, soon after their return, both François Jarret and his wife were called away. He had been ordered to duty in Quebec City and Marie was in Montreal. The armed soldiers had been redeployed to Montreal and area now that the harvest was completed. Thus, the only people left behind to defend the fort were Madeleine, her younger brothers, Pierre and Alexandre, two soldiers, an old man of 80, a family servant named Laviolette and a few women and children. It is questionable as to whether or not François would have left had he considered that there was a real danger of an Indian raid. However, he possessed a strong sense of duty to God and to King, and not likely would have hesitated to respond when his ruler needed him.

October 22 was a bright crisp day that began innocently enough for Madeleine. Early in the morning, she and Laviolette left the fort and travelled to the riverfront. It was her responsibility to check the moorings of the boats and Madeleine took no responsibility lightly. Suddenly, the terror began. A shot rang out and women appeared at the gate of the fort screaming of an attack. Madeleine desperately looked about; there was no time to think, only time to react as a number of Iroquois rushed at her. Madeleine took flight towards the fort, praying to God for strength and courage and hoping to avoid being caught.[8]

And it appeared that the Iroquois did want her alive. Although it would have been easy to have felled her with a rifle shot, the enemy continued to pursue her. The gate seemed so far away. The pounding of her heart was matched by the footsteps that seemed to beat closer and closer. She could hear the sound of breathing and feel the breath of one of them when suddenly a hand reached out and seized her by her shawl. Struggling frantically, Madeleine shook her wrap loose and lunged free. Shouting "To Arms," she reached the gate with a final surge and slammed the door shut. As she sobbed and gasped for air, any thought of rejoicing was dashed by the horrible cries of the habitants who were trapped outside in the fields. Madeleine knew that her only concern was for the safety of those in the fort. Nothing could help the souls beyond the gate. She had to present a cool resolve to calm the women and children – not for their sake, but to deny to the enemy any sign of weakness.

Looking first to the two soldiers for leadership, Madeleine saw panic and knew that the lives of every person in the fort depended upon her. Calmly she gathered the tense group around her and issued orders. Her quiet determination had a soothing effect and the others found themselves responding to her crisp orders. Emergency repairs were made to the stockade walls to prevent the enemy from getting inside. Then Madeleine ordered a cannon fired. She felt that this might not only frighten the Iroquois, but also alert any settlers to seek shelter and help persuade the enemy that Verchères was strongly defended.

At a time when she should have collapsed, the young teenager commanded the fort, issuing words of encouragement and praise to her small "army." Grabbing a soldier's helmet, she placed it on her head. Exhorting her two brothers to march with her, she led them in parade formation across the palisades, to present an image of strength and order. Shamed into action, the two soldiers joined in the charade and suddenly the attack stopped. The wary enemy backed away. The first battle was over! Yet the siege would continue. The Iroquois did not know what was behind the walled fort, but they were not prepared to retreat without some fighting. The day watch began.

In late afternoon, Madeleine was aware of a noise from the river. Craning her head, she saw that a neighbouring family, the Lafontaines, was arriving. Although there were no Iroquois in sight, Madeleine knew that they were watching in the woods and that the entire family could be captured. Without a moment's hesitation, she walked out of the security of the fort and marched the 140 metres to the riverfront. Quietly, she informed them of the situation and calmly she escorted them back to the safety of the fort. Madeleine's bold initiative had saved the family.

The day watch turned to a night watch. Snow and hail, accompanied by biting winds brought physical hardship to compound the mental agony they were enduring. Madeleine ordered the women and children to be taken to the strongest building on the fort, but there could be no rest for either her or her brothers. All night long, numb fingers clung to the rifles as they acted as sentinels. Regularly, shivering voices called "All's Well" to deceive the Iroquois. According to Madeleine's written account (it ultimately became an official report for the governor of New France in 1716[9]), a night attack had been planned, but was thwarted by the apparent strength of the fortified seigneury.

Around midnight, the strain became almost unbearable. Strange noises drifted into the fort above the raging winds. Was this the moment of attack? Again, the noises were heard, this time louder. Were the Iroquois getting closer? The noise became clear and it sounded like animals. Was it a trick or did some of the cattle wander to the gate? Madeleine made a careful, and potentially fatal, decision. While her brothers stood guard at the gate, she slipped outside and rescued some wayward livestock.

The night of terror had been too much for Madame Lafontaine. The next morning she pleaded with Madeleine and the others to desert the fort for safer grounds. In her mind, no one would survive an Iroquois attack at Verchères. Yet Madeleine knew that her duty was at the seigneury. She was the head of the family and responsible for the fort while her parents were absent. Also, if she should abandon Verchères with its weakened fortifications the vulnerable state of all the other seigneuries would become evident. There was no choice for young Madeleine. Others could leave if they wished, but she belonged at Verchères. While Madame Lafontaine and her children did sneak away to the safety of Controcoeur, her husband stayed behind to help defend the seigneury.

And so the siege continued. For eight days and eight nights, the brave teenager rallied her forces, but Madeleine never broke. She would not rest; she would never surrender, until help arrived. The Iroquois watched, wary of a trap. They would never know that a young girl and her straggly troop of eight were successfully defending Verchères. On the ninth day, forty soldiers arrived from Montreal to rescue them. At last, Madeleine could surrender her responsibility. The gate was flung open and a cheering group greeted the disbelieving soldiers. Thwarted by the reinforcements, the Iroquois disappeared into the woods.

Madeleine de Verchères is a stirring example of heroism in an age of heroes. Those terrifying and exhilarating eight days guaranteed for the heroine a place forever in Canadian history. After these unforgettable hours, Madeleine de Verchères matured into adulthood, continuing to demonstrate her strong sense of duty and responsibility. She was a widow when she met her second husband, Pierre-Thomas Tarieu de Perade. He and a group of his men were pursuing a band of Iroquois when they were suddenly trapped and seemingly doomed. Miraculously, Madeleine appeared, leading a contingent to his rescue. Sieur de Perade realized the value of having a famed "fighter" in the family and soon proposed to her.

A son, Daniel-Hyacinthe-Marie de Beaujeu was born to them on August 19, 1711. It is evident that his mother's heroism was passed on to

This still photograph taken during the filming of "Madeleine de Verchères" in 1922 depicts the conclusion of Madeleine's saga. *Courtesy of Library and Archives Canada/PA-028623.*

the next generation, for it was Daniel who defended the French Fort Duquesne (present-day Pittsburgh) when it was attacked by British troops.[10] The British seemed assured of victory. With 3,000 veteran soldiers led by General Edward Braddock and supported by the famous Virginia militia troops under the command of George Washington (he later would become the first President of the United States), their forces were far superior to those of the French. Yet de Beaujeu, with his 72 soldiers, 250 militia and 637 Native allies marched out of the fort to fight off the invaders. Madeleine's beloved son was killed during the third attack, but his forces were triumphant and Fort Duquesne remained in French hands. The lessons of the mother had been well learned by the son!

CHAPTER FOUR

John Tanner: Ojibwa Odyssey

hile the writer Morley Torgrov once said that Sault Ste. Marie was
a good place to come from, for John Tanner it was also a good
place to come to.¹ One spring morning in 1828 this exhausted
individual arrived in the small community. It was the end of an incredible odyssey that had begun on a similar spring day in Kentucky thirty
years earlier, when he was a pioneer lad barely nine years old.

Born of a Virginia clergyman in 1780, John was to have little recollection of his younger years. He remembered that his mother died when
he was just two years old and that shortly afterwards, his family moved
to Kentucky. John grew up at a time when white settlers and the
Shawnee First Nation of that region were engaged in recurring skirmishes. Indeed, one of his earliest memories is that of his father bursting into the cabin, proudly asserting victory over a group that had
attacked the village the previous night. Another of John's distant memories revolves around a family move up the Ohio River with livestock,
furniture and slaves. As John's family moved to Big Miami, Kentucky,
they travelled in flatboats that were stained with the blood of whites
and Natives alike. The new home was to be two log cabins that had

33

This photograph of a pioneer house could well represent the last visual impression of home for the young John Tanner as he was wrenched from his family and familiar surroundings in Kentucky. *Courtesy of the Archives of Ontario, RG 65-35.0, 11764-X4074.*

been deserted because of the incessant Indian attacks. Yet the Tanner family eagerly set about fortifying the buildings, repairing the fences and clearing the fields. The spring of 1789 was ripe with the anticipation of a new beginning in a new land.

It was a clear, warm day that spring, and John's father was eager to plant corn on the fertile soil. There had been recent sightings of Shawnee in the area so John's father and older brother took guns with them to the fields. John, his stepmother and the younger children were left behind with the stern warning not to leave the house. It was a warning that John would regret not heeding!

The house seemed so stuffy, so confining. The nearby woods beckoned, and seemed so inviting. If John could just sneak past his preoccupied stepmother, he might be able to capture a few minutes of liberty under the old walnut tree. Stealthily, he crept out the back door, out of sight of the group in the fields and the busy woman in the cabin. Suddenly free, John scurried about gathering walnuts and dreaming of lazy summer days at the fishing and swimming brook, when abruptly from nowhere, two pairs of strong hands seized and dragged him away.[2] For nine years, John had led a typical existence of a young pioneer in Kentucky. For the next thirty years, Shaw-shaw-wa be-na-se (the Falcon) grew up amongst the Ojibwa First Nation of Canada, in the northern area of Ontario between present-day Sault Ste. Marie and Sudbury, sharing the adventures and hardships of his new people. In the end, John Tanner was to become a tragic figure – a man with no country, no people, no family or friends – but his experiences were to provide for posterity a stirring saga of individual heroism and a rare glimpse of the fascinating world of the Native Peoples of North America.

A cruel and painful beginning marked his captivity. His captors hated the whites and were contemptuous of the young boy they had abducted. He was taken to replace the lost son of a Shawnee woman, but was not really wanted or loved. John recalled frequent tauntings and beatings and constant abuse:

> One morning, [my new father] got up, put on his moccasins, and went out; but presently returning, he caught me by the hair of my head, dragged me out, ... then tossed me by the hair into a snowbank.[3]

Other ways of tormenting John included telling him that his white family had all been slaughtered and punishing him severely for falling asleep while he was supposed to be working. Mercifully, John was soon sold as a son to Net-no-kwa, a chief of the Ottaway.[4]

For the rest of his childhood, John was to become "Falcon" and was accepted totally as one of the Ojibwa people. He learned to hunt and fish like an Ojibwa, to feast and fast like an Ojibwa, to engage in battle and think like an Ojibwa and when Falcon was to marry at the age of twenty, he was an Ojibwa.

Net-no-kwa and the rest of the family were kind and loving towards the new child. Gently, he was taught the Native ways by the same method that applied to all Ojibwa children. Little praise was given and rewards such as maple sugar or carved wooden toys were infrequent, but Falcon was never criticized or ridiculed. Falcon learned by listening and observing as the older members spoke of past customs and adventures. It was crucial to pay full attention when older people were talking, for anything less was a lack of courtesy. One day when Falcon was complaining about his older brother, Net-no-kwa pushed him away and the others walked away from him. Quickly he learned that Ojibwa children do not tell tales on others.

Yet the world into which John Tanner was plunged was different not only from what he was used to, but also from what he had imagined. As a youngster growing up on the frontier, John had sometimes fantasized about living with the Indians. It was daydream punctuated by glamour and adventure. The reality of his existence proved to be quite different. Although the Ojibwa Nation numbered up to 10,000, there was no main chief or leader of all the people. Rather, the main political and social unit was the band. There were approximately 20 of these bands, each with its own totem or sign such as the Loon or the Snake, each with its own chief, and each containing about 400 people. The male chief was also the war leader and made important decision in cases of conflict within the band. Yet for all this, the main structure was the family. For Falcon, Indian life invariably revolved around Net-no-kwa and her immediate relatives.

Living independently of others within the band, the family would vary in size from five to fifty people. Men would venture out daily to hunt for game. Other hunters might use their spears to jig for fish in the nearby rivers. The boys would hunt for squirrels or grouse, while the girls and women would set rabbit snares or gather berries. The entire life revolved around hunting for food and the individual who proved an adept provider was considered an important and successful person. Indeed, the coming of age for a boy of the band occurred when he killed his first bear or moose. After that, he no longer sat quietly while the elders talked, but as a man, shared in the discussions.

As a result of this constant struggle for survival, the Ojibwa had a strong notion of sharing. Falcon remembered one particularly cold and barren winter when his family was starving. A Cree whom they met took them into his lodge, shared all he had with them and cared for them the entire winter. So strong an impression did this spirit of caring and giving make upon Falcon, that he ignored an opportunity to return to the white world when he was 14 years of age: "Among the Indians, I saw that those who were too young, or too weak to hunt for themselves, were sure to find some one to provide for them."[5]

Another result of the daily preoccupation with food was the importance of feasts among the Ojibwa. Feasts came to be a favourite source of excitement and socializing and provided opportunities for clans to gather. Almost any occasion would justify calling for a feast. When a boy had killed his first bear, a feast would be held to celebrate his skill. Feasts for the dead would be called, where food was eaten at gravesites of deceased friends and portions of the food were thrown into the fire to attract the *Je-bi* or spirits. Feasts could result from dreams, for the Ojibwa firmly believed in the importance of dreams of prophecy and direction. Religious feasts called by medicine men invariably provided dogs as the main course. War feasts, feasts to celebrate winter's end or plentiful game, feasts to formally name a child – all were occasions of gathering, singing, dancing and smoking.

The greatest of them all was *Midewiwin*, a feast held at mid-summer to worship the Great Spirit and to initiate new members into the secret society of medicine men. Hundreds would gather at the beginning of the four-day festival, which might include a giant game of lacrosse involving all the men on an immense playing area. The referees were the medicine men and the cheerleaders were the women who beat the men with sticks to encourage them to play harder. Children could not participate, but had to content themselves with listening and learning, and running foot races among themselves.[6] These were happy times marked by a picnic atmosphere and the memories would remain with Falcon long after he returned to white society as John Tanner.

One morning, when he was about eleven, Falcon woke up to see Net-no-kwa holding breakfast in one hand and a piece of charcoal from the fire in the other. Falcon chose the charcoal and began an important ritual of all Ojibwa children – fasting. Pleasing his mother, he blackened his face to indicate that he would forego any food for the next few days. A child of four or five would only fast for a day, while a child from six to eight would go without food for up to four days. A child Falcon's age could fast for up to ten days, but this would not be expected of him since he was a relative newcomer. Falcon left his wigwam alone into the woods during his fast. He hoped that the Great Spirit would speak to him through his dreams so that he might know his future. He especially hoped the dreams would be of the sky or some type of bird because to dream of things above you meant a good life.

After three days, the Great Spirit did come to Falcon and reprimanded him for crying and complaining too much! Falcon now knew that if ever he was in danger of starvation during his lifetime, he could call on the Great Spirit and would be provided with food. He also knew that there was no reason to complain for he would never face death by starvation. He returned to his wigwam, a happy Ojibwa.

As a young teenager, Falcon proved to be a skilled hunter. Net-no-kwa had every reason to be proud of her new son. The first bear that he killed was the result of a dream of his mother. The Great Spirit had told her that a bear would be in a small round meadow with a path leading from it and that it could be killed the next day. Falcon's older brother ignored Net-no-kwa, but Falcon trusted her vision and found the bear exactly as she had described. By the age of 13, Falcon was providing for Net-no-kwa, as well as for her widowed daughter and three young children. As game animals became exhausted in one area, the family would move to another, demonstrating the importance of food in determining the lifestyle of the Ojibwa. The nomadic life was in some ways lonely, but in other ways it created a spirit of cooperation and sharing. Hunters would leave behind their traps for other hunters who might wish to use that area. There was no concern about theft among the Native Peoples themselves. The rightful owner would always be assured of his traps being returned to him. If a trap disappeared, it was an indication that white trappers had been in the vicinity.

When Falcon was about sixteen, he had an opportunity to go on his first skirmish against an enemy. As a young boy he had sat by the fireplace during feasts, enraptured by tales of bravery by the Ojibwa against their hated enemy, the Sioux. He had heard the tales of Bauswush and of Big Martin, two Ojibwa warriors who had fought against a vastly numerically superior Sioux raiding party. He was particularly stirred by the story of the "Big Ojibwa" who had demonstrated his heroism the previous summer.[7] Leading a band of 20 warriors, he tracked down over 200 Sioux. The small group fired on the fearsome enemy and fled, but the Big Ojibwa realized he was holding others back, for he had deliberately slowed down in order to embrace his destiny as told to him in a dream. Ordering them to continue he quietly sat down to wait for the war party of Sioux to reach him. The Sioux, suspecting some sort of a trap, cautiously surrounded the calm figure in the clearing. When they opened fire, he fell forward and the emboldened enemy rushed him. Suddenly, Big Ojibwa leaped up and shot the first Sioux to attack. He also managed to kill two others before a brutal blow that severed his head finally felled him. Even in his death, this brave warrior continued to smile, for his group had managed to escape. So overwhelmed were the Sioux with the strength of Big Ojibwa, that they paid him the ultimate tribute: the Sioux at a feast in his honour shared his heart, the symbol of his courage.

Like most other aspects of Ojibwa life, the war party was firmly directed by ritual. To the white man, it would appear disorganized and strange since no one was obliged to accompany the party and the chief exerted little real influence during the excursion. Anyone was free to return home at any time. Moreover, wars were not waged for land, power, conquest or wealth. Adventure, and sometimes revenge, were the motivating forces. Yet for the Ojibwa, there was an inherent logic and order. A newcomer to a war party would paint his face black and would always follow in the footsteps of the older warriors. He could not share his drinking vessel or knife with the veterans of previous war parties. At night camp, while the chiefs and older warriors sat at the entrance of the camp, facing the enemy, the younger warriors all huddled at the back of the compound, facing home.

For all of the warriors, there were firm rules during the march. No one was allowed to sit on the ground unless there was grass or brush beneath him. A warrior had to avoid getting his feet wet if at all possible and, if he was forced to go through a swamp, he was required to keep the rest of his clothes dry. No article could be stepped over by anyone other than the owner of the item. If this was done by accident, the owner had to throw the offender to the ground. Yet despite the rules, there was an element of individual freedom on a war party. In emergencies, all rules were disregarded, and at any time a warrior could turn around and go back to his family.[8]

It was evident that as Falcon was leaving his childhood and teenage years, he was in every way a man. It was natural that one day Net-no-kwa would say to him, "My son, you see that I am now become old; am scarce able to make you moccasins, to dress and preserve all your skins, and do all that is needful about your lodge. You are now about taking your place as a man and a hunter, and it is right you should have someone who is young and strong to look after your property and take care of your lodge." At this suggestion, Falcon acted in an unusual manner for an Ojibwa – he resisted the arranged marriage. Most partners had never spoken prior to their agreeing to live together. And most arranged marriages were accepted since either party could walk away from the relationship at any time. Moreover, Falcon could take additional wives as he got older.

Nevertheless, he balked at the formal ending of his childhood, feeling he was too young. What ultimately directed him into a marriage were the overtures of a celebrated Ojibwa chief called Wish-ko-bug (the sweet) who was a male, but decided he was a woman. Wish-ko-bug was about 50 years of age, and had lived with several husbands when he set his sights on Falcon. It was at this stage that Falcon determined that perhaps marriage with a younger girl was not so objectionable after all! Thus, he formally ended his Ojibwa childhood and ultimately would have three wives and several children.[9]

It would be pleasant to conclude Falcon's story at this juncture, but unfortunately, there are some sad postscripts to his life. While Falcon was working as a scout in the Red River territory in 1817, Lord Selkirk,[10] who had established a Scottish settlement in the area, realized that he was a white man and helped him contact his family in Kentucky. A

The piercing eyes and the proud aquiline nose of the adult John Tanner explain his receiving the Indian name of "Falcon." This photograph of a portrait of John Tanner is taken from the frontispiece of his book published in 1830. *Courtesy of the Toronto Reference Library (TRL) Baldwin Room.*

joyful reunion with his brother, stepmother and some nieces and nephews soon ended in the bitter realization that Falcon was not comfortable in the white society.

Yet tragically, John Tanner equally no longer felt comfortable in the Native society. For the next twenty years, Tanner lived in Sault Ste. Marie, lonely, friendless and held in contempt and fear by the white settlers. With the assistance of a local doctor, Tanner put his incredible saga into print in 1830 and in doing so, provided an eloquent voice for the dignity and worthiness of Native Peoples. At a time when the governments of North America were coming to regard these people as "savages" to be driven west of the Mississippi River, John Tanner presented a picture of a noble people of integrity and honour. His story, even today, provides us with invaluable insights into the lives and customs of the Native Peoples at the time of their initial contact with the white man. Tanner was to flee town of Sault under suspicion of murder in 1846, never to be seen again. (Sadly, an ex-army officer eventually confessed to the killing after a skeleton believed to be Tanner's was found in a swamp years later.) Yet the legacy of his life and his narrative will never die.

CHAPTER FIVE

Billy Green:
Hero of Stoney Creek

W hen Canada was attacked by the United States in what has become known as the War of 1812, she became engaged in what many consider to be one of our country's most important struggle. Over the next two centuries, thousands upon thousands more Canadians would sacrifice their lives in later conflicts. Canadian bodies would rest forever in Africa, Asia, Europe and India. Heroic Canadians would gather glory in the skies above Belgium, the mountains sloping down Korea, the swamps of Indochina, the deserts of the Middle East and the turbulent waters of three great oceans. Yet, for Canada, there remains but one war that was fought over the question of survival of our country – one war where defeat would mean that Canada could cease to exist. The War of 1812 not only assured that Canada would continue, it also gave our young community an early sense of identity. It was in this war that heroes and myths were born, and a pride of national spirit sprang forth during those early days of the nineteenth century when the country was threatened by a far more populous and far more powerful nation. Faced with the spectre of foreign invasion, Canadians were able to repulse the superior American forces, in victory after stirring victory. British North America emerged from the crucible of battle, not only victorious and proud, but as a community inspired and transformed – a collection of colonies (Nova Scotia, New Brunswick, Upper Canada and Lower Canada) had begun their march towards nationhood!

Yet there was no notion of optimism in Upper Canada when the war clouds were looming on the horizon. General Isaac Brock[1] had been sent over to govern the colony on behalf of the British Crown, taking over the position of provisional administrator of Upper Canada in 1811. He lamented what he saw as a collected sense of hopelessness and defeat in the face of a threatened U.S. attack. In a confidential letter to England prior to the war, Brock expressed dismay at the torpid attitude that infected the settlement. Upper Canada had been created in 1791 in response to the influx of some 10,000 refugees seeking safe haven in the Colony of Quebec from 1776 to 1784. Known as United Empire Loyalists, these individuals had rejected the American ideals and institutions in order to remain British subjects.[2] Enduring considerable hardship and sacrifice, these hardy pioneers created a new colony from the wilderness that was to become Ontario. Yet by 1812 their collective voice was no longer the voice of influence in the new colony. Later "land loyalists" – those Americans who settled in Upper Canada, not for loyalty nor for principles, but for cheap and fertile farmland – outnumbered the original Loyalist inhabitants, and radically altered the face of the young settlement. The earlier appeal for American settlers[3] made by Lieutenant Governor Simcoe, would come back to haunt the later governor, Brock. From his perspective. the possibility of survival if attacked by the Americans seemed bleak. Not surprisingly, boastful American politicians bragged of the prospect of an easy conquest of Canada. Thomas Jefferson[4] confidently asserted that the taking of the colony from British hands was "a mere matter of marching."[5] The situation did indeed appear hopeless when war broke out.

What rescued Upper Canada, of course, was the heroism of Isaac Brock, the valour of the local colonial militias, supplemented by British forces defending their soil, and the inestimable contributions of our First Nations allies and the Coloured Corps.[6] General Brock entered the War of 1812 leading 8,000 British and colonial soldiers against an army of 35,000 American troops. Brock had 20,000 militiamen to draw on against the hundreds of thousands that America could thrust into the fray. Yet, this remarkable general not only captured Fort Detroit from superior American forces without firing a shot, he also seized the initiative and rushed his regiment back to the Niagara area to engage the enemy in further battle.

Hopelessly outnumbered at Queenston Heights, Brock drew his sword and exhorted his men to follow him up the sharp incline. Despite being wounded, Brock continued to lead his men against insurmountable odds. Wounded a second time, this time fatally, Brock fell, but his inspiration remained.[7] Canadian farmers and shopkeepers rallied around Sir Roger Shaeffe, Brock's second-in-command, and with British soldiers and the Native and Coloured Corps support, they were able to hold Queenston Heights. Three hundred Americans lay dead or wounded and a further 1,000 were taken prisoner. About 1,000 British and local "Canadian" soldiers were killed, but Canada had its first important hero and its first important victory. For the first time, we realized that we could defeat the superior forces, that the invading Yankees could be repulsed and that there was a cause to rally to and a hero to emulate. A Canadian sense of identity was crystallizing. Throughout the Colony of Upper Canada, in particular, people responded to this awesome challenge with renewed vigour and a restored sense of purpose: We would not become Americans!

This resolve was already present in Billy Green's family. Adam Green had been born a British subject in New Jersey in 1739. During the American Revolutionary War, he had supported King George and assisted the British troops in their fight against rebellion. As a reward for his loyalty to the Crown, he was given 300 acres of land near Stoney Creek. In 1793, Adam and his wife Martha moved to Upper Canada with their nine children to begin a new life under the familiar British

Crown. One year later, a son Billy was born – the first white child to be born in Stoney Creek. Unfortunately it was a costly birth as Martha died from complications, but the new baby entered the world on February 4, 1794.

Growing up without the support of a mother in the expanding settlement, Billy was very much a loner; his nine siblings were all much older and many had already left home. Painfully shy, he preferred the solitude of the forests to the more boisterous human companionship. Billy loved to wander through the woods alone, forsaking the company of other children as he sought solace in becoming a part of the wilderness. In time, he taught himself to recognize all the roots, herbs and flowers in the area. He knew and could imitate the calls of any of the animals. He was able to distinguish tracks, climb trees and travel with ease through forest and swamp. At the time of Isaac Brock's exploits, Billy had already secured considerable local fame as "Billy the Scout" – an active, inventive, courageous youngster who thought nothing of hiking fifty kilometres a day through the hillside passes and secret trails that were mysteries to the other residents of Stoney Creek. This was the boy who not only thrilled at the heroism of Isaac Brock and cheered the victories of the Canadians in the first year of fighting, but also came to play the most crucial role in the story of our nationhood in the year 1813.

In 1813, the Americans launched a new offensive. The foreign troops had gone back home at the close of the first year of the struggle, but the following spring saw their return with an even greater determination to capture Upper Canada. The capital of the colony (York, now Toronto) had been seized and burned in late April and early May, and now the strategy was to sweep through the Niagara Peninsula and ultimately capture the entire heartland of Upper Canada. William Henry Harrison,[8] the formidable general of the invading army, had 4,500 Kentucky militiamen camping near Grimsby and readying for battle. Charged with the responsibility of defending this area, General John Vincent and Colonel John Harvey[9] had about 750 men at Burlington

Heights who were blissfully unaware of the powerful force so close to them. The fifth of June 1813 was to be one of the most important days in Canada's history.

For nineteen-year-old Billy, the day began at dawn when he heard rumours that many Americans were camping nearby. With his older brother Levi, the teenager set out on a day's adventure by making his way along the mountain towards the site of the enemy's camp.[10] It was a clear but muggy day and after a few hours, the heat and humidity started to slow Levi down to a more deliberate pace. He was beginning to doubt the truth to the rumours of an American presence when Billy pointed to the dust in the distance. Troops were marching towards them and judging by the dust it was a large force. Billy and Levi, from their vantage point higher on the mountain, greeted the marching militia with mock war cries. This, they knew, was the surefire way to strike terror into the hearts of the invaders. Nothing was stronger than the Americans' fear of Native Peoples during the war. Time after time, this ploy was used effectively by the British and Canadians against the Americans. The soldiers suddenly quickened their pace and the two brothers scrambled down the side of the mountain, enjoying the joke that they were playing. When Billy and Levi ventured too close, the American's realized the deception and shot at them as they scurried back up the mountainside, laughing and whooping.

As the Americans marched on, their ill humour increased and they actually opened fire on Levi's wife, Tina, who was holding her two-year-old daughter and watching the events from their farm on Stoney Ridge, atop the escarpment. Billy's harmless prank had become a declaration of war. He realized that it was now a question of survival. His initial levity turned to an even grimmer determination when he visited his sister, Kezia, in the early afternoon. Her husband, Isaac Corman, had been wounded in an earlier battle and was subsequently sent home. At this time he was recuperating on their farm, also on Stoney Ridge, mending his fence when the Americans marched past. One of the officers approached Isaac and started questioning him about the location of the British forces. Isaac's obvious reluctance to provide any information resulted in his arrest and detention by the Yankee troops. He was forced to accompany them on their march eastward. Billy learned this from his distraught sister and set off to rescue his brother-in-law. This decision marked the beginning of a remarkable series of events, circumstances and coincidences that seems almost providentially inspired and would secure for Canada one of the greatest heroes in the history of our country.

The American troops in Stoney Creek that day were Kentucky militia men, specifically chosen for their fighting spirit and their intense loyalty to the American general of all the forces in the western campaign, William Henry Harrison. Harrison was a Kentuckian, and a second cousin to the major who happened to be interrogating Isaac Corman. It is easy to imagine the major's astonishment when he discovered that his captive was not only Kentucky-born, but also a first cousin to Harrison! Isaac, as a young boy, had attended school and played with his mother's brother's son, William Henry Harrison. He was able to reveal details known only to family members. The Kentucky major was convinced that a horrible mistake had been made and ordered the release of his kin. He even gave Isaac the password – WIL HEN HAR – in order to safely get past the American lines.[11] A mistake had indeed been made that day, but it was committed by the major who not only released a staunch British patriot, but provided him with the key that Billy would employ so effectively later that night.

Meanwhile, Billy was continuing his search for his brother-in-law. Signalling his presence by whistling, Billy soon heard Isaac's owl-hoot reply and the two men conferred and decided on action. Isaac would return home and Billy would be responsible for warning the British troops who were resting several kilometres away. He borrowed Levi's horse "Tip" and "led him along the mountainside until I could get to the top. Then I rode him away around the gully when I dismounted and tied old Tip to the fence and left him there."[12] The rest of the journey was on foot and only Billy could have attempted it. By this time, it was growing dark and thunderclouds were threatening a storm over the area. "Billy the Scout" was the only inhabitant in the entire Niagara Peninsula who knew the terrain as well as other men knew their barnyards. Billy's years of navigating and exploring secret trails and passageways were about to be paid off in a miraculous journey for the British troops. Billy's long day would end about one hour before midnight when he stumbled into their camp at Burlington Heights.

The British troops were at first suspicious and concerned that Billy was an American spy. It took some fast and persuasive talking by Billy to save himself from being imprisoned or shot on the spot. Finally, he convinced Colonel Harvey that he was sincere and that he had valuable information to share. The British leaders, Harvey and Vincent, conferred briefly and immediately realized the full import of the military situation. They now knew that a massively superior American force was readying for an all-out assault that could turn the tide of the campaign and the war. They knew that the forces they had on hand were overwhelmingly outnumbered, and that no reinforcements could arrive in time to assist them.

On the other hand, they also soon understood that in Billy Green, they had a valuable resource. He represented the secret password that could get them past the American sentries and he represented the essential guide through the unknown wilds. If Billy were willing and able, he could lead the British forces on an all-night march against the enemy. But could they ask a youth who had been up for the last 17 hours, who had taken part in strenuous actions all day long, who had just completed a wearying journey, and who had already provided so much help to the grateful British? They had no choice. They had to use Billy or all would be lost. Colonel Harvey approached the exhausted young man and asked if he knew the land between Burlington Heights and Stoney Creek.

"Yes, every inch of it." Billy would be given a corporal's sword and put in charge of the safety of over 700 hundred soldiers. But the march had to begin immediately. With less than a half hour's rest for Billy, the troops set out for a surprise attack.

The night was dark, foggy and moonless. Angry flashes of heat lightning would light the sky for brief moments, but the most part of the journey had to be completed in pitch black. And it had to be completely quickly. Billy kept running back to urge the troops to march faster through the swamps and rocky ground. They had to arrive by daybreak. Passing over Red Hill Creek, three American sentries opened fire on them and they knew that the enemy was near. Behind every tree lurked possible death. Suddenly Billy saw an American sentry leaning against a tree. Whispering to Colonel Harvey, he asked what they should do. Harvey's reply: "Run him through."[13] For the fist time in his life, Billy used a weapon against another human, and with his new corporal's sword, silently dispatched the unsuspecting sentry.

The next sentry was by the church. Quietly, Billy moved forward and as he approached the Yankee, he gave the secret countersign. The sentry hesitated for one fatal moment, and Billy grabbed the sentry's gun and thrust his sword into him. He had taken two lives, but the enemy campfires were now in sight. Tomorrow Billy would feel remorse for the necessary killings, but that night there was not the time for the luxury of contemplation. Suddenly, the order was given, "Fix flint! Fire!" and Billy found himself in the middle of a bloody battle. He had led the British troops right into the centre of the unsuspecting Americans' campsite.

With fighting at such close quarter, it was a particularly gruesome and terrifying encounter. Billy's actual description is as accurate an account as any other: "We fired three rounds and advanced about one hundred yards. Then we banged away again. There was a rush in our middle flank. Their south flank charged, then came orders for our flank to charge. This is where we lost most of our men."[14]

The battle was fought in total darkness, resulting in considerable confusion by both sides. The British left flank held firm and about 500 Kentucky militiamen were put to flight. The British soon sensed that the Yankee centre flank was weak and vulnerable, but the main problem was how to capture the heavy American guns that were inflicting so much damage from their vantage point at the top of a high hill. Twenty volunteers charged up the hill and were successful in taking four of the six guns as well as about one hundred American prisoners.

Meanwhile, the American commander, General John Chandler had mistaken the British troops for his own and rushed into the centre in order to exhort "his" men to battle. The embarrassed American general was taken prisoner without any difficulty. Compounding the American problems was the loss of their second-in-command, General William Winder. He too had gotten lost and wandered into the centre of the British troops. A second eagle fell into the lion's den! On the British side, however, all was not going smoothly. General Vincent, without Billy the Scout at his side, wandered into the woods and got lost. He was not found until after daybreak and was both relieved and astounded when he learned that the Americans had been routed.

The Battle of Stoney Creek was a decisive British and Canadian victory. Although about 200 men were lost, the Americans lost their heavy artillery, two generals among the American prisoners and about 400 of their feared militiamen either dead or wounded. In a few hours, the perilous situation along the Niagara Peninsula had been reversed. Before the battle, the Yankees appeared to be in full possession of this vital land, outnumbering all the British and Canadian forces by better than three to one. The British commander was giving serious consideration to surrendering all of Upper Canada to the Yankees and pulling back to Kingston.[15] Suddenly, and irrevocably, the roles were reversed. The Americans were not only in retreat, they were in humiliating disarray. A jubilant Colonel Harvey was preparing an official report for the British government to inform them of the remarkable change of fortune. In his report, superior military strategy and bold action were highlighted. He neglected to mention the embarrassment of General Vincent and totally neglected the vital role of Billy Green in preventing the capture of Upper Canada. The

The Gage homestead (now Battlefield Museum) was the site of the
American encampment at the time of the Battle of Stoney Creek. After the
battle, the home became a hospital where Billy Green helped care for the
wounded soldiers. *Courtesy of the Archives of Ontario, RG 65-35-3, 11764-X3558.*

Americans, however, acknowledged his crucial role, referring to the
"treachery" of a spy who had secured their password and led the
British troops to the American encampment.

And the people of Stoney Creek knew what had happened. While
Billy remained at the Gage farmhouse[16] to help treat the wounded soldiers, the story of his heroism spread through the community and
within hours, Stoney Creek had its first local hero.

Billy eventually inherited his father's land and established a sawmill
near the scene of his glorious battle. He married Mary Summers,
became a widower and remarried a Mrs. Galbraith of Stoney Creek. In
all, he had six children and became a legend in the Niagara Peninsula.
Eventually, the Canadian government paid him a pension of about

twenty dollars a year in recognition for his services and erected a plaque acknowledging his contributions on the battlefield of Stoney Creek. For Billy, no thanks and no acknowledgement were necessary. When he died in his 84th year on March 5, 1877, he died with the corporal's lance still in his possession and the memory of an unforgettable experience emblazoned on his mind.

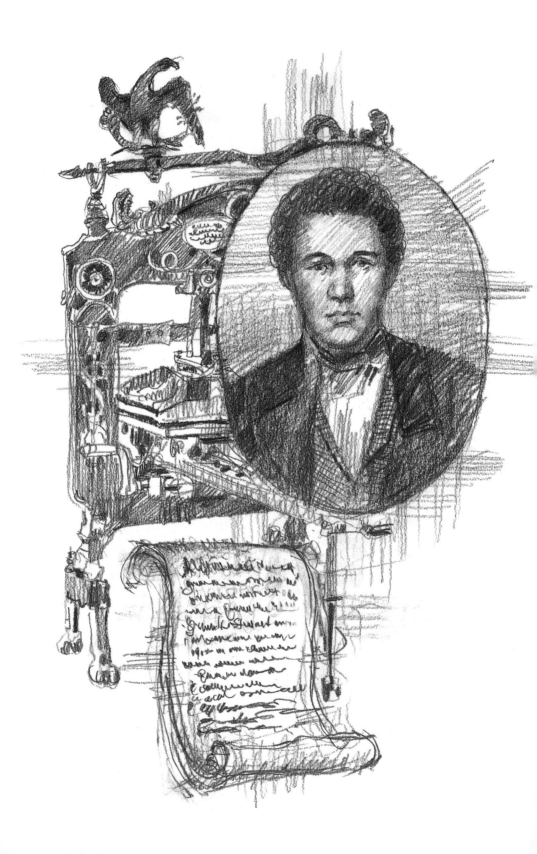

CHAPTER SIX

Osborne Anderson: Survivor of Harper's Ferry

O sborne Anderson grew up in turbulent times and his life was cut short far too early. Yet in his very brief existence, he demonstrated that the ordinary person can inject himself into the crucial issues of an era, interact with the great historical figures of the day and play a vital role in the unfolding pageant of history. Moreover, he was able to do this on a world stage that highlighted the fascinating interplay between events in America and the reactions to these events in Canada.

Osborne Anderson was of African descent, born in America in 1839. Fortunately for him, he was born north of the Mason-Dixon Line and that meant that he would not personally experience the most odious institution inflicted upon people in North America – slavery. The "abominable institution" was brought to the New World in the infancy of European exploration and development. The British raider Captain David Kirke,[1] owned a small six-year-old boy (later christened Olivier LeJeune) when he arrived in what is present-day Quebec City in 1628. LeJeune was the first slave to be brought to Canada.[2] By the time France surrendered New France to England after the Battle of the Plains of Abraham of 1759, she also surrendered about 5,000 slaves (both Black and Native) who now became part of the new English Colony of Quebec. After the American Revolution, hundreds of free Black Loyalists were joined by hundreds more Black slaves brought north by their United Empire Loyalist owners. Yet it would be a mistake to assert that slavery flourished in what was to become Canada in the same way as in the American South. A combination of climate and terrain made the deployment of large-scale slavery economically unfeasible and unnecessary. In most cases slaves in Canada were household slaves, farm hands and assistants in shops. In 1793, John Graves Simcoe, Lieutenant Governor of Upper Canada, became the first British official anywhere in the Empire to strike an initial blow against this wretched and reprehensible affront to human rights. Yet even this legislative act of 1793 would not be sudden and swift; no further slaves could be brought into Upper Canada (Ontario); children born of slaves in the province would gain their freedom at the age of 25; those presently "owned" by white masters in Upper Canada would die as property, not people. Feelings of moral outrage against slavery in the colony were not as strong as the influence of the existing slave owners such as Peter Russell, Administrator of Upper Canada following Simcoe's departure, and his sister Elizabeth. Their property would remain intact.[3]

Conditions in the southern United States were drastically different from the circumstances in Canada and the northern states. The plantation system had a firm grip on the economy, the politics, the society, and life in general in the Old South. Vast estates concentrated on one key export crop (primarily cotton, but also rice or indigo) and used hundreds of slaves on each plantation as an integral part of the process.[4] By 1860, there were 28 million people in the United States, and four million of them were owned as pieces of property and bound to perpetual servitude. A loathsome tragedy was inflicted upon an unsuspecting people. Hunted and ripped from their homeland, terrorized Africans were slapped into chains and dragged to the beaches to be bartered and sold. Chained together, they would lay in darkness during the six-week sea voyage. Their nightmare journey might be interrupted by being hauled on to the deck for a brief exercise period – still chained and with guns pointed at their bodies. Young girls would be hand-picked and delivered for the pleasure of the captain and officers. But other than that, the unfortunate victims lay in darkness, terror-stricken bodies pressed together, sometimes watching the person beside them retch and vomit while drawing his last breath. Twelve million souls were transported across the Atlantic Ocean to the Western Hemisphere before the abolition of the slave trade in 1820. Another six million never made it. Disease, starvation or suicide meant that one in three would never complete the nightmare voyage.[5]

Nor did arrival in the New World offer any ray of hope. Slave auctions were scenes of weird-looking people, wearing weird clothing and babbling in a weird tongue poking and prodding the frightened Africans. Teeth were examined, as lips were pried open and fingers thrust into the mouths. Bodies were stripped for closer examination and treated like packages being purchased. Instructions were given through gestures and mime for them to dance and shuffle to demonstrate their vigour and general health.

After the purchase, slaves were taken to their new home. Slave quarters on the plantation were often fetid, damp shacks. The bed might be a few pieces of plank; the pillow would be the sparse shirt worn during the day. Food would likely be scraps and, as long as there was daylight, time was spent bending over picking cotton. If there was a bright moon, the workday could extend into night. Sundays, if permitted by the master, was a day off, but every other day was spent under the malevolent gaze of the overseer. Slowing down meant a whipping. Talking back meant a whipping. Speaking to another slave meant a whipping. Trying to escape or being caught with reading material could mean dismemberment. A finger, a toe, perhaps a hand or foot, would be chopped off as a grim warning to others. Punishment could mean being sold down to the Deep South; children could be ripped from arms of slaves and given to someone as a wedding present; the white child a slave woman nursed and cared for along with her own children could grow up to be the cruel master who bartered in human flesh. There seemed no escape. There seemed no hope. The laws, culminating in the Fugitive Slave Act of 1850, were designed to perpetuate hell on earth. This act stated that any Black person anywhere in the United States could be declared a slave and returned to his "rightful" owner. If a slave catcher and another white person declared that you were a slave, you were. There was no trial by jury. There were no civil rights. Anyone assisting a slave could be punished by fines and imprisonment. The goal was to destroy every avenue of escape and end any hope for the enslaved souls.

This was the world into which Osborne Anderson was born. He grew up a free Black in Delaware, but after 1850, it was obvious that his freedom and his life were in peril. Along with Absalom Shadd and his family, young Osborne moved to Canada to help manage and work Shadd's two farms[6] near Chatham shortly after the passage of the notorious act.

It is interesting to note that the Fugitive Slave Act, designed to stamp out the last vestige of hope, added strength to two key anti-slavery movements that were both very prominent in Canada – the Abolition Movement and the Underground Railroad.[7] It was inevitable that an institution that slapped humanity and civilization in the face would be met with moral outrage. The Abolition Movement had long been a force of opposition to slavery; actually originating in the area that experienced this institution first-hand, the South. No thoughtful, no compassionate, no moral person could justify the continued existence of this evil war against human beings. Critics had long condemned the brutal, heartless system and even many of its apologists anticipated the eventual demise of slavery. Yet flaming emotions were stoked and rigidity on both sides became firmly ensconced. The Fugitive Slave Act was a part of the "Compromise of 1850"[8] which demonstrated just how inflexible feelings had become. The battle lines were clearly drawn and it was obvious that a middle ground did not exist. "A house divided cannot stand," but the house was divided before the secession of South Carolina and other slave states.[9] In both Canada and the United States, voices asserted that slavery must die.

Mary Ann Shadd of Chatham was one of the leading opponents of the odious practice.[10] The first female editor in all of North America, she used her paper, the *Provincial Freeman*, to articulate a powerful

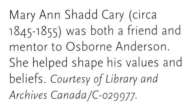

Mary Ann Shadd Cary (circa 1845-1855) was both a friend and mentor to Osborne Anderson. She helped shape his values and beliefs. *Courtesy of Library and Archives Canada/C-029977.*

indictment of slavery. Working beside this renowned writer was the young teenager, Osborne Anderson, who had left the farm to pursue his interest in printing. He had received an education in the United States (something denied to the Blacks born into slavery) and became the printer for the newspaper which was founded in 1853. His role in helping Mary Ann Shadd, allowed his education to continue. His views on women's rights, slavery, segregation, civil rights and a variety of other topics were honed and sharpened under her watchful tutelage. Soon, he too, became an ardent spokesperson on these issues.

Working with Mary Ann Shadd also provided Osborne with the opportunity of meeting key figures in the Abolition Movement. Although much of their energy was directed towards the role of Blacks in Canada, they could not ignore events unfolding south of the 49th parallel. Mary Ann herself had been educated by American Quakers and people like the Reverend William King,[11] Josiah Henson[12] and Henry Bibb[13] were a part of her life. George Brown,[14] editor of *The Globe* and a future father of Confederation, was perhaps among the most famous abolitionists in Canada, but countless other opponents of slavery from both sides of the border would drop into the printing shop in Chatham.

Working hand in glove in support of the Abolition Movement was the Underground Railroad. Particularly after 1850, fugitive slaves and free Blacks living under the shadow of the new law saw the North Star pointing to the final terminal in their escape to freedom. Abolitionists claimed that as many as 75,000 Blacks ultimately made it to Canada,[15] and although that figure is undoubtedly exaggerated, even the more realistic number of 40,000 to 50,000 is impressive. Land and jobs were plentiful during the economic boom years of the mid-century. Opportunities for an education and a new start were available for the eager Black immigrants. At that time, in Canada, a person of African descent could be a full citizen, enjoying all the rights and freedoms under the law that were exercised by his white counterparts. Small wonder it was that the arrival on British soil was such a powerfully emotional experience.

The Underground Railroad was a remarkable success story in the years before the Civil War. Free Blacks risked their lives and whites risked their personal freedom in their efforts to assist the fugitive slaves. Blacks born into slavery were not permitted to learn how to read or write. They were not permitted to congregate or communicate with one another. They needed a pass if they ever left their immediate area (which very, very few ever did). In geographic terms, they had no idea where they lived or where Canada was. They were told that Canada was a land of frigid cold and savage cannibals who ate slaves. Yet they nourished in their breasts a need to escape and many successfully accomplished this life-long dream. Slaves as old as seventy-seven and as young as suckling babies completed the hazardous journey. Spirituals sung by slaves in the fields were actually secret messages of escape and freedom.[16] Songs like "Steal Away," "Go Tell It On The Mountain," "Swing Low, Sweet Chariot," "Let My People Go" and "This Train's Bound For Glory" promised a better life and provided instructions on how to skilfully elude the hunters and bloodhounds.

People like Doctor Alexander Ross, born in Belleville, Upper Canada, would become famous for their acts of personal integrity and courage. Doctor Ross was a Canadian physician and naturalist who was acclaimed in many European nations for his scientific work. A world

John Brown, who, according to
Osborne Anderson, was "simply
the most spiritual man I have ever
met." *Courtesy of the Library of
Congress, Prints and Photographs
Division, LC-USZ-62-2472.*

famous ornithologist, he is said to have travelled throughout the plantations of the South, welcomed by the owners who were flattered that he had chosen their properties to observe birds and take notes on their patterns of existence. Unbeknownst to them, he was also meeting with pockets of slaves and helping them plan their escapes.[17]

On of the most famous of all the conductors on the Underground Railroad, leading dozens of slaves to freedom over numerous trips, was Harriet Tubman, known as the "Black Moses." Born into slavery in Maryland, she herself ran away when she learned she was going to be sold by her master. From her home in St. Catharines, Canada West, she would set out time after time to rescue more slaves. Despite a mind-boggling bounty of $40,000 for her capture, she was never caught and never lost a passenger during her secret journeys. Through swamps and forests, over mountains and fields, always travelling at night, she guided her passengers from station to station until they reached the land of freedom. It was small wonder that when slaves sang "Go Down Moses," while picking cotton under the watchful eye of the overseer, excitement shot through the fields like a jolt of lightning. This was the signal that Harriet Tubman was somewhere in the area.

Osborne Anderson knew of these people and helped write about them in the newspaper, The teenager's life was to change even more dramatically in late April of 1859, when John Brown arrived in the town of Chatham for a ten-day visit.

John Brown was arguably one of the most important Americans in the epic struggle against slavery prior to the Civil War.[18] A deeply religious man, he had taken an oath in church twenty years earlier to do all that he could to destroy the hated abomination of slavery. His religion was rigid and violent. He knew that he was God's agent of vengeance on earth and was fond of quoting his favourite section of the Bible: "Without the shedding of blood" there can be no remission of sin. Slavery and the slave owners were too evil and too engrained to go away peacefully. A prelude to John Brown's mission took place during the Kansas-Nebraska disputes in 1856. After 800 pro-slavers swept into the town of Lawrence, Kansas, to burn it down since it was one of the stations of the Underground Railroad, Brown retaliated with his band of followers by dragging five supporters of slavery from their beds and hacking them to death. "Bleeding Kansas" was John Brown's statement that Abolition was not a philosophy. It was a war.

Waging this war was his obsession. His long white beard added to his aura as a Biblical prophet and the fire burning in his eyes was a warning to his enemies and a beacon for his followers. One year after Kansas, he came to Canada to enlist Harriet Tubman's support in his secret plan. He needed her secret routes, names of supporters and her expertise for his scheme. Harriet Tubman indicated that if she were a man, she would have joined his crusade. Then he moved to Boston to apprise Frederick Douglass[19] of his mission. Again, this former slave, charismatic and eloquent, was swayed to Brown's side. He did not join Brown's "army" but always envied Brown's total commitment: "I live for the slaves; he dies for them."[20] Finally, late April 1859 brought him to his next-to-last stop – Chatham. It was here that he secured Mary Ann Shadd's assistance in the event that was a portend of the "irresistible conflict." The Shadd family housed John Brown and gave him free use of the printing press to enable him to spread his message to other supportive communities. Mary Shadd, like Harriet Tubman, would have joined the enterprise, had she been a man. Osborne Anderson was a man – a very young man – and he was a convert to John Brown's mission.

Brown's plan was simplicity itself. Inspired by the successful Black communities in Ontario (such as Josiah Henson's Dawn Settlement, Henry Bibb's Wilberforce Settlement and the world-famous Buxton Mission School of the Reverend King), Brown desired to impose these models on the evil slave owners. He would raise a small, select band of fighters who would serve as the vanguard of revolution. They would descend on the small town of Harper's Ferry, Virginia, seize the federal arsenal there with its fortune in army supplies and conduct raids on neighbouring plantations. The stronger slaves (both physically and morally) would join John Brown's army of avenging angels. Harriet Tubman and other conductors would lead the other slaves to freedom via the Underground Railroad. Slavery would be destroyed, and ultimately a new, Black nation would rise in the mountains of western Virginia.

John Brown spent his days in Chatham, holding meetings, conducting military drills, drawing up a constitution for his new nation and consolidating his plans. During that time, he demonstrated with resounding clarity those qualities which made him a feared fanatic and lunatic to his enemies and a devout agent of God to his followers. And there was no question as to which group Osborne Anderson belonged. Brown was impressed with the young printer and Anderson was equally overwhelmed by the compelling crusader from the States. As Anderson himself asserted, "...I was willing to give my life to the cause..."[21] In Brown, he saw a "strong and commanding intellect, high-toned morality and inflexibility of purpose...and a profound and holy reverence for God."[22] In John Brown's family and in John Brown's presence, there was true brotherhood of humanity. "Every heart beat in harmony for the suffering and pleading slave"[23] and hateful prejudice withered and died. Osborne Anderson was a believer and disciple, but he was also important to John Brown and the others. Recognizing his intellectual prowess, his total commitment and his courage and vitality, the others elected him as a congressman in the new provisional government which would lead to the Black nation. He became one of only two Canadians to be chosen to join John Brown's select band of fewer than 20 men to carry the war into the heart of slavery – into Virginia.

On Sunday, October 16, 1859, John Brown led five Blacks and sixteen whites, plus a wagon with 200 rifles, 200 pistols and 1,000 pikes, into Harper's Ferry. The group quickly seized control of an engine house and sent a small band out to proselytize the slaves on a neighbouring plantation and foment an uprising. From this point on, the plan collapsed. An outraged town took up arms and fired at the small group holed up in the engine house. Ten men, including two of John Brown's sons, were shot dead. The governor of Virginia called for the U.S. Marines, which were dispatched from Baltimore by train. This contingent of 90 soldiers, led by the up-and-coming Lieutenant Colonel Robert E. Lee, captured most of the remaining men. Brown himself almost welcomed capture and execution as the second best alternative to his original goal. As he was led to his gallows on December 2, 1859, less than two months after his initial attack, he slipped a note to his guard which stated: "the crimes of this guilty land will never be purged away but with blood."[24]

John Brown was the point of no return in the "irrepressible conflict." For the South, this was the realization of their greatest concern – the enemy abolitionists moving from the North into their homeland, and the spectre of their greatest fear – the rising in arms of millions of slaves, bent on revenge for the generations of injustices inflicted upon them. For the North, the death of Brown represented a strike at the forces of rightness. Henry David Thoreau compared Brown's hanging to the crucifixion of Christ, and Brown became immortalized in the rhyme that was the marching song of the Union soldiers during the Civil War. "John Brown's Body" was set to the tune of the "Battle Hymn of the Republic" and the greatest martyr of the Abolition Movement was born.

Even the death of John Brown did not end Osborne Anderson's story. He was one of only two men who were able to escape the capture as Brown had sent him on a mission just prior to the attack of the Marines. Using the redoubtable skills of the great conductor, Harriet Tubman, he followed her route to safety. Hiding in haystacks, travelling under turnips on wagons, using the stars and moss growing on the north side of the trees, he travelled by night. Miraculously, he made it back to Canada. His story had to be told and, with the help of Mary Ann Shadd, he wrote *A Voice from Harper's Ferry*. It was published in Boston in 1861, the same year that the Civil War broke out. Along with 50,000 other Canadians, Osborne Anderson once again marched south – this time as a soldier fighting in the Civil War. He became a non-commissioned officer in the epic struggle to destroy the institution that he hated with all his passion. His life was dedicated to wiping the blot of slavery from the brow of humanity and he would willingly die to help achieve it.

Sadly, Osborne Anderson died alone and penniless in the City of Washington in 1872. He had settled there after the war, but there was no employer willing to hire this educated, talented, experienced Black man. When Mary Ann Shadd heard about her protégé and friend, she was so distressed that she tried to raise money for his burial. Despite her efforts, she was unable to secure enough funds and Anderson's body lay unclaimed in a vault for several months before being consigned to a pauper's grave.[25] It was an unfitting and unfair finish for an individual who had left such an indelible imprint on the annals of both Canadian and American history. His idealism, his selflessness, his heroism deserved better.

CHAPTER SEVEN

Anna Swan: Nova Scotia's Giantess

On August 7, 1846, Alexander and Ann Swan greeted the birth of their third child with unconcealed delight. She was a beautiful girl with an ivory complexion, perfect features and lovely dark hair. Moreover, in an era of tragically high infant mortality, Anna appeared to be a robust and healthy baby. The parents had already lost their two previous babies to the ravages of primitive frontier life, so there was considerable relief at the sight of such a solid child. That night was an occasion for thanksgiving and celebration in the stolid Scottish farming community of Nova Scotia. Neighbours, friends and well-wishers gathered at the Swan farmhouse to share in the family's happiness and good fortune. This was a close-knit collection of pioneers who worked together, suffered together and celebrated joyous events together. Everyone in the small village felt genuine happiness that the Swan's good fortunes seemed to be moving upwards.

Not just for the Swans, but for all of Nova Scotia, these were prosperous times. It was the "Golden Age of Sail" when naval powers such as Great Britain were turning their attention from traditional heavy construction material like oak to the lighter timber of spruce and pine. The

Baltic Blockade, emanating from the Napoleonic Wars, put timber from Scandinavian countries out of reach. England then turned to her North American colonies to avail herself of the wealth of timber to be found there. The advantages that Canadian lumber had in naval construction made our ships world-renown for their beauty and their speed. Gnarled old sailors would turn poetic as they described the "ballerinas of the sea."[1] Hard-nosed businessmen would get misty-eyed after studying the ledgers and realizing how inexpensive it was to construct a "Bluenose Fleet." Gold in remote areas like California, Australia and South Africa beckoned to thousands of fortune seekers, while catastrophes such as the Irish Potato Famine and the Highland and Lowland Clearances of Scotland created generations of immigrants. By the middle of the nineteenth century, the increasing demand for ships built in the Maritimes had turned Nova Scotia into one of the jewels in the British Empire's crown. By 1850, Halifax, a city of 20,000, had become the commercial and military capital of this thriving region in British North America.

It was for a greater share of this prosperity that Alexander Swan moved his family to New Annan in central Nova Scotia. Although Swan was an established farmer, he was also a man of vision and ambition, not for himself, but for his growing family. Alexander dreamt of comfort and wealth. The timber of the Cobiquid Mountains represented an untapped potential for some enterprising entrepreneur. A family could supplement its income by moving to the local village and exploiting the natural resources of the area. It seemed almost sinful not to take advantage of God's gifts to His People. As a result, a not-so-tiny four-year-old child found herself in a new home in the village near the forested mountains.

Already, it was evident that Anna was not a normal girl. She weighed close to 100 pounds and had the wrists of an adult male. Her height at this age was starting to rival her mother's five feet, two inches. In hindsight, it seems obvious that Anna would never have enjoyed a normal childhood. Although her family loved her, doted on her and protected her, she could not share comfortably the social life of the neighbours. Too young to join the ladies in the quilting bees or corn-husking activities, she appeared too big to fit into the carefree play of other youngsters of her age. Anna was an outsider before she was old enough to enter school. Her size came to be an embarrassment for her parents and a torture to her! The Swan family (eventually there would be 13 children) was close-knit and loving, and Anna's parents were demonstrably proud as well as mildly embarrassed by Anna. Yet even in this refuge from a thoughtlessly cruel world outside of her family, Anna was aware of her differences. The family home was a simple one-and-a-half storey dwelling. It was a sparse structure that was ill-equipped to accommodate a "giantess." While other members of the family sat on chairs around the table at mealtime, Anna sat rigidly on the floor with her back against the wall. Indeed, by the time she was a teenager, sleeping on a bed several feet too short and stooping constantly to pass under doorways seriously impaired Anna's health. At the age of 14, Anna was seven feet tall and still growing.[2] Photographs of the day show her towering over her diminutive parents.

For Anna, though, the home provided relief from the pains suffered outside. When she started school, Anna was a bright girl who was anxious to learn. Unfortunately, life in the classroom was a humiliating ordeal. A special high stool and raised table assisted her in the schoolwork but did little to improve her social adjustment. Other children in the class could not understand why the biggest student was working at the same level as the youngest ones. The stares and giggles in the classroom were replaced by taunts in the schoolyard as unfeeling youngsters delighted in teasing the awkward outsider. Going and coming from school remained an agony for Anna as unthinking faces stared at her with curiosity, loathing and contempt. Anna knew she was different, but she could not adjust to being punished for it. It was impossible to convince the seven-year-old that she was not somehow to blame for the disgusted and disbelieving expressions. Even on the streets of New Annan, Anna came to be at first embarrassed and later annoyed at the rude comments and questions. Strangers gave little consideration to the turbulent emotions of a young girl growing up in a hostile environment.

For Alexander Swan, these too were troublesome times. Somehow, the anticipated wealth did not come. The family income was growing with the supplement earned by selling timber from his property to the local mill, but so too were the number of children. In addition, the special needs of his eldest daughter created additional expenses. Alexander remained a man of vision, hope and ambition, but God's gifts did not produce the anticipated result. It was in the face of this frustration that Alexander reappraised his beloved Anna. At the time, she was four years of age and the pride of her father's existence. The thought occurred to him that Anna too was a special gift from God, a natural thought that would readily come to mind in this deeply religious Christian community. What would be the harm in travelling to Halifax and through Nova Scotia to put Anna on display? The child would be too young to realize the implications of the tour and the customers. She could be assured that people were coming to see her because she was special – for special she was! If people are going to stare at his daughter, let them pay for the privilege. By March of 1851, at the age of four, Anna was being exhibited in towns throughout the colony. Harnessed to her father's dreams, she sat in tents and halls in village after village.

"Pay your admission and step inside to secure a glimpse of the 'Infant Giantess.' " These words rang and reverberated in Anna's ears as she was placed on display. No matter how many curious eyes stared or rude mouths gaped open, Anna could not get used to the attention. Very quickly excitement in anticipation of a new adventure turned to bitter humiliation for the sensitive child. Mercifully, the ordeal ended at the end of summer when her father brought Anna home as the profits did not materialize as he had hoped. The bruised youngster returned to the security of her quiet home.

Childhood for Anna would have more than its share of unhappy memories. Yet Anna was strong and able to survive the pains she encountered. At the age of fourteen, Anna had six younger brothers and sisters of normal size, while she was seven feet tall and just entering puberty. It was around this time that she left home to go to Truro, Nova Scotia, in order to attend classes for teachers. Anna knew she was different, but was determined to carve out a normal career for herself. Perhaps her future was in teaching.

But again, in the midst of strangers, she endured humiliations and hardships. Travelling to school through back alleys and little-known routes, Anna did her work on a specially constructed desk. In the safe refuge of the classroom, Anna could cope. It was in the open streets that the experiences overwhelmed her. The effort finally ended in an unhappy defeat for Anna when she left early and she returned home even more uncertain about her future.[3] There appeared to be no market for a seven-and-one-half foot burden on those she loved.

The Maritimes during this time period were a part of Britain's North American colonies and possessions that primarily represented, in terms of population, little more than a rural collection of farms, villages and frontier settlements, despite the timber resources. For the most part, the colonies remained self-contained backwards communities with scattered pockets of urban bustle. Maritimers were aware of unusual discoveries and developments in the other colonies – oil in Canada West, Métis discontent in the Prairies, camels being imported to the West Coast to travel the gold routes of the Caribou Trail. Generally, however, people living inland, were too preoccupied with their harsh existence on the farms to take notice of the events of the day. Men laboured long hours ripping out stumps, clearing swamps and scratching a living from the land. Women worked hard and died young as a result of backbreaking chores assigned to the "weaker sex." Local politicians did not imagine that in a few short years all of these independent communities would be forged into a single nation that would stretch from sea to sea.

Indeed, the great political concern of the day was not in British North America, but in the carnage of the American Civil War to the south.[4] As brother was pitted against brother in a senseless bloodletting, there was a fear that events might spill over into own backyards. It seemed inevitable by the summer of 1862 that England's colonies would be sucked into the nightmare. Already, British troops had been rushed across the Atlantic to strengthen the local militia at Halifax. Abraham Lincoln, President of the United States, regarded the Confederate spies and agents from the South who had relocated in Canada as thorns in the Union side. Congressmen in Washington, DC, exhorted Lincoln to unleash the Union army so that it might sweep

Phineas T. Barnum became a sponsor, employer, friend and exploiter of Anna Swan. *Courtesy of the Library of Congress, Prints and Photographs Division, LC-BH82-4961.*

northward to destroy the hotbeds of political intrigue. With the a continent in such turmoil, people sought diversion from the tragedies unfolding in the daily newspaper headlines.

Phineas T. Barnum, the master showman, was a genius in providing this diversion. His protégé, Tom Thumb,[5] his New York museum of unusual phenomena and his later touring circus would all thrill a world hungry for human interest stories. During that summer of 1862, he was preparing to introduce his latest acquisition to his collection of "freaks and oddities" – Anna Swan, a painfully shy 16-years-old, was about to be thrust into international notoriety.

For Anna, P.T. Barnum represented a solution to her personal dilemma, yet it must have been a solution that was a two-edged sword. Being on display would assure Anna of a secure future for herself and her family. It would end forever the dreaded uncertainty of what lay ahead. But it would also be the final admission that she was not normal and could never live a life of blissful obscurity. The public spotlight, which she had grown to despise, would shine forever on her.

Barnum described his first encounter with Anna Swan in his autobiography:

> ... She was the tallest of women. I first heard of her
> through a Quaker who came into my office one day
> and told me of a wonderful girl, seventeen years of age,

who resided near him at Pictou, Nova Scotia, and was
probably the tallest girl in the world… I at once sent an
agent who in due time came back with Ann Swan. She
was an intelligent and by no means ill-looking girl, and
during the long while she was in my employ she was
visited by thousands of persons.[6]

Exactly what Barnum had in mind for Anna Swan was evident soon
after she arrived with her parents in New York. A visit to the museum
owned by Barnum revealed to her the role she was to play. In all, the
showman had over 600,000 exhibits. Anna's place was to be on the third
floor in the "Large Curiosities" section. Competing with her for the customers' attention were such notable displays as an African who invented
a weed that "turned all coloured folks white;" young Herman who could
inflate his chest from 38" to 60"; Madame Josephine Fortune Clofullia,
the bearded lady; Chang and Eng, the Siamese Twins; the fat lady and
the fat boy; the albino family; the monkey man and the living skeleton.
In addition, the museum boasted of important items like the largest
ball of earwax in the world and the contents from a shark's stomach.[7]
And this was to become home for the teenager from Nova Scotia!

Yet even in her new home, misfortune continued to stalk Anna. On
November 25, 1864, fire struck Barnum's museum, entrapping the
frightened 18-year-old. The story behind the fire is as incredible as the
story of the fire itself.

Jacob Thompson was a wealthy lawyer, a Congressman and a former
cabinet minister in President James Buchanan's administration.[8] He was
also a Confederate spy located in Toronto during the American Civil War.
In 1864, he and a group of Confederate agents were given $1 million by
Jefferson Davis[9] in a plot to destroy New York City and instigate riots
against Abraham Lincoln's re-election. Led by a Captain Robert Cobb
Kennedy, the agents were to set the nineteen most important hotels in
the city ablaze.[10] The plot failed, but a fire set in the morning did
spread to P.T. Barnum's Museum of Freaks and Oddities, attracting
thousands of spectators.

A portrait of Mr. and Mrs. Van Buren Bates, both of whom were eight feet, one inch tall and weighed five hundred pounds (circa 1878-1888). Shown here with a friend, Anna and Martin found it difficult to adjust to and live in a "normal" society. *Courtesy of Library and Archives Canada/PA-051546.*

Whether this story of the plot is true or apocryphal, the havoc that resulted from the fire is undeniable. According to eyewitness accounts, the main entrance to the museum was thick with smoke. Firemen rescued some of the patrons by ladder, but Anna Swan appeared to be too formidable for even the Fire Department to assist. Finally, six men managed to subdue and sedate the hysterical teenager and rescue her from the blazing inferno.

Before Anna had sufficiently recovered from the first tragedy, a second fire struck the museum. In July of 1865, the New York Fire Department was again called to an alarm on Broadway Avenue near the Astor Hotel. This time, Anna Swan was trapped on the third-floor staircase, overcome by the smoke and virtually unconscious. There appeared to be no escape for the young performer as the stairs were engulfed in flames and in danger of collapsing. Her friend, Isaac Sprague, the living skeleton, had remained with her as long as he dared, but eventually he had to flee for his own safety. In desperation, someone remembered a giant derrick, which was being used at a nearby construction site. As the crowd gathered in wonderment at the spectacle, the derrick was erected along the museum wall. With 18 men firmly grasping one end, a harness was secured around Anna and she was swung over the cheering crowd. Gently, she was lowered to the ground. Her entire life savings were destroyed in the fire, but Anna Swan emerged unharmed.[11]

The remainder of Anna's brief life was a curious blend of triumph and tragedy. Barnum closed his museum forever after the second fire and for a time, the situation confronting Anna was grim. Again, P.T. Barnum came to her rescue with an offer to tour Europe along with other members of his entourage. The ship set sail on April 22, 1871, and was noteworthy for a couple of important episodes in Anna Swan's life. In June she had the opportunity of being presented to Queen Victoria and was privileged with a private reception with His Royal Highness, The Prince of Wales. More significantly, on June 17 at St. Martin's-In-The-Field Cathedral in London, Anna Swan was married to Captain Martin Van Buren Bates – the Kentucky Giant, whom she met while on the European tour. The ceremony was attended by hundreds of curious onlookers. Even Queen Victoria had sent a wedding gift to the two giants she had recently entertained. The wedding itself was a gala show and business event, with reporters jostling one another for a better description of the activities. Yet, along with the circus atmosphere came a curious calm to Anna. For the first time since her childhood, she could dream of a private life. When the tour was completed, she and her husband could retire to relative obscurity. They would seek out a sleepy little hamlet in middle America and be forgotten by all.

To some extent, Anna did realize her dream. She and Captain Bates settled in a quiet town in Ohio and enjoyed a degree of contentment that Anna had long forgotten. She had become pregnant shortly after her marriage and, in the following year, Anna gave birth to an eighteen-and-one-half pound girl. Unfortunately, the child was stillborn. A new year, 1878, also saw Anna give birth again. In January, a boy was born, weighing almost 24 pounds! Again, tragedy would not leave Anna and the youngster died within hours.[12] Life could still dole its cruelties to the vulnerable giantess. At last, on August 5, 1888, Anna was beyond tears. At the age of 41, she quietly surrendered to death in her sleep. Doctors stated that her heart gave out – weary from carrying the large woman for a lifetime, but also perhaps weary of the grievous pains inflicted by a harsh world!

CHAPTER EIGHT

Fred Bagley: Youngest Mountie

On September 22, 1858, at a remote military outpost in St. Lucia, the British West Indies, a baby boy, Fredrick Augustus Bagley, entered this world. The son of an Imperial Officer in Her Majesty, Queen Victoria's army, young Fred would spend his early years moving from posting to posting. It was not until 1868 that Fred Bagley Sr. retired from military life and moved his family to a permanent residence in the fledgling young Dominion of Canada.

Growing up in Toronto, the youthful Fred found few things more pleasing than curling up under his covers and thrilling to the exciting exploits of his favourite author, James Fenimore Cooper.[1] The pages would leap to life with stories of noble Indians, brave white men and tales of courage and danger. Dreamily, Fred would be transported to a heroic age that seemed to be fast vanishing. Little did the youngster realize that in five short years, he would embark on his own adventure that would surpass everything that he had devoured as a wide-eyed youth. At the age of fifteen, Fred would march into Canada's vast untamed wilderness. There he would meet the notorious bank robber, Frank James. There he would come face to face with Sitting Bull, fresh

77

from the Battle of the Little Big Horn (Custer's Last Stand).[2] Crowfoot and Poundmaker,[3] two of the most famous First Nations men ever to cross the annals of Canadian history, as well as countless rogues and outlaws, were to become a part of Fred's life. For Fred was the youngest recruit of one of the most famous symbols of law and order that was ever created – the Canadian Mounties then known as the North West Mounted Police and later renamed the Royal Canadian Mounted Police.

The American West of the 1870s was a land filled with gunslingers and outlaws. It was the land of Billy the Kid, Geronimo, Belle Starr, Wild Bill Hickok and the shootout at the OK Corral. But perhaps the most hated, the most contemptible and the most dangerous of all the thugs and brigands to ply their trade in the wild West were the "Whisky Traders." These jackals brought their guns and their firewater, a deadly combination of cheap booze, chewing tobacco, molasses, soap, red ink and hot pepper to establish a lucrative trade with the Native Peoples. Disregarding the fatal consequences, they supplied enough booze to the Natives to reduce them to abject objects of desperation. They would trade anything – their furs, their houses, their wives and daughters – to gain another bottle of the potent poison. Drunken, they would fight and kill and sell their souls for another drink. The whisky traders transformed the land into a powder keg wherever they went.

And now, unfortunately, the stain was spreading into Canada. By early 1873, more than twelve forts were set up on Canadian soil by renegade whisky traders from Montana. Colourful names such as Robbers' Roost, Fort Standoff, Fort Slideout and the notorious Fort Whoop-Up, provided a graphic commentary on the outlaw establishments. "Rotgut" whisky was traded for quality furs and the tragic result usually led to mass orgies followed by mass passing out. As one missionary reported, "Within a few miles of us, forty-two able bodied men were victims among themselves, all slain in drunken rows."[4] Compounding the tragedy being foisted on the Canadian Plains Natives was a smallpox epidemic that swept across the prairies in 1869 and 1870 and the ruthless fur trappers who spread strychnine-laced buffalo carcasses across the land to poison wolves for their fur. A proud people were being reduced to debasement. The mighty Blood, Cree, Assiniboine, Piegan, Sarcee and

Blackfoot Nations were fighting their last futile battle. As the great leader Crowfoot sadly lamented: "We are powerless before this evil."⁵

The powder keg exploded in May of 1873 with the Cypress Hills Massacre. Ten wolf hunters from Montana had their horses stolen one night on the Prairies. Outraged, they stormed into an Assiniboine camp of about 40 lodges demanding the return of their steeds. The Assiniboine, under Chief Little Soldier, said that the Cree had taken the horses and tempers seemed soothed. A night of drinking and boisterous campfire stories followed and the situation was evidently resolved. Yet tragedy struck in the morning when words turned harsh and one of the hunters opened fire. What followed was a massacre of 36 Natives (with only one dead hunter) that electrified the Canadian populace back East. The prime minister of Canada, John A. Macdonald, had just passed a bill on May 23, creating a force of "Mounted Police" (the name had been changed from the original "Mounted Rifles" to placate the American government, thus replacing the spectre of soldiers with the more benign image of a group of men monitoring the safety of the region). As always, Macdonald remained vigilant of the persisting American threat to the Canadian West.

Seven hundred and seventy-six thousand, seven hundred square kilometres of land seemed in danger of falling into a replication of the American Wild West, with the American desperadoes and seething Natives heading for a confrontation. This immense tract of land, almost the size of all of Europe, had few settlers and no railway (despite the promise to British Columbia in 1871) and was facing the sorry prospect of falling under American domination. Action was needed immediately, and the response was the decision to raise a force of 300 men who would be paid 75 cents a day to patrol the "Great Lone Land," bring Canadian law, order and good government to the wilderness and preserve the region for the new Dominion. The Mounties were born.

And what a seductive siren song this new force presented to a young impressionable teenager. Dreaming of action in the land of buffalo, romancing beautiful Indian princesses, fighting American desperadoes and riding across the Prairies on his buckskin mustang, Fred knew he had to be a part of this grand adventure. But his father knew he was too young to join up. Fred, however, was determined and a compromise was reached with Colonel George Arthur French. Not only was French the head of this new police force, but he was also an old army buddy of Fred's father. Fred could join for six months maximum as a trumpeter. After his taste of excitement was satisfied, Fred would return home. Neither father nor son knew on that fateful day in May 1874 that Fred was embarking on a career that would see him serve in the Mounties until the turn of the century when he would enlist to fight in the Boer War in South Africa.

At age 15 Fred Bagley was the youngest member of the famous group of 300 who took part in the "Long March" on their way to tame the West. Excitement was hanging in the air that late spring morning when this select group gathered at Toronto.[6] Bartenders, schoolteacher, telegraphers and lumberjacks – they came from all walks of life, and even included the son of famous English novelist, Charles Dickens. Yet none stood more proudly than young Frederick Augustus Bagley, resplendent in his spanking "new uniform of scarlet cloth, Norfolk jacket, blue cloth white banded "pill box" cap, overalls of the same colour and material with double white cloth stripes down the outside seams."[7] Clutching his brand new bugle and brand new trumpet, Fred stood proudly at attention as he posed for a photograph to give to his family. As Fred said, "A feeling of intense elation buoyed us up as our train pulled out of the station, and we started on our way West bound for the Great Adventure."[8] Sixteen officers, 201 men and 244 horses, along with nine boxcars of supplies left that Toronto station. Bagley's group of 150 men were bound for Detroit, Chicago and St. Paul and finally to Fargo, North Dakota, where the march was to begin. Once they set foot on American soil when they got off the train at Fargo, the uniforms had to be removed so as not to offend the American hosts.[9] In Chicago, Fred came face to face with his first figure from the pages of the pulp fiction novels that he had devoured just weeks before. Frank James, brother of Jesse the convicted bank robber and armed desperado, was sitting on a verandah with his feet propped up, idly whittling on a piece of wood while he eyed the raw greenhorns.[10] Civilization had truly been left behind and the long march was about to begin!

The first leg of the march became 258 kilometres on horseback from Fargo, to the newly established Fort Dufferin on the Red River just over the border on the Canadian soil of Manitoba. For five exhausting days reveille would jar Fred out of a sound sleep at 4:00 a.m. and push him into the mind-numbing and body-wearying tedium of endless riding through barren land. Finally on June 19 at 4:00 p.m., the troops arrived at Fort Dufferin and it seemed like a brief respite might be in order for the worn-out men and horses.

Nature had a different idea. Fred was lying in his tent about 8:00 o'clock the next evening, too tired to even turn the pages of his beloved *The Last of the Mohicans*, when an explosion jolted him out of his cot. Then the heavens opened and water came cascading down on hapless recruits. Rivers of water poured through the tents as lightning illuminated the great Western sky and thunder pounded out its majestic symphony. The tents were first flattened, then swept away by the powerful wind. The thunder was so loud that shouting officers could not be heard more than one foot away. So heavy was the rain that Mounties discovered their boots were filled with water as they hastily dressed. But at this time, Fred was thinking not of his own discomfort, but of the horses. Although he was the youngest recruit in the force, ironically Fred was one of the most expert horsemen. So skilled was he, that he actually gave lessons to some of the city-bred Mounted Police recruits who had never ridden in their lives. His knowledge of horses caused him to look towards the corral, where his worst fears were being realized. In a panic, the horses had stampeded and broken the fence. Two hundred and fifty of the three hundred horses had galloped off in a terrified frenzy, leaving only a few behind for the Mounties to saddle up and begin the search for the runaways. It is a testament to Fred and the others that they were able to round every single horse, save one, even though some had scattered as far as 80 miles back into American Territory. There can be no doubt that Fred earned his 75 cents that day when he rode back to camp after midnight "fast asleep in the saddle, and had to be lifted off and put to bed. Not much Fenimore Cooper romance about this, but rather strenuous for a slip of a boy as I am."[11]

A few days later, Fred's expertise as a horseman was again put to the test when he spotted the horse of his dreams. A beautiful buckskin mustang right out of the pages of one of Fenimore Cooper's novels was

The deceptively innocuous-looking Fort Whoop-Up, often the scene of rampant lawlessness in the Canadian West, as photographed by George Mercer Dawson in 1881. *Courtesy of Library and Archives Canada/PA-051172.*

haughtily pawing the ground in front of him. The only problem was that it belonged to a Mountie in B Troop. Fred offered the other Mountie 50 cents to go and get a drink while he minded the horse. Off went the thirsty Mountie, and off went Fred in the other direction, back to D troop with his proud new steed. At the end of the day Fred was a horse thief, but also the owner of his beloved "Old Buck," who would share his adventures for years to come. The other Mountie was furious but had no comeback. He dared not complain because he would get into trouble for drinking while on duty during the day. Helplessly he realized that he had been buffaloed by the youngest member of the forces.

The march continued. The month of July was sweltering hot as the men rode forward. Grasshoppers filled the air and floated in drinking ponds, forming a thick scum over the surface. The mosquitoes and blackflies had been a persistent nuisance, swarming around in clouds, but the grasshoppers were even worse. Millions crossed the Prairies like a dust storm. They covered the tents, the wagons and the ground. Fred even saw a sleeping Mountie completely blanketed by the pests. As the force rode along, they left behind a thick brown liquid juice that was disgusting to smell. Walking through one of the waves of grasshoppers created a crunching sound enough to set one's teeth on edge. There had been no mention of these pests in the romantic stories of Fred's earlier youth. Finally on July 18, the troops reached the Souris River, over 434 kilometres from Fort Dufferin and about one-third of the way to their final destination of Fort Whoop-Up, near present-day

Lethbridge, Alberta. The men were parched. For days the only water available had been from alkaline ponds that caused dysentery to sweep through the ranks. Upon reaching the river the men fell into the flowing water, fully clothed, and thirstily gulped the refreshing drink. Washing themselves and their clothes after days of dust, blackflies, grasshoppers and mosquitoes, the men had never been happier. They had earned this oasis, but adventure still lay ahead.

Assistant Commissioner James Macleod[12] was tall and tough. Although through his full beard his face could easily break into a smile, he was renowned as a two-fisted drinker who could put any drinking partner under the table and still be clamouring for more. He invoked a fierce loyalty from his men because of his bravery and his sense of fair play. He stood up for them in the most dangerous circumstances and they would go to the wall for him. It was Macleod who would forge a lasting friendship with Crowfoot and receive from his ally the Native name *Stamix-otaken* or "Bull-Head." Because of Macleod, the Blackfoot accepted the authority of the North West Mounted Police in their land.

Sam Steele[13] was another daunting figure in the Mounties. His physical strength and remarkable endurance were already the talk of the camp and the beginning of epic stories around the fire. The sergeant major gained later fame in the Riel Rebellion of 1885 and as commander of the Mounties during the wild days of the Yukon Gold Rush.

But perhaps the most compelling character was the "half-breed" scout, Jerry Potts.[14] Short, muscular and bow-legged, he was a staunch defender of his Blood family and Blackfoot allies. A fierce warrior, Jerry had taken sixteen victims in battle against the Assiniboine and the Cree. Now he was working with the Mounties to rid the West of the common scourge of all the Indians – the whisky traders. It would be Potts who would ultimately lead the Mounties to Fort Whoop-Up in early October of 1874 and then to the site of the bastion, Fort Macleod. These legendary figures of the Canadian West were bound to have made a strong impression on Fred, but, as he wrote in his diary, he still anxiously awaited his first sight of the Indians.

That was to come in August. After enduring days more of riding and marching in boiling hot temperatures the troops arrived at Old Wives

Creek and spotted about fifty Sioux lodges camped there. A Sioux scout informed them of the war in Cypress Hills, where the Blackfoot had attacked the Sioux, but had been beaten off. To Colonel French, the parched land seemed like a tinderbox for future battles, and he called for a powwow with the Sioux chiefs to take place in two days time.

On August 13, 1874, the day of the powwow, Fred marvelled at the formal ceremony that took place. The Mounties presented presents of tobacco, flints and clothing, while the Sioux performed the "scalp dance" and presented a bow-and-arrow exhibit. Then, with Fred sitting in the tent, Colonel French made his important speech to the Sioux. He proclaimed that the Great White Mother has red children, black children and white children. Despite the facetious comment of one Sioux brave that the Great Mother must be a lady of easy virtue (according to two eyewitness accounts), the Natives were impressed with the sincerity and courage of the Mounties. Both sides left the meeting filled with optimism for the future of the Great Land and its inhabitants.[15] As an added bonus, Fred even managed to trade for some buffalo moccasins from his new friends.

August 28 saw another crucial development for Fred and the others. They were now in Cypress Hills – fighting grounds for Native tribes who had endured a long history of enmity among themselves – Gros Ventre, Sioux, Blackfoot, Cree, Blood and Sarcee, as well as others. This was hostile enemy territory! In deference to the danger, the number of sentries increased substantially and the horses were more carefully guarded. The recruits now slept in their clothing with weapons by their sides. Perhaps sensing the danger in the air, the horses stampeded and escaped on August 30. Again, the determination and skill of the Mounties was put to the test and they were able to round up virtually every steed.

On September 2, Fred saw his next notable sight – six buffalo. It was a poignant image for Fred because what he witnessed was merely the straggling remains of the great herds that had once dominated the plain in the West, but were in the process of being annihilated by white "civilization." At one time, herds of up to 80,000 roamed freely over the land. Now the sight a mere six served as not only a message from the past, but also a portend for the future. Even this insignificant number did not stop Colonel French from ordering the slaughter of two of them for food for his troops.

The Mounties had their own artist accompany them on the "Long March."
This sketch is entitled *Six Months in the Wilds of the North-West* and documents
their crossing of a river in September 1874. *Courtesy of Library and Archives
Canada/PA-200864.*

September 13 was for Fred one of the most inspiring days of the
odyssey – it was then that he had his first sight of the majestic Rocky
Mountains. "As we stood there, after months of weary travel, and saw their
snow-capped summits glittering in the bright sunlight about 100 miles
[away] … while almost at our feet the prairie as far as the eye could see …
was covered by countless numbers of buffalo, elk and antelope."[16] The
storms, the heat, the dust, the mosquitoes, the exhaustion – all swept
away in the face of this splendid sight. The Long March was well worth it.

A few days and 1,600 kilometres later, September 22 (Fred's 16th
birthday) saw the Mounties split into two sections. Troops B, C and F
were to remain in the West. With winter fast closing in, this group was
to clean up Fort Whoop-Up and establish Canadian law in the wilderness. Upon arriving at the fort, the Mounties discovered that the cow-
ardly whisky traders had fled. Moving 30 miles northwest, the Mounties
established Fort Macleod and began law enforcement in earnest.

Meanwhile, Fred was a part of Troops D and E who were to continue
the march under Colonel French – this time moving eastward to open
new headquarters north of the Assiniboine River. By New Year's Day, the

Long March was over. Fred had travelled over four months and 3200 kilo-metres to reinforce the original group at Fort Dufferin near Emerson, Manitoba, about 100 kilometres south of Winnipeg. E Division was at Swan Lake (Saskatchewan); A Division in Fort Edmonton (Alberta); and B, C and F in Fort Macleod (Alberta). Frederick Augustus Bagley had joined his 300 compatriots to participate in an exciting chapter in Canadian history. In the process, he had experienced a summer and fall of excitement and heroism that seemed incomprehensible when put down on paper. Remarkably, Fred's adventures were not over yet.

The year 1876 saw the Battle of the Little Big Horn and the complete destruction of General George Armstrong Custer and every one of the Cavalry Long Swords under his leadership. Sitting Bull, the great Sioux leader in the battle against Custer, and traditional enemy of the Blackfoot, arrived in Canada with 5,000 of his followers. With only four constables and two scouts, Inspector James Walsh,[17] leader of B Division, rode into Sitting Bull's camp and lectured him sternly on the need to obey Canadian law. Sitting Bull and Walsh became such good friends, each extending to the other a well-deserved respect, that when American diplomats attempted to persuade Sitting Bull to return to the United States, he retorted:

> For sixty-four years you have persecuted my people. I was compelled to forsake my lands and come here. We did not give you our country; you took it from us. This land (Canada) is a medicine house, where men speak with unforked tongues, and you come here to tell us lies. We do not want to hear them. You can go back. I will stay with the White Mother.[18]

Meanwhile, Canada had her own brilliant Native leader. Crowfoot was born a Blood Indian around 1830, but grew up a Blackfoot. He had been involved in 19 wars, had been wounded six times and, armed only with a lance, had attacked and killed a grizzly bear that was threatening his people's camp. Such was his valour that by 1870, he was one of the three main leaders of the 6,000 strong Blackfoot Nation. When the Mounties arrived West in 1874, Fred met Crowfoot. Like Walsh and

Sitting Bull, Crowfoot and Macleod became friends and allies based on their mutual respect. When Crowfoot's brother was sold whisky, Crowfoot informed Macleod, who arrested, tried and fined the outlaws. It was obvious to Crowfoot that this law was to protect, not oppress his people.

As a result, Crowfoot led his people to Blackfoot Crossing on the Bow River in September of 1877. More than 4,000 Indians, 1,000 teepees and 1,000 warriors were on hand. Also on hand were the Lieutenant Governor of the North-West Territories, some government agents and a number of Mounties, including young Fred Bagley. They were there to take part in the signing of one of the most important treaties ever negotiated between the First Nations and the Canadian government. Treaty 7 ceded virtually all of southern Alberta to Canada in exchange for a pittance and a string of soon-to-be-broken promises. Crowfoot, relying on the honesty and integrity of the North West Mounted Police, whom he had come to respect, led his people into an agreement which assured the peaceful development of the Canadian West.

Fred's adventures continued during his career as a Mountie. Still a teenager, he was entrusted with guarding the notorious Kah-kee-see-choo-chin from the Cree Nation. This man killed, then ate, his mother, his wife, his brother and five of his children during the bitter winter of 1877-1878. A massive man, standing over six-and-one-half feet tall and weighing over 200 pounds, Kah-kee-see-choo-chin befriended the young guard and presented him with some gifts before leaving his cell to become the first legally executed individual in the North-West Territories.

Six years later, an even more famous execution occurred at Regina, where Louis Riel was hanged. Again, Fred Bagley was a part of the forces that battled against Riel and the Métis during the North West Rebellion.

Fred was to remain a Mountie until he resigned in 1899 to enlist to fight in the Boer War. He resumed his military service during the First World War and in peacetime settled in Alberta where he became active in the Calgary Citizen's Band and the Museum of Natural History. Married and the father of six daughters, Fred died a respected citizen of the West in 1945. Yet, he was so much more – he was the teenager who became one of its founders!

CHAPTER NINE

George Green:
A Home Child in Ontario

George Green stood on the deck with an excited group of boys. They were in the fog-enshrouded iceberg corridor just off Newfoundland and they could see the massive castle-like shapes floating by the ship. Perhaps it was a good luck omen for a boy who hadn't enjoyed a great deal of good fortune in his 15 years. Born in the slums of East London, blind in one eye, George was part of a remarkable program that saw over 100,000 young children taken from the rat-infested streets and courts of the urban centres of England and Scotland and sent to Canada to be taken in by families who lived in the land of opportunity.

The Industrial Revolution[1] that transformed the economy in the nineteenth century also drastically changed the society. In particular, the poorer rural people who migrated to the cities would feel the cruel pinch of privation. Captured in print for posterity by Charles Dickens, the plight of children in Victorian England has been well-documented. Youngsters not shipped off to poor houses or toiling in the mines and factories, were witness to a brutal existence in slums teeming with rats, gin parlours and brothels. Open sewage flowed through the streets where destitute children were reduced to begging, stealing and prostitution in their daily struggle to survive. Desperate mothers literally sold young children to strangers for the price of a glass of gin – it was better than enduring one more mouth to feed when there was already an inadequate amount of food to share. During the mid-to-late 1800s, a child, born to one of the 30% of the British population living in poverty, had a life expectancy of 36 years. There was one chance in four that he or she would be dead before being able to "celebrate" a first birthday. Although efforts were being made by the British government to ensure that every child receive an education to the age of 14, these reforms were meaningless in places like Whitechapel (hunting grounds in London for the notorious Jack the Ripper[2]). Yes, young children were sent to school from the ages of four to six but only because it was a cheap alternative to paying neighbours to look after them. But once a child reached the age of six, he or she was an essential cog in the slum family. Single mothers needed the older children to care for their younger brothers and sisters, to do cooking scrubbing and washing while the wage earners struggled through their fourteen-hour day, to take family possessions to the pawnshop or to find any employment that would bring a few pence more into a starving household. Statistics from the day show that half the children under 14 years of age who were living in the poorer districts did not attend school and that 20% of all children in these districts that did attend also worked. It was a cruel existence, but unfortunately, an all too common existence in Victorian England.

If the slum-infested streets were breeding grounds for rats, they were also breeding grounds for a new type of social reformer. Appalled by the unspeakable images of suffering and prompted by a Christian conscience that demanded action, middle and upper-class reformers, both men and women, sought to eradicate the worst of the abuses. Temperance movements, aimed at eliminating drunkenness and spousal and child abuse, became part of the mainstream of national policies. William Booth[3] founded the Salvation Army to wage a war for the body and souls of the downtrodden. The Social Gospel[4] movement preached an active commitment to charity work and direct involvement with the victims of the system. Evangelicalism[5] demanded improvements in workhouses, orphanages, factories, jails and hospitals. Everywhere, there was an impulse to rescue the oppressed.

Into this milieu, stepped Thomas John Barnardo. Although not the first, he was certainly among the most famous of the reformers who came up with the ingenious method of saving the slum children. If the city was the symbol of depravity and corruption, the countryside represented purity, simplicity and a higher moral order. What better solution to the dilemma of dirty little urchins, unwanted and unloved, running through the streets of the vilest slums, then to sweep them up, clean them up and ship them off for a fresh start! Thus was born the movement known as the "Home Children."[6] From 1830s to the 1930s, children were taken from shelters, orphanages and homes to be given a new life overseas in either Canada or Australia. Theoretically with the approval of the parent or parents (although none of the reformers were overly zealous in complying with this provision), children would be sent to eager households to start a new life. This was viewed as a win-win-win situation where everyone involved would benefit. England is afforded a safety valve. The most desperate, the most deprived, the most hopeless, and potentially, the most dangerous youngsters are taken out of the hellholes that defined their lives. Canada would receive hundreds of thousands of eager and able farmhands and domestic helpers who were all English speaking and who would all serve to strengthen imperial ties between colony and mother country. And the children would be offered the opportunity to escape from the poverty cycle and become productive contributors to a thriving economy. All of this, while at the same time rescuing children from near certain damnation and purifying their souls for eternity! At least that was what the propaganda said. Sometimes it proved to be the case.

This was why George Green and his brother, along with 237 other boys were shipped from England to Canada in early March 1895.[7] His widowed mother could not afford to care for herself, let alone two growing boys. With a dull sadness but a firm resolve, she took them to

18 Stepney Causeway, where a sign outside the "always open" door proclaimed: "NO DESTITUTE BOY OR GIRL EVER REFUSED ADMISSION." Barnardo was ready to receive his two new charges. When George's mother signed the legal document, agreeing that her boys would be sent to Canada and that she would never again attempt any contact with them, she trudged away with a heavy heart. For George, it was not only the end of his old life but the beginning of the end of his very existence.

A thorough medical examination by the attending House Medical Officer revealed that George was in good health. He was blind in one eye and his other eye was crossed inward, but other than that (and the usual fleas and bites) he was in sound condition. George was then taken to be photographed. This was a very important procedure for Barnardo since he would use "before and after" photos to nudge potential contributors to dig even deeper into their pockets to support the noble enterprise. After this, George was given a thorough scrubbing, a short haircut, a spanking new uniform and a number. He returned to the studio for the "after" shot and was then escorted to his assigned bed and locker.

Bugle call at 5:30 a.m. aroused George to early Morning Prayer, which was followed by a thirty-minute drill in the wall-enclosed courtyard. Breakfast in the common room with all the other boys was served on the long plank tables framed by wooded benches. Meals were simple – porridge and bread for breakfast, soup at mid-afternoon and a supper that would typically consist of bread, a fresh fruit and a cup of cocoa, but on Sundays after worship, you could always count on a meat dinner. After breakfast came classroom instruction, a trade shop session, chores (such as scrubbing the floors and making your bed) and exercise, all punctuated throughout the day and evening by prayers. At 9:00 p.m. lights went out, and George and the other 15 boys in his dormitory fell into a sound sleep.

This was George's routine until that fateful day in March when he was given his personal travel bag and marched "two by two" with the other boys to board the "Barnardo Special" – the train that would take them to the steamship. It had been a pleasant enough time for George. The day-to-day repetition was comforting, accommodations were better than anything he had ever experienced and the people were kindly towards him. Even though there were no demonstrations of affection, he was never mistreated and there was always food. He would miss this reassuring existence and couldn't help but feel apprehensive about leaving England forever.

The boat trip did nothing to alleviate his misgivings. George was one of the unfortunate ones who suffered terribly from seasickness. The steerage accommodations were cramped, dank and unsanitary. Hundreds of boys were crammed into the lower berth in accommodations designed for about half the number of passengers. The pervasive smell of body odour, urine and vomit did little to ease the seasickness, and the constant dampness aggravated the precarious health of the youngsters. He wanted to lie down and die, but the supervisor who accompanied him made him stand at attention, sing a hymn and drink tepid tea. It seemed like a voyage that would never end. Perhaps that explains George's added enthusiasm when he saw the icebergs off Newfoundland – they were nearing land and his new home.

Finally at 5:00 a.m. on March 29, he and the others were awakened, told to wash up and come up on the deck to retrieve their luggage. They had arrived at Quebec City. Going down the gangplank, George knew that Barnardo had three homes in Canada – in Peterborough, Toronto and Winnipeg. He didn't know anything about any of them and was still uncertain as to where he would be sent. After another medical examination, he was lined up and had a number placed on his back and herded towards a train with a large group of boys. He happened to hear someone say "Toronto" and he now knew his destination. George arrived late that night and was taken to 214 Farley Avenue. An address was to serve as his legal guardian until he reached the age of 18, an administrative convenience since Barnardo himself did not reside in Canada. All George had to do now was wait for a placement.

It would not be long in coming for George. Farmers were anxious to get strong young boys to work with them on their farms especially with spring seeding on the horizon, and a 15-year-old was big enough to do a man's job, yet young enough to provide three years of cheap labour until he turned 18. Within days, a request for George was processed. If you wanted a "home child" you sent in your application with a letter from your clergymen. There was no time, there was no need for an interview. The sooner the boy was placed, the sooner Barnardo could bring over another. The doctor at 214 Farley had examined him, proclaimed him fit for farmwork and sent him to Norfolk County to work on W.A. Cranston's farm.[8] The solitude and loneliness was the most severe adjustment for George. Raised in the cities he had never imagined such total darkness as that which engulfed him on the cool spring nights. He could walk as far as he could see and never encounter another human being. In London, England, on a typical day, he would come into contact with hundreds of people. On the Norfolk County farm, his only contact was the bachelor farmer, Cranston. And the work! For a boy who had known only rats, dogs and cats, these cows were intimidating. He was a strong boy, but the piling of wood, the cleaning of stables, the building of rail fences, the clearing of rocks, the plowing of fields – all were strange and difficult, almost impossible tasks. But Cranston was patient and kindly and George was eager to learn and please. Shy, painfully quiet, but always polite and obedient, George struggled to fit in. It was a hopeless effort. After a trial period of four weeks, Cranston sent George back. He said that the boy was strong and healthy, clean and polite, but his vision made him totally unsuitable for farmwork. He couldn't even manage a team of horses and would never be able to adapt.

Discouraged, humiliated and thoroughly embarrassed, George returned to Farley Avenue. Failure compounded his shyness and it was impossible to get him to talk to strangers. But George was soon given a second chance. A 41-year-old spinster, Helen Finlay, had requested a homeboy to work on her farm in Big Bay Keppel near Owen Sound.[9] She had emigrated from Scotland with her parents and brother 26 years earlier, but with all three of them now dead, she desperately needed

A farm scene, possibly similar to this photograph of a deserted farm home, would had added to George Green's dismay when he arrived at Helen Finlay's farmhouse. *Courtesy of the Archives of Ontario, F 1075-H1197.*

help on her 100-acre farm. With 30 acres of oats, hay and vegetables, 18 cattle, 12 hogs, 11 sheep and three horses she could not manage with just the one servant girl, Mary Brown, to help her. She needed a strong capable worker and she needed him now.

When the stage pulled into Big Bay Keppel on Georgian Bay, about 20 kilometres from Owen Sound, that fateful day on May 7, it was difficult to determine who received the greater shock. Helen Finlay gazed at a boy who was blind in one eye, crossed in the other and seemed stupid, slow and surly in his silence. The accompanying letter, stating that he was deficient in eyesight but capable of doing the chores, did little to assuage her misgivings. For George, it was even more traumatic. He was greeted by a tall, severe "Amazonian" (as one neighbour described her) woman with a strong sharp chin, iron grey hair and weathered skin. Her steely frown did nothing to encourage the poor boy to respond in any way but a nervous mumble. It was an inauspicious introduction to an experience that could only be described as six months of unspeakable torture.

George cried in his room that night. It would certainly not be the last time in his too short life, but it was an early indicator of the misery he was enduring. The isolation and loneliness seemed even more engulfing. He knew that he had displeased Helen Finlay, but she spoke so fast and demanded so much. He wanted to please but was always a few steps behind. And the duties she outlined for him were impossible. He knew he could never handle all the work she insisted had to be done. He also knew that there was no escape. An inspector was supposed to visit once a year, but given the remote distance and Canadian weather conditions, these overworked employees could not be relied upon. Even if they did visit, the inspections were perfunctory and the children infrequently consulted. If Helen Finlay decided to keep him, he was here until he turned 18 and had bleak hope for support or sympathy from anyone. He had never felt so alone in his life.

Helen did decide to keep him. After three weeks, she signed a document placing George Green under her unchallenged authority for three years. When he turned 18, he would be given $75 and his freedom. Until then, he was her beast of burden on the farm.

From that point, Helen's contempt and disgust for poor George accelerated. Frustrated by his inability to complete the chores, she became aggressively demanding and visibly angry. Complaining frequently to him and to anyone who would listen, she railed on about being saddled with a defective cross-eyed humpback. He was skinny and weak, she bitterly asserted, and his teeth did not meet because his lower jaw protruded. He walked funny and he was left-handed. He was an imbecile who was surly and unresponsive. He couldn't do anything right. To a neighbour, William Shier, she was heard to explode in rage: "I wish the brute would die or get better."[10] This was not the help that Helen had expected.

George was living in a nightmare. Mary Brown, the young servant girl, knew he was a good boy, but he was not fast enough to suit her mistress, Helen Finlay. William McKinley, a neighbour who dropped by the farm one day saw a strong and healthy boy who seemed eager to please, but was incredibly clumsy. Around Helen, George became even

The days were long and work was exhausting for George Green. This photograph depicts a young man behind a scuffler, uprooting weeds between the rows. *Courtesy of the Archives of Ontario, C 223-3-0-0-18.*

clumsier and slower. Terrified of her, he was paralyzed in his responses. While loading a cart one day, he accidentally hit Mary with one of the pieces of wood. Enraged, Helen grabbed the log and beat George with it. On other occasions, people saw George running in the field crying with Helen in hot pursuit, wielding an axe handle and screaming at him. She prodded him with a pitchfork, kicked him with her boots, grabbed him by the neck and shook him, threatened him constantly, verbally assailed him and was always striking him with the nearest available weapon. She actually told a neighbour that she enjoyed beating him.[11]

George's only friend in the world was Mary Brown. Mary wanted to help him when Helen kicked or beat him. She watched in horror one day when Helen smashed him across the back of the head with her nail-studded slipper. As George lay on the ground bleeding, she stood helplessly back. As much as she liked George, she did not dare defy Helen.

The abuse even invaded George's one sanctuary – his room. One night, Helen dragged him from his bedroom and threw him into the stable with the hogs. For two nights he lay in wide-eyed terror waiting for the dreaded footsteps. His diet was mash bran porridge with an occasional slice of bread, which he often had to eat standing up. With fall and winter approaching, he could never feel warm in his torn, ragged summer clothes. George was weary. He was a broken child who was too weak to drag himself into another day of taunts, threats, beatings and torture. Physically, emotionally and spiritually he was drained.

One cold November morning, his body finally joined his spirit in death. Doctor Allan Cameron, the coroner from Owen Sound, was called to a scene that would haunt him the rest of his life. In 40 years of medical practice, including working in the slums of Glasgow, Doctor Cameron had never encountered such squalid conditions. The room was filthy and foul smelling. The only furniture was two boards on which the frail body of George lay and a straw mattress with a ten-inch hole carved out in the centre. It was soon evident that this mattress was both bed and toilet for George in his last days. Weakened from the beatings and diarrhea, malnourished with visible wounds, George lay on the straw with the hole and himself reeking of feces. It was a cruel, sad death that Doctor Cameron, after an autopsy, concluded was the result of a combination of neglect, beatings and starvation. Helen Finlay was charged with murder, later reduced to manslaughter, and would stand trial for her brutality.

The headlines of the *Owen Sound Times* on November 14, 1895, were an indication of the sombre mood that greeted the trial:

ANOTHER KEPPEL TRAGEDY
A BARNARDO BOY DIES UNDER SUSPICIOUS CIRCUM-
STANCES
HELEN FINLAY, HIS EMPLOYER ARRESTED[12]

As the trial progressed, the quiet community was rocked by the testimony of the witnesses. More than a dozen neighbours took the oath and described the savage beatings and cruel mistreatment they had seen. Two other doctors, in addition to Doctor Cameron, provided appalling details about the condition of George's room when they found him and the heart-wrenching conditions of his body. Yet when Helen Finlay took the stand, she blithely contradicted the eyewitnesses to her brutality – she never mistreated him, perhaps just shouted at him because he was so slow. Furthermore, she asserted, George's room was not the squalid fetid accommodation described by the doctors. It was clean and tidy. Helen's testimony probably had little impact on the outcome, but the defence strategy that followed completely turned the trial upside down.

In a surprise move, the defence secured an order to exhume George's body for an examination by their doctors. The grave and the coffin were both filled with water, but that did nothing to deter the medical practitioners from arriving at their conclusions. They testified that the body of the Barnardo boy was tainted by heredity. It was a defective body before any encounter with Helen Finlay. One of the doctors, who had refused to examine the boy when he was alive because he regarded him as a London slum urchin, did not even examine him after his death. Yet this did not dissuade him from arriving at his reasoned conclusion: the boy had hereditary defects consistent with the offshoot of syphilis. It was his bad background that created this cursed misfit. The change in mood was evidenced by the front-page coverage in the *Owen Sound Times* of November 21, 1895:

> Nothing extraordinary has transpired during the past week in the Big Bay manslaughter case…. The greatest crime is being perpetrated against Canada by the dumping of the diseased off – scouring of the hot-beds of hellish slumdom of England amongst the rising generation of this country. From the vilest and most pernicious surroundings these exports of Barnardo are sent into homes where young Canadian children are growing up…. It is nothing less than damnable that the future of Canada should be blighted by the dumping of the Barnardo waifs on her shores to live in crime or die with abuse, and in either case leaving a trail of immorality behind.[13]

Pent-up resentment and hostility, which had been seething for years, bubbled over the surface. The late nineteenth century was witnessing the increasing urbanization of Canada. The rural community felt its influence waning under the onslaught of the immoral and disease-ridden urban centres, as they were viewed at the time. The myth of a pastoral country that was superior in all ways to its evil cousin, the city, took firm hold and the home children provided an easy target in the pulpits, the press and the parliament of Canada. By December 19, Helen Finlay was not longer on trial – the jury was deadlocked and unable to reach a decision. She was set free.

But the trial of George Green and all the home children was just getting started. The *Toronto Evening Star* chose as its headline, "A REPULSIVE BOY." In smaller print the subheading was "DISOBEDIENT, DIRTY, UNABLE TO WORK, BUT A BIG EATER."[14] The House of Commons, our national parliament, referred to them as the offal of the most depraved characters in the cities of the Old Country. Criticism even found its way into an icon of Canadian literature, *Anne of Green Gables*:

> "At first, Matthew suggested getting a Barnardo boy. But I said 'no' flat to that…. no London street arabs for me…"[15]

Public opinion rallied against the home children, but economic considerations kept the program alive. George Green may have been a more dramatic victim of the abuse endured by tens of thousands of those youngsters, but many of the children would acknowledge that their lives were better as a result of their forced migrations.[16] Canada received up to 100,000 worthwhile and contributing citizens from the 1830s to 1939.

Today the descendants of home children enrich the fabric of Canadian life from the Atlantic to the Pacific. Yet when a ship arrived in Canada with 28 youngsters in July of 1939 (just before the outbreak of the Second World War), it marked the final voyage of an experiment with the lives of children that cannot help but reduce our nation to a sense of remorse and shame. That may be of slight solace to George Green – a boy whose body and soul searched so desperately for peace during a brief lifetime.

CHAPTER TEN

Alan McLeod: First World War Air Ace

The guns of August, which precipitated the most devastating blood-bath in the history of mankind, caught a Canada unprepared but enthusiastic. When war came in 914, the country had an army of approximately 3,000, a "tin-pot" navy of 350 men and two ancient cruisers, and no air force at all. England's Royal Flying Corps was formed in 1912. Germany's air force also consisted of Zeppelins as well as air planes. Canada spent $11,000,000 on her defence budget in 1914, while Germany was allocating $5,540,000,000 in preparation for the carnage.[1]

Nevertheless, news of the war was greeted with a fervour in Canada. "WAR," proclaimed the bold and proud headline in the *Toronto Star* on August 5, 1914. Crowds milled and cheered spontaneously as the word spread and lusty choruses of "God Save the King" or "Rule Britannia" rang out in city streets across the nation. Politicians and people were one in their patriotism. Such diverse individuals as Sam Hughes,[2] Clifford Sifton,[3] Henri Bourassa[4] and Wilfrid Laurier[5] endorsed the view of the Prime Minister Robert Borden that Canada's place was "shoulder to shoulder" with Britain during the struggle. In villages, towns and cities of every province young men who were eager to be a part of this exciting new adventure thronged to recruiting stations. Girls kissed their fiancés goodbye with the comforting thought that they would be home by Christmas. A nation marched confidently to war!

Alan Arnett McLeod, grandson of immigrants from Scotland, shared fully the enthusiasm for war. Born on April 20 in the last year of the nineteenth century, Alan grew up in Stonewall, Manitoba, with daily doses of Rudyard Kipling,[6] tales of imperial exploits and regular cadet training as an integral part of his school curriculum. So imbued with military spirit was Alan that at the age of 14, he lied about his age and attempted to join the local militia. When authorities in Winnipeg discovered that a mere youngster was in their ranks, they promptly shipped him home to school, but young Alan remained undaunted. Impatiently he waited until he finally reached the minimum recruiting age in 1917, then immediately volunteered for service overseas with the Royal Flying Corps. On April 23, 1917, Alan was formally accepted and on his way to flying training in Mimico, just west of Toronto.

His stay in the Toronto area was too brief to allow him much of an opportunity for sightseeing. Before the end of the summer he was transferred first to Camp Borden at Angus, Ontario, then to England. Had he stayed a bit longer in Toronto, he would have enjoyed the fascinating experience of the sights and sounds of the homefront during wartime.

Workers were still adjusting to the government's brand new method of raising money – the income tax. It was easier to accept since the Prime Minister had promised that this was to be a strictly temporary measure to help finance the war. When the war was over, the income tax would be forever forgotten! These same workers were part of an effort that saw a nation of seven million eventually pledge over $1 billion dollars to purchase Victory Bonds. Everywhere, an extensive poster campaign urged the people at home to do their share to defeat the hated enemy. Such lines as "Hun or Home?," "Let's Finish the Job" and "What did you do in the Great War, Daddy?" exhorted Canadians to meet their moral obligations. Pictures of pillaging fiends and vulnerable womanhood also stirred the conscience of any potential shirker. Torontonians also thrilled to the sight of "America's Sweetheart"

Canada did much more than provide people to serve in the carnage of battle. During the First World War, there were numerous factories producing ammunition for the Allied Forces. This photograph is an interior shot of an aircraft factory, circa 1918. *Courtesy of the Archives of Ontario, C 224-0-0-11-63.*

returning to her birthplace to address a patriotic rally. Mary Pickford[7] – the most famous movie star in the world – had come home.

Since more than 600,000 men volunteered to fight in Europe, someone had to replace them at home. Women in the workforce became at first a unique phenomenon, but eventually a commonplace occurrence. Whether they were toiling in factories making shells, labouring in farm fields to harvest crops for the Allies or conducting a streetcar through the streets, women were making their presence and their abilities felt everywhere. Perhaps this contribution more than anything else finally won them the right to vote by war's end.

Women also helped by knitting clothing and socks for the soldiers, rolling bandages for the wounded and shaming young men into joining the army by means of the notorious "chicken brigade" – countless women marching through the streets armed with chicken feathers. Their function was to embarrass civilians into joining the army by placing a chicken feather on any young man who was not in uniform.

At home, front lawns were converted into "Victory Gardens" so that families raising their own vegetables would not have to take food intended for overseas. Often family members would gather around the piano in the parlour to sing such patriotic ditties as "Over There," "I'll Never Forget You, Soldier Boy" and "Would You Rather be a Colonel with an Eagle on his Shoulder or a Private with a Chicken on His Knee?" It would have been evident to Alan McLeod that the war being fought 2,000 miles away was very close to the people at home.

Meanwhile, he was encountering his most profound disappointment since his dismissal from the Fort Garry Horse Militia in 1913. His pilot's training completed, Alan was assigned to the 82nd Squadron of the Royal Flying Corps. His plane was to be an Armstrong Whitworth Fk8 – a reconnaissance plane contemptuously referred to as the "Big Ack" because of its awkward appearance and its cumbersome nature.

The First World War[8] was one of the most tragic episodes in the story of humankind. The most lasting impressions of the survivors of this squalid experience, largely fought in the trenches of Western Europe along the long line called the Western Front in France and Belgium, were mud, lice and vermin. The smell of death in the air mingled with the odour of stale urine and disease. Rotting corpses oozed out of the mud where they had been lost for days, weeks or even months. Rats grew sleek, fat and arrogant on human flesh and human waste. Boldly they scurried over the faces and bodies of weary soldiers. When fighting erupted there was no escape from the total insanity of the hellhole. Maimed and mangled bodies, shell-shocked youngsters, veterans screaming in agony – these sights and sounds were as common as the daily rations of bullybeef and hardtack.

If there was any glamour to be found in the Great War, it would not be in the craters and mud, but in the skies above. Because the Wright Brothers[9] had not ushered in the age of flight until 1903, there was no previous history of aerial combat. Generals on both sides saw the advantages of aerial photography and surveillance in order to pinpoint troop movement and enemy defenses. Moreover, the unwieldy two-seater planes could be used for bombing enemy targets beyond the army's range. Each side, in an effort to countermand the aerial bombing and photography, developed the fighter plane – a lighter, more manoeuverable single-seater aircraft with machine guns mounted in the cockpit. This enabled the pilot to navigate and attack simultaneously. With the evolution of the fighter plane came the romance of the "dog fight" – a modern gladiator in the sky, pitting his skills and his life against his single opponent. Twentieth-century knights of the air duelled against enemy "aces" – a term previously reserved for dashing sports heroes. Before long, every nation had claimed its share of legendary aces. Their names were better known than the sports stars and the movie stars of the era. Their exploits were described to the finest detail and people at home thrilled to the telling and re-telling of aerial battles.

Canada, more than any other nation, produced its share of heroes. Led by Billy Bishop[10] (and his 72 victories), Canadians occupied ten spots in the top 27 aces of the Royal Air Force. Every one of the ten pilots had at least 30 victories against the enemy. Billy Bishop was the third leading ace among pilots of all nationalities and Ray Collishaw[11] (60 victories) was fifth. There was no doubt that the most glamorous – if also the most dangerous – spot in the First World War was in the cockpit of a single-seater fighter plane.

This accounts for the disappointment felt by Alan McLeod on being assigned to the "Big Ack." He had come to Europe to fight, not to take pictures. Nevertheless, he carried out his duties with care and precision. On one of his routine missions he could not withstand the temptation to treat his bulky bomber as if it were a darting fighter plane. Recklessly, he attacked eight German planes flying in formation. Not only did he escape unscathed, but he also managed to secure a casualty on the enemy's side. On several other missions, the young pilot repeated this audacious act. Before long he had secured a reputation as a "young fire-eater." Yet these forays were mere rehearsals for one of the most incredible sagas to emerge from the First World War.

In early 1918, the Germans were preparing for an all-out offensive, which they hoped would break the stalemate in the trenches and end the war. The Bolshevik Revolution[12] and the subsequent peace treaty between the two belligerents had knocked Russia out of the Allied Effort in December 1917. As a result, Germany was able to transfer her forces from the East to the Western Front using Germany as the focus (the Western Front refers to the fighting that occurred between Germany and the Western allies, while the Eastern Front was the fighting that occurred between Germany and Austria-Hungary against Russia). In the same year as Russia withdrew from the fighting, United States entered the war on the Allied side. However, in early 1918, the American troops were just arriving in Europe and were often inadequately trained for battle. Consequently, Germany enjoyed a distinct manpower advantage over the Allies. With this in mind, Germany struck out with sudden vigour at two British armies in France, north of Paris by the Somme River, on March 21, 1918. This bold assault was met with overwhelming success as German troops swept through the Allied lines. To assure the success of this new offensive, German air support was flown in – four elite divisions of Fokker triplanes led by the greatest ace of World War I, Manfred von Richtofen![13] Allied pilots both admired and feared the famous "Red Baron" and his "Flying Circus." Highly visible in his bright red triplane, the Red Baron presented an exciting picture as he reeled off victory after victory against the Allied Forces. He would score a total of 80 successive "hits" before being shot down by the Canadian ace Roy Brown on April 21, 1918.[14] On the day of von Richtofen's fateful encounter with Alan McLeod, he was at the apex of his career.

It was a misty grey overcast day – the seventh day of the German assault – when the 18-year-old second lieutenant was sent on a bombing mission near Albert, France. His observer was a trusted companion from past duties, Lieutenant A.W. Hammond. The bleak weather conditions did not augur well for the team. Hammond complained repeatedly of the difficulty of any intelligible sighting in the fog and mist. By mid-afternoon, the 18-year-old pilot reluctantly decided to return to the base. The exercise appeared to be a futile failure. Suddenly, Hammond spotted a lone Fokker protecting an observation balloon. Ignoring the fact that his plane had the "aerodynamics of a cow" and was capable only of a lumbering speed of 90 m.p.h., young McLeod pulled his plane into a climb. Flying directly at the Fokker triplane, the cool pilot held his

An aerial photograph of a Kite balloon over the site of Alan McLeod's fateful encounter with von Richtofen's Flying Circus. *Courtesy of the Archives of Ontario, C 224-0-0-10-47.*

course steadily while Lieutenant Hammond opened fire and sent the enemy plunging to the ground. They had scored another hit! But there was no opportunity to savour the victory. Emerging from the clouds came an entire formation of von Richtofen's "Flying Circus" – eight Fokker triplanes determined to avenge the death of their comrade. In a letter to his parents, Alan McLeod described the development modestly, explaining that he and Hammond foolishly " decided to take on the enemy and flew upwards to confront them head-on."[15] He also dismissively commented on his being hit once or twice.

McLeod did not mention in his letter the fact that he and Hammond had scored another hit before their plane was ripped from propeller to rudder. Suddenly they were flying in a plane whose bottom had been gutted and whose fuel tank was on fire. With cool decisiveness, Alan McLeod climbed from the cockpit to the wing of his plane. Hammond followed suit and crawled to a perching position outside his observation seat. From here McLeod not only continued the dog fight, but actually shot down a third triplane that had moved in for the kill. The plane was spiralling down to the earth, but both men continued to fly and fight. By now, the "Big Ack" was a blazing inferno. McLeod tried hopelessly to put out the fire, which was now engulfing him. With his boots and uniform in fiery tatters, he calmly glided his plane towards the ground. By this time, Hammond had received six wounds, while McLeod had been hit five times. Miraculously, the pilot landed the plane with a dull crash – directly in the centre of a raging battle. McLeod and Hammond were in dreaded "No Man's Land"[16] and the plane could blow up any minute.

When the fire reached the bombs on the plane, the war would come to an abrupt and cruel finish for both men.

Despite his wounds, the young lieutenant was able to crawl to safety. Hammond, however, was unconscious and had a shattered leg. With a total disregard for his personal safety, McLeod concentrated on rescuing his companion. Alternately crawling and scraping, he pulled the inert form from the charred wreckage, then began dragging his observer on his back towards the British lines. As he clawed his way inch by agonizing inch, Alan was hit a sixth time. Yet never did he consider abandoning Hammond so that he might reach safety. The Allied troops prayed and cheered for the valiant pilot, but none dared to venture on to the battlefield to help him. It appeared to be certain suicide. Finally, McLeod and Hammond reached the front line of the Allied forces. McLeod – hair burnt, uniform shredded, wounded six times – collapsed from exhaustion, shock and severe loss of blood. For another five hours the two men lay still and precariously close to death. It wasn't until nightfall that the troops were able to evacuate them by stretcher to the nearest first-aid station. After this three-mile ordeal, they were patched up and shipped to the nearest hospital in Amiens, France. The incredible day was drawing to a close!

The next morning, March 28, Alan McLeod was sent to the Prince of Wales Hospital in London, England. He was not expected to live, but his courageous deeds had earned him the best possible medical attention. The doctors notified Alan's family of his critical condition and suggested that a loved one should be with him at the end. Alan's father travelled to London, praying that his son would survive until he arrived. Once again, the mistake was made of underestimating Alan's fighting spirit. The doctors were as amazed as the German pilots by Alan's tenacious struggle for life. For two months, his father remained by his bedside while Alan's condition hovered between life and death. During his lonely vigil, the father learned that his son was to receive the Victoria Cross – the highest decoration or honour that could be bestowed upon a soldier of the British Commonwealth. For displaying supreme valour in the face of the enemy, for disregarding personal safety to rescue a comrade, Alan was to be personally honoured by King George V – if he survived!

On September 4, 1918, an emotional scene took place at Buckingham Palace. Lieutenant A.W. Hammond – whose shattered leg was amputated – was wheeled before the King to receive a bar to his Military Cross. By his side was a gaunt, pain-ridden nineteen-year-old who hobbled forwards with the support of two canes – Alan Arnett McLeod had come to claim his Victoria Cross!

Immediately afterwards, Alan was flown back to Canada to begin his arduous road to recovery. It appeared that the worst was over. Day by day he gradually gained strength and started to dream of new worlds to conquer. His days as a fighter pilot were over as it was evident that the war was fast approaching its conclusion. The German offensive was turned back and the Allies were driving to victory. Canada had entered the war as a colony but was emerging as a nation – proud, confident and prosperous. Opportunities seemed to abound as a nation was awakened to its fantastic strength and potential. The economy was thriving, the mood was enthusiastic and production was at an all-time high. There were no clouds on the horizon.

Then, unbelievably, the world was hit by the worst epidemic since the terrifying Black Death of the Middle Ages. Spanish Flu was sweeping across Canada creating a reign of terror. Men turned up at work with gauze masks covering their faces. Schools were converted to hospitals in a futile effort to handle the overflow of death. Movie theatres shut down because people were horror-stricken at the thought of being in a large crowd. The situation was so severe that the cities across Canada enacted numerous bylaws in an attempt to stem the tide: in Regina, a person was liable to a $50 fine for sneezing in public; in Edmonton, stores were forbidden to open before 12:30 p.m. each day; in Montreal, the stores had to shut down by 4:00 p.m.; in Toronto, barbers wore surgical masks to combat the dread disease.[17] All was to no avail. The Great War, which raged from 1914 to 1918 would claim 60,000 Canadian lives. The Spanish Flu which seized the nation in its grip for six horrifying months would claim 65,000 Canadian lives. One of those occurred on November 5, 1918. Six days before the Armistice ending the First World War and six months before his twentieth birthday, Alan McLeod lost his final battle.

CHAPTER ELEVEN

Armand Bombardier: Inventor of the Snowmobile

*C*anada emerged from the First World War as not one, but two distinct entities. Fortunately for Armand Bombardier – but even more fortunately for Canada – he straddled both cultural communities.

For English Canada, the 1920s were years of unbridled optimism and confidence. Tired of four weary years of the dirtiest and most devastating war that the world had ever encountered, the people eagerly embraced a decade of fun, spending and material accumulation. Literally and figuratively motored by the automobile, Canadians drove into a decade never before experienced by this staid, conservative country. Jobs were plentiful, spending was up and people had more free time then ever before to enjoy their new wealth.

The automobile was at the vanguard in the revolution in transportation and the economy. Henry Ford's[1] shrewd use of the assembly line and mass production made the Model T the symbol of the era and resulted in the price of the "newfangled contraption" tumbling down. In neighbourhoods all across Canada, cars suddenly appeared in garages, freeing the working man and enabling him to live miles from his place of employment. Thus, suburbs started to develop and a housing boom erupted on the outskirts of cities. Young people took advantage of the freedom of the automobile to go to parties and dates unchaperoned. The scandalous new music (jazz) and dances (such as the Charleston) that were sweeping across the continent assisted the ensuing change in morality. Vacations in faraway places became a reality rather than a dream and everywhere there were "jobs, jobs, jobs." Whether it was paving the new roads, opening service stations or motels, selling fashionable accessories for summer and winter drives or building new homes with garages, there was work, and fun, to be found for anyone who wanted it.

The aeroplane also contributed to the "shrinking world." It was still too early for extensive passenger air travel, but Canada had been inspired by the heroics of the glamorous "aces" of the First World War. Led by Billy Bishop, Canadian pilots provided heroes during the bleak war years and inspiration for the adventurers of the 1920s. Individuals such as "Wop" May[2] represented a new breed that was born in Canada – the bush pilot. These were the men who opened our northland, flying in medical supplies and making us aware of the opportunities of exploration and exploitation of untapped resources. Canada enjoyed a boom economy as a hungry America greedily gulped up more and more of our minerals, our pulp and paper and our hydroelectric power. Again, jobs, money and opportunities awaited the adventurous spirits of Canada.

Even the Canadian government was swept up by the buoyant enthusiasm. Taking on increased responsibilities because of wartime demands, Parliament established the National Research Council in 1916. For the first time, the government would actively fund scientific investigations and activities. The inventive Canadian mind, unfettered by regulations and restrictions, could push to new frontiers during this exuberant and confident decade. Businessmen like Charlie Trudeau (father of a future prime minister) would make their fortunes from the new technology. And Canadian inventors and innovations would provide much of this new technology to the world. Sam McLaughlin[3] would have 13,000 people in his employ when he sold his Buick and his expertise to General Motors; Reginald Fessenden[4] helped to develop the principle of amplitude modulation (AM) that was vital to both radio and television broadcasting, while Ted Rogers,[5] with his alternating current radio tube would put this wireless, battery-free, device in every home. In the world of medicine, Banting and Best[6] would receive global acclaim and the gratitude of millions of diabetics for their development of insulin. Small wonder that, for many in Canada, the 1920s were the "Golden Twenties."

But if English Canada emerged from the war confident and assertive, French Canada remained bitter and wary. Ontario Regulation 17, banning the use of French in schools, enlistment and training tactics and thus denying recognition of French Canadians' as worthy partners in the national endeavour, plus the Conscription Crisis of 1917[7] drove French Canadians further into a suspicious attitude towards English Canada. Past experience with change led them to view change as a threat. Shunning the world of technology and progress, French Canada of the day remained defined by the village priest and the family. Cautious to the point of being ultra conservative, French Canadians emphasized the traditional values of a rural and devout community. The Church not only held sway in the village, but also was the unchallenged leader in all public issues of the day. With its iron grip on education, it continued to provide the young people of Quebec with a classical education. Latin, religion, oratory and classical history were worthy subjects to pursue, while the sciences and technology were largely ignored. Quebec was the only province that would continue to deny women the right to vote for a further two decades and a "woman," as defined by the family, was firmly and legally enshrined – she could not sell property, sign a contract or even undergo surgery without her husband's written consent.[8]

Yet collectively, French Canadians in the 1920s did not see themselves as an oppressed people in their relationship to the Church or their own government. The Church was a vital force in their lives. Spiritual comfort and salvation were important, but that is not all that the Roman Catholic Church provided. The hospitals, the schools, the

The spiritual side of Armand Bombardier is evident in this formal photograph taken when he was nine years old. *Courtesy of the Musée J. Armand Bombardier.*

charitable institutions were all staffed by devout Catholics. Virtually every father and mother aspired to see one of their children become a nun or a priest. The Church had respect because it had earned and deserved that respect. It was the rock of stability that served as an anchor for a people besieged by an onslaught of change.

Into both of these societies, French-Canadian and English-Canadian, strode a young teenager, Joseph-Armand Bombardier. Born on April 16, 1907, of devout Catholic parents, Armand (as he was called) could trace his family's presence in Canada back seven generations to André Bombardier, a soldier from France who had settled in Montreal after helping to found what would become the City of Detroit. The eldest child, Armand was born into a family strong in piety and duty. His father, Joseph-Alfred, took over the family farm at the age of 14, when his father died unexpectedly. Alfred was renowned in the community for his strong personality and his highly developed sense of responsibility. He methodically added both a woodworking shop and a blacksmith shop to his farm and eventually purchased the general store in Valcourt in order to provide for his wife Anna and their growing family. It seemed that Armand had inherited his father's temper and his father's sense of duty, but had added an incredibly inquisitive and probing mind.

By the age of nine, Armand was systematically helping with the repairs of the farm equipment. The boy was gifted with a mechanical genius that was able to dismantle and re-assemble the machinery of the tractors and threshers owned by the family. By the age of 14, Armand had built his own wood lathe and was turning out miniature motor-boats, trains and even tractors with working engines. The youngster was a celebrity in the small village of Valcourt, admired for his remark-able abilities as well as his fun-loving, yet devout character.

When his father bought the general store, Armand was able to draw from both of Canada's two national heritages. In keeping with his French-Canadian heritage, he not only attended mass regularly and aspired to be a conscientious Catholic, but was also paid the princely sum of five cents each week for assisting the priest in serving mass on Sundays. Yet with respect to the English-Canadian spirit of technology and progress, Armand haunted the local clock repair store owned by an individual named Drainville. It was here that the young boy watched with fascination at the repairs of the intricate mechanism. Using his money, he bought sprockets, ratchets, gears and tiny wheels from the store. Driven by a compulsion to create and invent, Armand used these pieces of clockwork to propel the toys that he had made. When the father (an avid gun collector) of one of his friends gave him what he thought was a useless old gun, Armand re-fashioned it into a small cannon. Fascinated, the father gave him some gunpowder to see what would happen. The explosion from Armand's cannon brought neigh-bours scurrying from all directions and a pledge from the young boy that he would never fire it again.[9]

Yet as proud and supportive as he was, Alfred had other dreams for his first-born. Armand had always been a firm and enthusiastic Roman Catholic. His first paying job – helping to serve mass – was no more than an extension of his everyday religious feelings. Armand rarely missed Saturday confession or Sunday Mass and he made every effort to live his life as a devout Catholic. Thus, it seemed natural to Alfred that his son should pursue his calling and become a priest. In September of 1921, when Armand was 14 years old, he was sent to neighbouring Sherbrooke, Quebec, to attend St. Charles Borromée Seminary. There the youngster would be afforded a classical education in Greek, Latin, religion and other subjects that would prepare him for his vocation in conservative Catholic Quebec.

The problem was that Armand did not feel any calling. He accepted the teachings of the Church with a resolute faith and always endeavoured to live as God would expect of him, but he felt no desire to be a priest. His dreams lay not at the altar as a village cure, but with his hands on machinery and his mind scheming and probing for mechanical innovations. On trips home during holidays, Armand would be found in his father's garage, tinkering around, or down at the train station gazing in fascination at the steam engines there. For Armand, there was no crisis in faith, but definitely a crisis in career. The ultimate expression of this strong-willed boy's determination came over the Christmas holidays of 1922. Alfred had bought an old Model T from a local junkyard for his son and Armand had fixed up the motor, as he had done numerous times before with his father's machinery. But now he was going to take a giant leap forward from his past mechanical accomplishments.

The Quebec winters could be dismal bleak seasons. The great Voltaire[10] had described the land as "a few acres of worthless snow" when the King of France was establishing a new colony. The winters could isolate communities behind walls of snow that were impenetrable by car, by horse and cutter, and sometimes even by foot. Ted Rogers' development of the wireless radio would bring the world into these villages later on, but that day had not yet arrived.

But Armand had a vision. A fifteen-year-old with a passion for mechanics saw a way of breaking down the snow-banked fortresses. With the help of his younger brother, Leopold, New Year's Eve of 1922 was to be a night to remember for Armand. Using the frame of his Model T and a wooden propeller crafted from pieces of wood from the storage shed, and bolting them onto a two-passenger sled, Armand started the engine. His first snow vehicle shot out of the garage with

This is the technological innovation that transformed Canada's winter landscape – the first snowmobile developed by Armand Bombardier, 1922. *Courtesy of the Musée J. Armand Bombardier.*

two terrified but excited and proud brothers hanging on for their ride of a lifetime. With Armand at the throttle and Leopold steering the skis the contraption actually travelled about one kilometre. Alfred, however, was furious. Picturing pieces of his sons flying from "the propeller" machine into snowdrifts, he demanded that they dismantle it.

Armand himself had long dreamed of inventing a machine that would conquer the snow. In those days, of course, there were no snowploughs in rural areas, so when heavy winter set in people were trapped. In sudden snowstorms, farmers couldn't get outside to save stranded cattle; police cars, ambulances and fire trucks couldn't get through the drifts; people even had difficulty getting such basics as mail and food supplies. Armand knew he could help his community and others like it throughout Quebec.

Though Armand would dismantle the machine, he would never abandon the vision. His life was inalterably headed towards a future in technology rather than the Church. He never stopped thinking about his machines. His father, in the face of such determined resolve, agreed to let him leave the seminary and study to become a mechanic, and sent his sixteen-year-old son to apprentice at Gosselin's Garage in a neighbouring community. Quickly moving beyond that, Armand furthered his apprenticeship in Montreal. Wherever he went, he was respected as a mechanical wizard – deftly repairing, in record time, engines that had baffled older and more experienced mechanics. With a voracious appetite for self-improvement, Armand took courses in electricity and mechanics. Devouring all the reading material he could get his hands on, the teenager taught himself English since that was the language of most of the science and technology journals he read.

In April of 1926, the circle was complete. Still a teenager, Armand moved back home to Valcourt. His father had purchased land for him so he could build his own garage and continue his mechanical wizardry in his own backyard – surrounded by the friends and family members who were so important to his sense of personal self. In the summer of 1926, Garage Bombardier was opened, providing Imperial oil and gasoline for the automobiles and providing repairs not only to cars, but to any machinery that found its way into Armand's shop. While still a teenager, Armand Bombardier established the vision of a new method of travel and also built his first snow machine, changing not only his life, but the world forever.

He would go on to live a simple personal life in the finest French Catholic tradition. Marrying the great love of his life, Yvonne Labrecque, when he was 22, he would become patriarch over a close-knit family of six children that were an integral part of his business. In his spare time he loved fishing and hunting in the woods of Quebec, and of course there was always time for his religion. Faithfully attending mass, he also sang in the choir. A speech given to his employees in 1952 (the 10th anniversary of his company L'Auto-Neige Bombardier Limitée) sums up the values, which guided his life: "this torch, gentlemen, this flame, is the desire to help my compatriots succeed in life and to prove once again that the French Canadians are better than mere carriers of water."[11]

He explained that the flame mentioned was:

Love of work.
Love of your children and the future.
Love of God.[12]

Thus, Armand Bombardier demonstrated that a French Canadian could remain true to his heritage while succeeding in the English-Canadian world of science and technology. And succeed he did – probably even beyond anything this man of vision could possibly envision. In his too short lifetime, he was granted over 40 patents by the Canadian government. The Ski-Doo snowmobile is known throughout the world, but is just one part of the Bombardier financial empire. The company he founded, Bombardier Inc., is involved in aerospace, rail transportation equipment, motorized recreational products and in both military and industrial vehicles.

In December 2003, the recreational products segment of the company was sold to a group of investors, including the Bombardier family. This segment remains active on three continents and more than 80 countries, employing 7,000 workers and continuing a tradition of innovation that spans more than 60 years. Bombardier is a Canadian success story.

Even while dying, lying on a hospital bed being fed by intravenous tubes, Armand's active and inventive mind continued to project into the future. Aware of his own plight and thinking of others, he demonstrated his innovative spirit by working out in his mind a method of regulating the intravenous feeding tubes.[13]

He died on February 18, 1964, just as snow started to fall in his beloved village of Valcourt. He was laid to rest three days later, again, fittingly, while it was snowing. In his last will, he said to his children, "I now put my trust entirely in my Creator. I thank Him for having given me the faith to go through this trial..."[14]

CHAPTER TWELVE

Toy Jin "Jean" Wong: Spirit of the Dragon

T oy Jin Wong was born on July 30, 1919, but her story really begins in 1880 when Andrew Onderdonk arrived at a desperate decision in order to salvage his contract with John A. Macdonald.[1]

The story of the Chinese in Canada is not a story that instills a great deal of pride in our national psyche, but it remains a story that must be told. Although some historians assert that Buddhist monks sailed to British Columbia from China one thousand years before Christopher Columbus,[2] the first documented Chinese to Canada were a group of fifty artisans who settled at Nootka Sound about 270 kilometres northwest of Victoria in 1788 and built a two-storey house and a forty-ton schooner called the *NorthWest America*.[3] This colony did not last, however, and the chapter on Chinese in Canada really begins with the discovery of gold in the Fraser Valley in British Columbia in the 1850s and the influx of settlers – both white and Chinese – searching for wealth. Yet there was still no flurry of immigration from China until Onderdonk's decision in 1880.

Andrew Onderdonk, an American contractor, had been given the contract to build a railway for a vital 620-kilometre stretch of land from

Port Moody on the Pacific Ocean to Eagle Pass (near Revelstoke, the site of the "Last Spike," marking the completion of the Canadian Pacific Railway). Prime Minister John A. Macdonald had promised the railway to entice British Columbia into Confederation and complete his vision of a dominion from "sea unto sea." Onderdonk was the man who would deliver that dream, but he was faced with a massive financial headache. To secure the contract, he had to cut expenses to the bone and it was estimated that he was as much as two million dollars short of the capital needed.[4] His solution? He would import thousands of Chinese "coolies" (labourers) and pay them less than half what he would have to pay white workers. Connecting with the Lian Chang Company[5] and others, Onderdonk arranged for 2,000 Chinese to come from the Province of Kwang Tung[6] (whose main port was Canton) as the vanguard of the movement. In Kwang Tung, the average wage was seven cents a day for the peasant farmers, while the "Golden Mountain" (the name given by the Chinese to express their optimism about finding wealth in North America, specifically to the west coasts of Canada and the United States) offered a staggering $1 a day. Little wonder that a people beset by fourteen major floods, seven typhoons, four earthquakes, two droughts, four plagues and five famines as well as local wars[7] were flocking to answer the call. The dream was to save $300 and return to China to retire. The reality was far different for the 15,000 labourers[8] who arrived over the next five years.

Hostility and hardship greeted them. If they could read or understand English, they would have read this in the *Port Moody Gazette*:

> "Necessity compels us to tolerate a few Mongolians in
> the community, but let them herd themselves and not
> attempt to mix in with the whites. There is no affinity
> between the races, nor ever can be, in spite of all that is
> preached about the universal brotherhood of man."[9]

They were not wanted, but they were needed – and cheated. The $25 a month salary was reduced to about $40 annually. From their $1 a day,

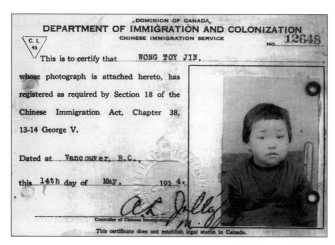

Like all the Chinese living in Canada after the Exclusion Act was enacted in 1923, Toy Jin (Jean) had to be registered and receive a certificate. *Courtesy of Arlene Chan.*

they had to pay for their tools, their rent, their clothes, their taxes, their food, oil and water, and even their fare over from China. The railway store enjoyed a monopoly in providing the essentials and the prices were exorbitant. Their diet of rice and stale salmon enhanced their chances of contracting scurvy, thus adding to their medical expenses. Naturally, there was no pay for the three months a year when work was impossible and the dream of returning home grew increasingly elusive. Naturally, too, the Chinese were assigned the most dangerous jobs – the tunneling, the dynamiting and the work in landslide areas. Little wonder that the Chinese assert that four men died for each mile of track.[10]

Thus, they were trapped when the railway was completed in 1885. Thousands of Chinese men had no prospect of returning home or finding a Chinese bride in Canada. They were unwelcome aliens in a hostile land. The same year that the last spike was driven into the ties (a ceremony to which no Chinese were invited), a "Head Tax" of $50 was imposed on any new Chinese immigrant to Canada – a staggering amount for that year. Moreover, any Chinese wishing to return to China was subject to an exit tax. Fun Gee Wong, who had just arrived as a labourer in Nanaimo, British Columbia, paid his $50. His wife, Mah Hong Wong who arrived in 1898 was not so fortunate. She and her infant son were both subject to the $100 Head Tax.[11] As Chinese immigration continued to trickle in, the discrimination increased. By 1903, the Head Tax was a staggering $500 per person. But the Chinese still came, leading to one of the most outrageous pieces of legislation ever enacted in Canada – the Exclusion Act of 1923. This legislation effectively terminated immigration to Canada for one specific group of people, the Chinese. After July 1, 1923, virtually all Chinese were forbidden entry. Moreover, any Chinese living in Canada had to register and receive a certificate. Any Chinese who was not, at that time, a Canadian citizen (by virtue of being born in Canada) was to be forever barred from that opportunity. The Chinese were to understand emphatically that they were not welcome in Canada.

This was the world into which Toy Jin Wong was born in 1919 and grew up during the 1920s and 1930s. Jean (as she came to be called) was the sixth of twelve children born to Fun Gee Wong and Mah Hong Wong. She was a young girl from a remarkable family whose courage, determination and indomitable spirit were forged in the fire of growing up "outside the circle."

The memory of the Vancouver Riot of 1907 still burned in the minds of Fung Gee and Mah Hong. Who could forget the spectre of six thousand thugs storming through Chinatown, smashing windows and screaming slogans like "White Canada Forever"? Who could forget the fear and humiliation of organized public meetings of the Asiatic Exclusion League, exhorting the youth of Vancouver to mayhem and violence? Jean was told from her earliest memory that white people were *fan gui* – devils. Fear them; avoid them; stay with your own. The advice was easy to follow since Jean was growing up in a Chinese ghetto. Nanaimo on Vancouver Island in 1920 was little more than a frontier village, small enough to still have dirt roads, but large enough to have its own Chinatown. This was home to the unwelcome intruders on white society. They could venture out to do the gardening on white estates, to pick up the laundry from the wealthy matrons and to babysit the precious children, but they belonged in the ghetto. Canada taught them they could not count on society for help so they turned to each other. This was an easy transition for a people steeped in Confucianism.[12]

They were taught that family was everything and that a stable family was the foundation of a stable society. Each person knew his or her role. Each person was well aware of his or her duties. Harmony and stability were the basis of family life. There remained a sense of fatalism – an acceptance of one's burdens – but there also remained a strong sense of hope. Through education, each person could advance. Learning was vital. It may be your destiny to endure the hardships, but you have the power to change that destiny. Jean knew her role and embraced it without question.

Her father worked in the coal mines until 1928; her mother bore children and looked after her husband's home, while Jean was the obedient daughter, always keen to be dutiful and helpful. When each younger sibling was added to the family, Fun Gee would explain that he went to the railway tracks and picked up a baby. Jean accepted this without question. Eleven children and Jean never once realized her mother was pregnant! These were hard times, but happy times. Firecrackers welcomed the Chinese New Year and children loved to watch the dragons in the parades. Afterwards, they would open their little red packages and treasure their newfound wealth – sometimes as much as five cents! The family did not have a lot of money, but they never lacked necessities. Material possessions were not important. The human being is what counted. In the darkest days of the Great Depression, when 80% of the residents of Chinatown were unemployed and when Fung Gee lost his 100-room hotel in Nanaimo because he couldn't keep up the rent (letting relatives, friends and people in distress stay for free definitely played havoc with the profit margin!), Jean and her family never went hungry. There was always food on the table and love in their hearts. Jean's mother often said that no child should cry. She never wanted to hear her children crying for any reason. This instilled in Jean a bright outlook and an appreciation for what the family had.

School was another source of joy for Jean. When Jean was five years old and ready to start school in Vancouver, a Vancouver school trustee was quoted in the paper as saying, "As a father, I object to my little girl

In the Wong household, the sense of family was central to making everything else worthwhile. Pictured here are Toy Jin (Jean), on the right, and her sister Toy Ying (Edna) in Nanaimo, circa 1931. *Courtesy of Arlene Chan.*

sitting next to a Chinese boy in school…I would keep Canada a white Canada as a heritage to my children."[13] There could be no question of where Jean would attend school. Each day, she would leaver her home on Pender Street and walk past the neighbouring white schools enduring the taunts and catcalls ("Chinky, Chinky, Chinaman" being one of the milder epithets) in order to arrive at the segregated school of Chinese, a few Japanese and Native Canadian children. In school, Jean excelled. She actually skipped a grade and was in the same class as her older brothers. That explains her heartache at the age of 12 when her father told her she could no longer attend school. The family had opened a small fruit store and needed someone to work in the shop. Robert, her brother, would stay in school because it was important for a boy to secure an education. Jean, a girl, did not need any more schooling since she would be marrying in a few years in any case. It was the first time that Jean could remember crying. Her mother's admonition of never crying seemed futile in the face of this devastating decision. Fun Gee was baffled by his daughter's reaction, but when Mah Hong explained to him that Jean loved school he quickly arrived at a decision – Jean's schooling would end, but her education would continue. Using her brother's texts, Fung Gee patiently, lovingly served as Jean's tutor for three years. In the day she would work; at night she would study. By the age of 15, Jean had a firmer grasp of the Chinese language than her brothers and a solid background in the Canadian school subjects. A window had opened when the door was closed. An added advantage for Jean was the opportunity to become even closer to her father, a man she would love, revere and idolize all her years.

Then, at age 15, another momentous event occurred in Jean's life. An older sister had married and she and her husband owned a fruit store in Toronto. They needed someone to help them and Jean was the obvious answer. Dutiful, but terrified of leaving the only life she had known, Jean accepted her responsibility. She would take the train to Toronto and help her sister. Then her mother made a surprising announcement. Jean would take her eight-year-old sister, Dorothy, with her. It would be one less mouth to feed for the Wong family in Vancouver.

Thus, in the summer of 1934, two terrified but excited young girls were taken to the train station. Fun Gee gave Jean some bread, a bit of ham and one dollar for drinks. Then, after hugs, kisses and tears, the girls embarked on a three-night, four-day trip on a hard bench across the vast country. A proud teenager gave her older sister the seventy-five cents change from the dollar when they arrived in Toronto.

Toronto was different for Jean. There were fewer Chinese and the prejudice was not as overt. It existed; it was obvious that the Chinese were not welcome in certain areas. But the underlying tensions, the annual Halloween invasion of Chinatown by teenage hoodlums and the blatant name-calling, were not present. Yet she could not stay in Toronto. The fruit store was not doing well, so they all moved to Sudbury and opened a restaurant – the Hollywood Grill. The restaurant did fairly well, but the isolation haunted Jean. At the age of seventeen, she decided to take Dorothy back to Toronto to work with her cousin and uncle at a fruit stand.

The Depression was hard on everybody in Canada, but it was harder on the Chinese. Little relief was available for a people who were neither wanted nor welcomed. When a church set up a soup kitchen in Vancouver's Chinatown, it was only given half the funds provided to "white" soup kitchens. One dollar and twelve cents per week was expected to provide fourteen meals for the Chinese supplicant. Little wonder that from 1931 to 1935 more than 100 Chinese died of starvation in Canada.[14] Little wonder too that Jean's father was struggling to support his family on a small pig farm he was operating. The dutiful teenager made a fateful decision. Borrowing two hundred dollars, Jean opened a fruit store at Bathurst and St. Clair in Toronto. Soon it was doing well enough for her to send for the rest of her family, whom she missed desperately. She missed her kind father who used to sit outside the home and smoke his pipe to reassure the children that no ghosts lingered in the vacant lot next door. She missed her gentle mother who would sit back in the evenings and listen to Chinese records on her gramophone, a calm and relaxed moment in her hectic life. She needed to be with them and she wanted to support them in their new life. So the family arrived and Jean found herself putting another brother through school at an expense of $100 per month. It was expensive, but there would be no complaints from a buoyant Jean, who was thrilled to be back with her family.

Shortly after her arrival, Mah Hong voiced a concern. Her daughter was still a teenager, but in a year's time she would be twenty. Did Jean have a man in her life? A girl who had been working the hours she put in for the past seven years had no time to consider romance and Jean told her mother there was no one. For a traditional Chinese woman like Mah Hong, that was no problem. Approaching a matchmaker in Chinatown, she asked her to find a suitable mate for her beloved daughter. The matchmaker came back with a promising prospect – this man didn't smoke, drink, gamble or fool around with other women. Moreover, he had $1,000 in his bank account. He sounded good, so Mah Hong invited Doyle Lumb to their home for tea. She told Jean that if she approved, then they would pursue the match. If she didn't like him, then they would find another. This was certainly a progressive approach for such a traditional woman, but Jean was special.

Doyle showed up at the house with his spats, his black coat and his fedora. Jean had only one reaction: "Wow!"[15] And it turned out that Doyle was as nice on the inside as he looked on the outside. He was quiet, but that was a nice yang to the yin of the outgoing, bubbly personality of Jean. Respectful of her parents, of her family and of Jean, Doyle would take her for walks, chaperoned by her brothers and sisters. When it came time to buy Jean an ice cream cone, Doyle had to dig deeper into his pockets to buy ice cream for everyone. But Jean was worth it. She was also worth the two hundred dollars he paid for a ring and the five hundred dollars he paid to the family as a dowry. He would gain a wife, but literally go bankrupt in the process (since he had borrowed money from friends to inflate his bank account in order to impress the matchmaker). It didn't matter. Doyle knew that Jean was special.

Still a teenager, it was now time for Jean to plan her wedding. The one vital component that she would insist upon was a Christian church. The "Church" was the only friend from Canadian society that reached out to the Chinese community during the dark days of racism. Through Sunday School, through services, through picnics and social gatherings, the Church gave the Chinese a glimpse of the white society that had closed its doors to them. Indeed, it was the Church that re-christened Toy Jin to the more Canadianized "Jean." All her life, Jean and her brothers and sisters had been active members of the church community. This was more than her spiritual haven; Jean realized it was her door to getting inside the circle. Thus in April 1939, while in the final months of her teenage years, Jean Wong gained a new name, but lost her old citizenship. Jean Wong was now Jean Lumb, but because Doyle was not born in Canada, he was not a Canadian citizen. Jean, born in Canada in 1919, was forced by law to take on the status of her husband. She would enter a new decade as a wife without a country.

Jean was determined that the injustices of her childhood would be overturned. She and Doyle would own a fruit store and later open the

Kwong Chow Restaurant on Elizabeth Street in Toronto's Chinatown. They would raise six children and Jean made certain that they were all active in High Park United Church – in the Sunday School program, in the choir, in the boy scouts, in the girl guides. Her children would walk through doors that had been shut in her face.

Jean would also fight against the gross injustices against the Chinese. The Exclusion Act of 1923 was finally overturned in 1947, but restrictions still remained. Families had obstacles in their efforts to reunite, and for Jean, family was everything. Throwing herself enthusiastically into the struggle for human rights, Jean was the only woman in a forty-person delegation to Ottawa to meet the Prime Minister in 1957. This was her chance, thought Jean, for a Conservative government was now in power. The Liberals were loathe to change the legislation that they had enacted, but the Conservative Party, under John Diefenbaker, represented a new opportunity. Jean sat immediately to the left of the Prime Minister. The man presenting the brief sat to his right and unknown to both delegates, Diefenbaker was deaf in his right ear. He kept asking Jean what the brief said, and Jean (who knew it by heart) kept informing him. Then, in the question period, a number of people directed their questions about the wives in China to the only female delegate – Jean Lumb. As a result, the unofficial spokesperson for the Chinese community was born. The odious legislation was overturned and Jean's role was invaluable. (As an added benefit, Jean was also able to be sworn in as a Canadian citizen once again.)

Jean fought other battles. Her efforts were largely responsible for saving Toronto's Chinatown from the developer's wrecking ball. She was given the Fran Deck Award as outstanding restaurateur in Toronto and the Award of Merit, the city's top honour; she was presented to the Queen on her Silver Jubilee and named Citizenship Judge for her community work. Perhaps the highlight of her accomplishments occurred in 1976 when Jean Lumb became the first Chinese-Canadian woman to be inducted into the Order of Canada. But perhaps, Jean's greatest honour is not any award she has earned, nor any battle she has fought and won. For Jean, it was a simple choice; "If I didn't have the family behind me, I really couldn't have done it. Because if your family isn't with you, beside you always, you really can't do anything. And if your family is strong, this will make our country strong, too!"[16]

CHAPTER THIRTEEN

The Baby Derby:
Escaping the Great Depression

*I*t might have happened in any decade; but it seems appropriate that the story of the baby derby unfolded during the dark days of the "hungry thirties."[1] It was a product of the 1920s and it acknowledged two symbols of that roaring, fun-filled decade: bequests involving horse racing and booze were important clauses in the will of Charles Vance Millar, a prominent, but rather eccentric bachelor lawyer who practised in Toronto. Yet the most famous provision of what Millar modestly asserted was a "necessarily uncommon and capricious" document was succinctly summarized in the following gem of legal brevity and clarity: "...at the expiration of ten years from my death to give [the bulk of my estate]...to the Mother who has since my death given birth in Toronto to the greatest number of children, as shown by the Registration under the Vital Statistics Act."[2] The death of Charles Vance Millar at 4:30 p.m. on October 31, 1926, launched the world famous baby derby or "Great Stork Derby" that would see its important final race against the clock dominate headlines during our country's most desperate years. The baby derby would meet two of the most compelling needs of Canadians during the 1930s: the need to forget about the terrible lean years that stalked the nation and the need to believe that even the poorest, most downtrodden citizen might have a chance to strike it rich. And in the process, the 118 children (of whom only 80 were eligible for various reasons) born to the top ten contenders came to symbolize both the despair and the hope of the Great Depression.

Nothing like this depth of despair and hardship had ever occurred in our Canadian history. Milk was only a dime a quart. Bread, fresh from the baker's oven, sold for about a nickel a loaf. Roast beef could be bought for twelve cents a pound. Altogether, the weekly grocery bill for a family of five might run to $5.00 or $6.00. But who could afford these prices if you were a construction worker earning $5.00 a week, a factory worker earning $10.00 a week or even an office worker earning $15.00 a week? These lean, hungry years were known as "hard times" for both those clinging to their jobs and the 35% of the workforce who could not find any work anywhere. When a help-wanted sign was posted, dozens of eager applicants scrambled to apply for the jobs. The decision by a father to buy a pack of smokes was enough to ignite a family blow-up. Arguments would accelerate as feelings of failure and hopelessness set in. Humiliation and shame burned on the faces of people standing in relief lines,[3] prevalent on city streets in those days before unemployment insurance. It didn't matter where you lived in Canada during the 1930s, life was a struggle.

The struggle was perhaps most brutal for the two million Canadians who lived in area known as the Palliser Triangle, a great piece of land that centred in Saskatchewan, but stretched into Alberta and Manitoba.[4] A drought had set in and an arid desert climate crept over the once lush, prosperous wheat farms that had flourished in the 1920s. Sad, weary eyes would gaze on the fields and see nothing but acres of parched sod. A farmer could pick up a clump of his barren, brown soil and watch the wind pick up the dust and blow it away. The dust storms were so bad that families had to sit inside in total darkness as the wind and dust assaulted their forlorn farmhouses.

Then the grasshoppers came – millions upon millions of them! Trains couldn't run because the squashed insects prevented the wheels

The drought and the sandstorms in the Prairies aggravated the suffering of the battered farmers in the "dirty thirties." The photograph shows a tractor and threshing machine partially buried in the drifted sandy soil, 1934. *Courtesy of Library and Archives Canada/PA-139647.*

from gaining any traction on the rails. The grasshoppers left a juice that turned barns and houses brown. If a farmer's wife left her broom outside, only the handle would remain, and even that was so badly chewed it was unrecognizable. Any farmer who was lucky enough to squeeze a sparse crop from the dry, cracked soil would bid it farewell when the grasshopper clouds loomed on the horizon.

Nor did winters provide any relief. The temperatures seemed to be always below freezing and the snowdrifts reached heights of twenty feet. The nearest neighbour might be miles down the road. Schools would close down in late January when communities ran out of money for fuel or for paying the teachers. This meant that young boys like Gordie Howe could play more hockey, but certainly not with the modern-day equipment we now enjoy. *Eaton's Catalogue* would do as the hockey pads and frozen horse manure (known as road apples) had to serve as the puck.

It is little wonder that these people sought an escape. Farmers who were proud and independent were reduced to standing in line at relief depots, throwing themselves at the mercy of the men behind the counter who would dispense food and hand-me-down clothing to the beaten breadwinners. They were living on farmland so worthless that the banks didn't bother to foreclose on the mortgages. Transportation for a people who couldn't afford the price of gasoline became the "Bennett Buggy"[5] (named after the Prime Minister of the time), those cars that had the motors removed and were then hitched to a team of starving horses.

Not that life in the cities of central Canada was much better. The obsession there during the thirties was getting, or holding on to, a job. Certainly during the Great Depression,[6] there were many companies who tried to be fair to their long time employees. Owners would feel genuine dismay at having to lay anyone off work. Yet just as certainly, there was a vicious, unscrupulous number of businessmen who used the hardships of others for their personal gain. There was a minimum wage for a 60-hour week in Ontario of $12.50, (about $0.20 an hour), but owners ignored the legislation, for no one would dare complain. Employers would expect their workers to provide extra help at their homes on weekends – as bartenders or waiters at a party, as gardeners, as baby-sitters or whatever. Again, no one would dare complain.

Complaining meant losing your job and facing the humiliating spectre of going on relief. Probably no word in that decade was capable of generating as much fear and disgust as the word "relief" or going "on the dole." To be eligible, a person had to live in the city paying the relief for a minimum of one year prior to applying. The attitude of those who had money was that Canada was in danger of being turned into a nation of lazy "dole-bums" who would drink away the money sent to them. Consequently, when a person applied for relief, his (or her) liquor permit[7] was confiscated. Without this permit, a person could not purchase any type of alcohol. Usually, one's phone would be disconnected since it was expected that there would be no time to gossip with friends when you should be out looking for a job. Likewise license plates and driver's licenses were taken away. A person was expected to walk or take the streetcar when going out to look for work. Investigators hired by the municipalities could enter a home without warning and demand reports on an individual from previous employers. And if a person was reported as seen in a tavern, then his relief was immediately cut off. Even the radio was usually confiscated.[8] Entertainment was not a commodity for those on relief.

Nor did the humiliation end with being eligible for relief. It continued with the first payment and every subsequent payment. For no one on relief could be trusted with money. Instead, vouchers were distributed – small cards listing the amount of fuel, rent, food and clothing that each family was entitled to receive. Lucy Alice Timleck, one of the finalists in the baby derby, together with her husband Arthur and their 14 children, received vouchers for only $15 a month from the City of Toronto. This was pitifully little but other families on relief also had to make do on less then forty dollars a month, with no provision for clothing until after the first year. These people too sought an escape from a life that seemed determined to bear down on them and break them.

In eastern Canada, the Maritimes experienced a particularly acute pinch of privation. This proud, prosperous and self-sufficient society enjoyed one of the best standards of living in all of British North America prior to Confederation.[9] Yet their economy seemed to spiral downward after joining with Ontario and Quebec to create a new nation in 1867 and resentment set in with poverty. The Depression exacerbated an already suffering situation. As factories closed down in central Canada and as the United States erected a wall of tariffs on imports, the Maritime economy stuttered to a halt. The pulp and paper industry was gathering cobwebs, the coal mines were shutting down and about one-third of the fishermen (a seasonal occupation in the best of times) were totally unemployed. Farmers in Prince Edward Island saw their income fall by 75% over five years. Newfoundland (which had opted not to join Confederation in 1867) was so destitute, it was reduced to becoming a

Families evicted with possessions piled around them were an all too common sight on city streets during the lean years of the Depression, photograph circa 1930. *Courtesy of Library and Archives Canada, Edith Gould Ottawa Acquisition, C-030811.*

British colony under the care of England. Thousands of Maritimers were thrown "on the dole" at a time when their local economies could not help them. Thus, while Ontario was paying an average of $8.00 monthly for relief, the average in Prince Edward Island was less than $2.00, and in New Brunswick only $1.67. Small wonder that scores of Maritimers gave up hope and left home for the United States or to "ride the rods"[10] across Canada, becoming a part of that phenomenon of the Depression years – the hoboes. Living in cardboard and tin shacks hastily thrown together near railway depots of towns and cities (bitterly referred to as "Bennettvilles") these vagabonds would wander through neighbourhoods looking for any small chores, line up at the "soup lines" of the local Sally Ann (Salvation Army) or hop a ride on the freight train to the next town in their futile quest for some work and some meaning in their lives. Sadly typical of the Maritime plight were the circumstances of a miner in Nova Scotia. He had worked the mines from the age of 14 to the age of 68. Then the mines were shut down and there was no pension available. He had paid into a pension program all his working years, but the money was not protected. It had gone into dividends for stock-holders during the heady days of the roaring twenties. The profits were there, but not the money for the workers. After more than 50 years of toiling in unventilated, dangerous pits, he was reduced to a government pension of about $14.00 a month.

Life was cruel. All across Canada and elsewhere in the industrial world there was a need for dreams and a need to escape. As the Depression continued to pound a bludgeoned nation, headlines from outside Canada did little to ease the oppression. That comic-appearing little man with the Charlie Chaplin moustache, Adolf Hitler,[11] no longer seemed so funny as he foamed and ranted against the Jews and embarked on his mad scheme of a powerful Germany ruling the world. Mussolini[12] was no longer a noble descendant of the great Roman Emperors, but a strutting, pompous bully who was determined to beat tiny Ethiopia into submission. The madman Stalin[13] in Russia was embarking on his murderous purges to root out and destroy all of his real or perceived enemies and Spain was engulfed in a bloody civil war. Meanwhile, Japanese soldiers had thrust through China, leaving a tragic trail of rape and butchery. The world seemed to be marching relent-lessly towards the second major war in less than a generation after "the war to end all wars." It was little wonder that these years came to be known as "the low, dishonest decade."

Escape of some nature became important. Hollywood was "king" during the 1930s. By now the movies could "talk" and they called to every member of the family. And although some of the movies did fea-ture the hard times ("I Was a Fugitive From a Chain Gang") people gen-erally did not want to plunk down their 25 cents to be reminded about what their life was like. The Hollywood "Dream Factory" churned out the adventures, the westerns, the romances and the screwball come-dies. You went to the show to forget about your troubles.

That was why people tuned their radios to "Amos 'n Andy," Fred Allen or the Jack Benny Show. Radio made you laugh and helped you forget. Of course, Saturday nights belonged to the most famous voice in Canada – Foster Hewitt.[14] His greetings of "Good evening, hockey fans in Canada and those in Newfoundland and the United States" brought the heroes into the homes. King Clancy,[15] Eddie Shore[16] and the famous Kid Line[17] of Charlie Conacher, Joe Primeau and Busher Jackson thrilled a generation and somehow made the unbearable bearable. This was a time period when people desperately searched for stories that could give them hope or help them through their darkest days. Human-interest stories abounded – from the Dionnes[18] to the abdication of Edward VIII;[19] from Grey Owl[20] to Gable and Lombard.[21] But none captured the spirit of the era as much as the story of destitute mothers scrambling to escape their poverty by winning the substantial reward accumulated for the baby derby victor. As the calendar and biological clocks ticked relentlessly closer to the hour of decision, newspapers intensified their glare of publicity. By 1932, the courts had seemingly silenced the cousins and half-aunts who had challenged the term of the will. The attorney general of Ontario had introduced a bill to send all the money to the University of Toronto, but backed down in the face of outraged opposition from political parties, the press, women's organizations and public opinion. The raunchy and headline-seeking bachelor premier of Ontario, Mitch Hepburn, could fulminate that it was "disgusting" and "revolting" and "an affront to the time honoured institution of motherhood,"[22] but anyone aware of his scandalous private lifestyle or the public mess that his government had made of the Dionne Quintuplets would only shake their heads at his hypocrisy. Attention was focused on the 17 claimants getting ready to collect, and particularly on the six finalists who had received so much publicity in the closing years of the baby derby: Annie Katherine Smith, Isabel Mary Maclean, Lucy Alice Timleck, Kathleen Ellen Nagle, Pauline Mae Clarke and Lillie Kenny. Collectively, they represented the drama of the Depression.

Of the six mothers, Isabel Mary Maclean stood apart. She registered late in the baby derby (October 30, 1936 – the day before the conclusion) and had managed to avoid all the press coverage of the earlier years. The mother of ten children, nine of whom were registered for the derby, her family was comparatively more affluent than the other contenders. Her husband John's job as a clerk with the provincial Highways Department guaranteed a steady income of $250 monthly and a home with their own private phone line! She continued to remain aloof from the other contestants, shunning interviews and quietly waiting for the court's final ruling.

Three of the other mothers had developed a close personal relationship during the derby. The Timlecks, Nagles and Smiths had been brought together by the newspapers for publicity purposes, but soon discovered they shared common values and common dreams. Alfred and Annie Smith enjoyed a steady income from his job as a fireman, but giving birth to nine children in ten years had been a drain on their meagre income. The hospital bills (aggravated by the tragic death of three of her children) also sapped their resources. Their dream was to buy a home, buy a car and share the winnings with some of the other families in the race.[23]

The Timlecks were somewhat between of the Smiths and Nagles in terms of money. Arthur had a job with city parks, but being the head of a family of 14 children (nine of them registered in the derby) forced the family onto welfare intermittently during the dark days of the thirties. One bleak winter saw Lucy Alice, Arthur and their three youngest children sleeping in the living room with a fireplace – the only heat in the entire house. The other ten children had to sleep in the unheated rooms. Tragedy seemed to stalk this family, as their baby Blanche was buried on the same day as the derby officially ended. Yet nothing could deter their hopes and aspirations. They wanted a home and a cottage for their children, a new car and presents for everyone that first Christmas. It was a natural dream for a girl who came to Canada as an indentured servant from Ireland at the age of six, ran away as a teenager and worked in a munitions factory during the war and had only glimpsed at prosperity on the movie screen. Interestingly, Lucy Alice had one other dream if she were to win – she would like to get a job as a birth control advocate.

The Nagles were the third family in the triumvirate. John was an unemployed carpenter at a time when there was no demand for his skills. Living on welfare, the Nagles found life to be a daily struggle. But if life was physically hard for his wife Kathleen, her spirit remained indomitable. She had a dream of having enough money so her children would all be able to receive an education. They would own their own house if they won, and never have to rely on public relief, and all its humiliation, again. It was Kathleen Nagle, in particular, who seemed to be the linchpin that kept not just her family, but all three families, close-knit. For instance, she suggested (when it appeared that she would be one of the winners) that all the winners chip in $5,000.00 each for the other mothers. This was embraced by the Smiths and the Timlecks almost immediately.

The final two finalists provided the most colour to the baby derby. Lillie Kenny wanted no part of any partnership. She saw herself as the one who was most like Charles Vance Millar (a gambler) and the one who most deserved to be the only declared winner. She was known in the press as "One Punch Kenny" because of an apocryphal story in which she took a swing at a news photographer and accidentally decked her husband with one swing. Living on relief, she and her husband had either eleven or twelve children and seemed certain winners. Unfortunately, one set of twins was mistakenly registered as one child and two other of her children were never registered at all. Nevertheless, she remained a reporter's dream with her boisterous sense of humour and her aggressive personality. While other mothers talked about security and education, she had a different idea of how to spend her winnings. She would hire a band and take it down to play at Charles Vance Millar's grave. Then she might buy Mary Pickford's frame house on University Avenue and open a museum. While the reporters were quoting one mother saying: "I would be satisfied with part of the money. We have been through terribly hard times, and I suppose some of the other mothers have had the same experiences. I would like them, as well as ourselves, to have a chance at a brighter future,"[24] Lillie was having none of that: "I'm not splitting the pot with anybody. I get it all or nothing."[25]

The winnings of over $500,000 were substantial. In today's currency, that amount would make you a multimillionaire. Small wonder that the derby aroused so much excitement in a vicarious public and so many dreams among the contestants. But what if the judge should rule against Lillie? "If the judge dares to say I am not the sole winner of the five hundred thousand dollars, I'll slap his face in court."[26] That comment reflected an earlier quote by one of the frontrunners in the derby. The mother of 23 children in all, two of her nine were not registered. When informed of this, she asserted that she would tear the Parliament Buildings apart before she gave up. Just before the judge's ruling, Lillie ran afoul with "Toronto's Finest" when she assaulted a timid American photographer with a statue of Charles Vance Millar that she was carving. It seems he tried to take her picture without offering to pay her. The police claimed she was drunk; Lillie asserted it was the cough medicine they smelled on her breath.

Finally, there was Mrs. X or Mrs. A. This attractive 24-year-old redhead would soon be revealed as Pauline Mae Clarke. Her social worker first informed her of the baby derby in the summer of 1935 so she was a late but enthusiastic, entrant. Her ten children placed her in a very solid position, but there were a couple of glitches to her claim. For a time, her residence was 571 Beresford and 533 Beresford represented the city limits. Even more perplexing were the ten children themselves. Five of them were products of her marriage to her husband. The last five were the children of her boyfriend, while she was still married, but separated from her husband. They were born in wedlock, but were they legitimate? It was an important issue because in legal terms, "children" refers only to legitimate offspring. Is this what the will meant?

Ultimately the will fell into the lap of Mr. Justice William Edward Middleton, born in Toronto in 1860, the eldest in a family of nine children, and one of the most brilliant, most common-sensible, and most respected legal minds on the bench in Canada. In simple, direct, but compellingly logical wording, he cut through the legal tangle confronting him. With appeals all the way to the Supreme Court of Canada, it would not be until March of 1938 that the issues would be resolved. If there was one group that did not experience the pangs of hunger during these lean years, it was the lawyers. Between the twenty mothers and thirteen next of kin, 33 lawyers were gainfully and giddily employed. In all, 28 would argue before the courts at one point or another – each for a fee regardless of the outcome!

And what was the final resolution of how to distribute the fortune of $568,106? Annie Smith, Isabel Maclean, Lucy Timleck and Kathleen Nagle would share the accumulated capital from Millar's estate – just over $135,000 each. Lillie Kenny and Pauline Mae Clarke would agree to $12,500.00 each ($2,500 of it just for lawyers of course) and drop any further claims to a share of the inheritance. The baby derby, except for its denouement, was over.

The four winners, true to their words, continued to live frugally, but comfortably. The only difference seemed to be the security that they had achieved. The City of Toronto had the effrontery to publicly demand welfare repayment from Arthur Timleck and John Nagle. Despite the fact that the city had no legal or moral right to any of the money, both families readily paid the "amount owing" and spent a small amount on new cars, new homes and cottages and new lives. The money was spent on small farms in the country, a small-town hotel or a restaurant in Toronto. Life continued as before, only without the worries. As one of the children recalled, fifty years later, "Our first Christmas in the new house I was twelve. We got everything: hockey sweaters, skates, bicycles. My father bought the first station wagon in Toronto. All I know is his money did us nothing but good."[27]

Ignoring the city's demand for repayment, ignoring her boyfriend, her husband and some of her children, Pauline Mae Clarke, still beautiful and now rich at the age of 26, moved to Detroit and was never heard from again.

Lillie Kenny bought herself a sealskin coat and took cab rides to tourist locales like Niagara Falls. When her money ran out, she opened a small museum in her home on Adelaide Street. For 25 cents (5 cents for children) people could see a statue of Charles Vance Millar, carved by Lillie, newspaper clippings and a chance to talk to one of the contestants in the baby derby. And visitors could remember when the notorious story provided them a glimpse of hope and dreams – a chance for the average Joe, or in this case, the average Jane – to escape the gruelling poverty of the Great Depression.

CHAPTER FOURTEEN

Erwin Schild: Accidental Immigrant

T hroughout our history, there have been many eras and innumerable instances that have made us proud to call ourselves Canadians. Our immigration policy of the past, however, is not one of them. Casually cruel, we imposed a crippling Head Tax[1] on people whose skin was a different colour from the Anglo-Saxon majority. For many Blacks, the Underground Railroad, marking the way to Canada for fugitive slaves before the American Civil War was as often a journey to a more subtle oppression as it was a passage to freedom. With colossal cynicism, government bureaucrats adapted our policy to domestic economic requirements, while ignoring the genuine plight of suffering refugees. Perhaps the height of our arrogant insularity occurred when an immigration official was queried as to how many Jews Canada would take in as they fled from the nightmare of Nazi Germany. His off-handed reply? "None is too many."[2] Canada, in the days before and during the Second World War, was largely an exclusive Gentile preserve that remained tantalizingly attractive, but prohibitively unreachable for countless victims of the Holocaust. It is a bitter comment on our national attitude that at the concentration camp in

A shot of Erwin Schild (centre) and friends in happier days before Hitler came to power. The only survivors of the people in the photograph are Erwin and Martha Simons (to his left). *Courtesy of Erwin Schild.*

Auschwitz, "Canada" was a metaphor representing an abundance of supplies that was closely guarded and off-limits to the prisoners.[3]

Yet despite the restrictions a number of Jews did come to Canada, settled here after the war, and contributed to the well being and prestige of our society. Erwin Schild was one of them. His story remains a fascinating account of about 2,200 Jews who have been termed our "accidental immigrants."[4]

Born in Cologne, Germany, in the early 1920s, Erwin seemed destined to lead a comfortable, sheltered existence. His warm family life revolved around his father, Hermann, a successful businessman who had risen to a leading position in the community. Hermann was respected for his integrity and compassion, and was active in civic, social and cultural causes and events.

At school, Erwin excelled. He was a gifted scholar who was popular with both teachers and students. He was also one of those lucky individuals who found the academic life interesting and rewarding. It was small wonder that the childhood memories for Erwin remain loving and untroubled. Erwin was twelve years old on January 30, 1933, when Adolf Hitler came to power in Germany and altered Erwin's life – and the entire course of world history – forever.

For years after Hitler's accession to office, the Schild family remained optimistic. "Hitler will pass," Hermann confidently asserted and "his bark is worse than his bite." The family genuinely believed that if you were a good citizen, paid your taxes, obeyed the law and contributed to your country, then no harm would come to you. There was a God and He was a just God. Even when Nazi soldiers broke an international agreement and marched into the Rhineland, where Cologne was located, in 1936, the Schilds remained hopeful. Surely now, the British and French soldiers would come and restore order – and sanity – to the German nation!

Yet help was not forthcoming, and the nightmare accelerated. By 1938, Erwin was away from home preparing for his university entrance exams and beginning to realize that the new Germany no longer could be a homeland for a Jew. The Schild family still felt no sense of urgency, but it did seem time to consider another country in which to start a fresh life.

Canada was certainly not on the list of possible destinations. This was the nation that had signs posted on public beaches in Toronto and Montreal: "No dogs or Jews Allowed." This was the nation of the shameful riots against Jews,[5] of Adrian Arcand[6] and his Canadian Fascist Party,[7] of F.C. Blair, the narrow anti-Semite who wielded such influence in the Immigration department. This was the nation whose Prime Minister (William Lyon Mackenzie King) enthusiastically embraced Adolf Hitler with such fulsome phrases as "appealing and affectionate," "truly loves his fellow man," "keen perception and profound sympathy," "a profound love for the man" and "there will not be war."[8] This was the nation that admitted five thousand Jews in the same years that United States admitted two hundred and forty thousand.[9] Jews who wanted to immigrate to Canada were told to lie. If they claimed that they were Christian, or claimed to be farmers, they might sneak past the ever-vigilant administrators. Otherwise, regardless of their education, regardless of their skills, regardless of their wealth, they were not welcome.

Kristallnacht (Night of the Broken Glass) on November 9, 1938, plunged Erwin into the clutches of a national insanity. This was the night that the Nazis unleashed their brutal thugs to destroy and loot building and beat and kill helpless people. Jews were stripped of their property, their money, their livelihoods, their right to attend school, their citizenship, as a world watched aghast. Erwin describes waking in the middle of the night as Nazis "invaded us with axes and other weapons. I thought they were going to kill us."[10]

Instead, Erwin Schild was dragged away to Dachau Concentration Camp.[11] The grip of the nightmare tightened when Erwin learned two days later that his father was also at Dachau. Now they had to get out of Germany. But how?

> By the end of 1938, the International refugee problem
> loomed so large that all countries closed their borders
> to German Jews. With increasing desperation, I wrote
> letters, sent telegrams, applied to rescue agencies
> abroad, enlisted in emigration schemes. No success ....
> The days go by; the panic at the pit of the stomach
> grows like a cancer.[12]

For Erwin, a miracle occurred. A sympathetic individual, with the Dominican Republic consulate in Cologne, and Erwin's enterprising and energetic mother combined to secure the release of Erwin and Hermann Schild from Dachau. Now, it was imperative to flee Germany forever. In January 1939, Erwin Schild saw his parents for the last time as he boarded a train that would take him to Holland, from where he would leave for England and freedom.

It is interesting, at this juncture, to consider the reaction in Canada to the horrors of the Night of the Broken Glass, for we were not unaware. The front page of our "national newspaper," the *Globe and Mail*, carried three stories a few days after this episode. One of these dealt with a speech by Hitler denouncing Canada's treatment of her Native Peoples and our government's response to his speech. A second concerned an interview with a group of Jewish refugees stopping off in Canada while on the way to Australia and New Zealand. Talking to reporters in Montreal, they warned of the persecutions and of the concentration camps and noted, "God knows what will happen to our people. We are lost in Germany."[13] The final story was the reaction of the influential Canadian Corps, an organization that was dedicated to restrictions on immigration and was quite influential in the 1930s, to suggestions that Canadian immigration laws be relaxed. The reaction of the Corps was one of outrage. There were stern warnings that any future citizens to Canada must be predominantly British. The Jews could be sent to Africa, but they must not be permitted to threaten "the democracy and civilization" of Canada. Tragically, although many Canadians were probably sympathetic to the Jewish plight, editorials across the nation continued to urge the government to stand firm.

The year that Erwin Schild arrived in England to continue his studies was also the year that Hitler invaded Poland, turning the world upside down. One week after England went to war, Canada too declared war on Germany. Ours was not a crusade against Nazi aggression and expansion. It was not a war against anti-Semitism. It was not a resolve to defend principles or powerless nations. It was a war because England was at war. More than a partner, Canada was determined to pronounce her loyalty to her mother country and to demonstrate her desire to help in any way she could.

The request for help was not long in coming. When invasion of Britain appeared imminent, the government of Winston Churchill[14] rounded up people living in England who had been born in enemy territory. This seemed a reasonable and obvious security measure by a nation that was terrified of the spectre of a Nazi "Fifth Column" of infiltrators and spies. Again, it was natural to include as many people as possible in the net of national security – including refugees. They could be sorted out in internment camps. Thus, on May 16, 1940, Erwin Schild ate his usual sparse breakfast and was about to leave for the study hall when two police officers came to the door and put him under arrest. They assured him he would be back to his room in a few days. It was the beginning of two years of absurd captivity that ended with Erwin Schild choosing Canada as his homeland. He is probably one of the few Canadians who spent time in both a German concentration camp and a Canadian internment camp during the World War II.

Classified as a "B" category internee, Erwin was officially labelled a "friendly alien" who was subject to a few restrictions, such as not being able to travel 25 miles out of London. He had every reason to assume his loss of liberty would be short-lived. The concern, of course, for England was the tremendous drain on manpower required to guard about 30,000 internees at a time when every able body was needed for the imminent invasion.

England's solution was an appeal to her former colonies to share the burden. As a means of assisting the war effort, Canada agreed to accept 7,000 category "A" prisoners – the hardened Nazis and prison-ers-of-war (POWs) who were considered the most dangerous. The embarrassment for England was that she did not have enough from this category to fill the quota. Thus it was that about 2,250 refugees from the Nazi terrors found themselves being shovelled out of England to an unsuspecting Canada. Erwin had no idea where he was headed as he boarded the ship *Sobieski* at Liverpool. On board were 548 Nazis and war captives and 982 refugees who had been interned. The accommodations provided were ironical but an appropriate indication of what lay ahead. The terms of the Geneva Convention[15] assured the Nazis of first-class compartments since they were classified as POWs. Meanwhile, the refugees were packed into the steerage, surrounded by barbed wire and machine guns.[16]

It was a confusing, and somewhat frightening, reception that awaited these people at Canada. Herded onto shore, the internees were ordered to empty their pockets. What they did not realize was that any valuables would be "confiscated" by the guards as souvenirs for wives and girlfriends. Fortunately for Erwin and his group, there happened to be a Jewish sergeant major as part of the Canadian detachment. When he saw the Hassidic Jews[17] with their black hats, beards and prayer shawls, he astutely realized that these were not dangerous Nazis. "Empty your pockets," he gruffly ordered in English, "But keep your valuable possessions hidden," he added in Yiddish.[18]

The bewilderment of the arrival very soon gave way to genuine terror as the internees were marched up to the detention camp. As Erwin Schild and the other Yeshiva (young devout Jews) were prodded by bayonets in Camp T (at Trois-Rivières, Quebec), Nazi POWs jeered them and broke into a particularly vicious marching song which promised that Jewish blood would spurt from their knives. For a frightening moment, it seemed to Erwin that he had been thrust back into Hitler's Germany. The anxieties and tensions were compounded as Nazis taunted Jews in the camps and disrupted their Sabbath. At this point, the Jewish internees insisted that they were not Nazis and should be separated. The result, ultimately, was segregated camps, but a segregation in which the Canadian officers seemed to favour the Nazis over the Jews.

This favouritism highlighted the main frustration of the Jewish internees. The physical loss of freedom was a terrible experience, but, in actual fact, conditions in internment camps were quite acceptable when one considers that we were a nation at war. What was not acceptable was the ongoing psychological distress that was a constant burden for the internees. Simplistic camp officers openly sympathized with the Nazis who were captured while fighting for their country. For the Jews, there was scant support and outright hostility. They were either disloyal traitors – "scum" was the most common noun – for not fighting for their country, or they were sneaky potential spies on the off-chance that they might still favour Germany. In either case, they were not good

This photograph from a Second World War internment camp in Quebec, circa 1940-42, is indicative of the menial and meaningless labour extracted from the men. *Courtesy of Library and Archives Canada (Marcell Seidler photographer), PA-143492.*

citizens in Canada. Erwin and a group of Jews approached the camp commander one day to ask if they would ever be allowed to settle in this new land. "There is only one way you will be allowed to stay in Canada," was his blunt reply, "Six feet under the ground."[19] What this mentality could never begin to comprehend was that a Jew, by definition, had to be an enemy of Nazism. Desperately, the internees sought to be regarded as friends. Tragically, they were persistently cast as enemies. Wanting to help in the war against Hitler, they were scorned and rebuffed. The government preferred to use them as cheap labour for trivial contract work, while they yearned to be a part of the crucial struggle against fascist totalitarianism. They could not join the army. They could not help produce war supplies. They could not grow foodstuffs for the Allied cause. Instead, they were marched into the forests to cut down trees for 20 cents a day.

Compounding this daily reminder of their status were the petty aggravations of camp life. Although technically they were aliens, they were classified as POWs upon arrival in Canada, and as such were subject to POW restrictions. Erwin was allowed only one letter a week. This was particularly cruel for someone shut off from his family and friends and who spent every waking day hour terrified of what was happening to his loved ones still enmeshed in the vicious web of Hitler-controlled Europe. As internees, Erwin's group had to fight for the right to observe their Sabbath and dietary laws. For some, this meant two weeks of starvation until the government relented and permitted a local rabbi to supply kosher food.

Life in the camp moved at a snail's pace. After the first struggle to be separated from the Nazis, the next struggle was to win classification as refugees rather than prisoners-of-war. Again, the government machinery crawled along slowly. After more than a year of negotiations and wrangling, the Jewish prisoners were finally granted refugee status. Yet, this only heightened, for the internees, the absurdity of their plight. Why remain in internment camps when there is a war to be fought? The answer, for Canada, was that Jews were still not wanted as immigrants. To release them would be to permit them to stay in Canada. The government attempted to work out an arrangement with the United States, whereby that nation would accept them, but this broke down when U.S. immigration laws required these refugees to be free for one year prior to immigration.

With remarkable resilience, the internees adjusted. Schools were established and correspondences courses made available. Although Erwin had already completed his university entrance courses, there still remained a splendid diversity of classes to select from. In addition to matriculation programs, courses ranging from English to Physics, History to Philosophy, Latin to Mathematics were all offered. With few books available, the fertile minds of the teachers (the other inmates and students) were the most valuable resource. Camp life was indeed culturally rich with art classes, music recitals and full theatre productions revealing an incredible wealth of talent. For Erwin, now about twenty years of age, these could not be totally lost years, since so much of his energy was directed towards self-improvement and growth. Yet they remain stolen years that could never be recaptured.

The idealism of youth was forcibly channelled towards himself rather than helping others.

So the weeks passed into months. Erwin was shuffled from Camp T in Trois-Rivières to Camp B, near Fredericton in New Brunswick. For him, the journey was marked by a march under the blazing sun, all the while carrying his supplies. When he arrived, famished and thirsty, he was dismayed to discover that the camp was in a very primitive state of construction. It was expected that the prisoners would do most of the work. From Camp B, Erwin eventually moved to Camp I (an island that is the present site of Fort Lennox near Montreal) and his eventual freedom.

For most of the internees, the months became years. It was not until December of 1943 that the gates were finally swung open and the refugee camps forever dissolved. Earlier that year, Erwin had been part of a fortunate group that was permitted early release in order to pursue rabbinical studies in Toronto. The ordeal – and the triumph – of Erwin Schild was completed!

The alumni of the internment camps represent an exceptional roster of achievement. Successful architects, doctors, lawyers and university professors are typical occupations for this most atypical group. Among them are counted Nobel Prize winners, physicists, authors and self-made millionaires. The accomplishments of these individuals far surpass any similar cross-section of Canadian society. The remarkable Erwin Schild is a case study in point. Arriving in Toronto, he completed his rabbinical studies and pursued a further education at the University of Toronto. He served as a respected and beloved rabbi at the Adath Israel Congregation in suburban Toronto for over forty years. A literary contributor to the journals and a keynote speaker at international synods, Rabbi Schild enjoys the esteem of people both inside and outside of Canada, culminating in his call to the Order of Canada in 2001. When he looks back on the years of internment, there is no bitterness in Rabbi Schild's heart. Instead, he regards his adoptive nation with gratitude and love. He says that he is most fortunate to be a part of this precious country, but the truth is that this country is fortunate to have secured Erwin Schild and the other "accidental immigrants."

CHAPTER FIFTEEN

Steven Truscott: A Struggle for Justice

T o grow up in Canada after the Second World War was to be a part of a generation that seemed truly blessed. These were the golden years for our nation, both in the world and at home, and so much of the attention and affluence seemed to be directed to the very young.

Canada emerged from the war as a significant player in the world arena. The country was an active partner in the ultimate defeat of the evil axis of aggression, and the Canadian army had been forged in the fires of Hong Kong, Dieppe, Ortona and Normandy. Canadian soldiers had driven the Nazi menace out of Holland and liberated a grateful people. The Canadian air force was the second largest in the world and the navy had demonstrated itself capable of defending the nation in two oceans.

Moreover, Canadian diplomats presided over what has been called Canada's "Golden Age of Diplomacy." Quietly, but effectively adapting to a new world order, Canada affirmed her increasingly close ties to the United States, while simultaneously working to develop strong multinational institutions. Perhaps nowhere was this more evident than in Canadian commitment to the United Nations.[1] The esteem extended by other countries was accepted. Canada was now a nation with wealth and technology, a nation that could provide leadership to the "middle powers." The recognition accorded to Canada allowed it to have a role in key decisions made by the fledgling world government. The first director of the World Health Organization was a Canadian, Brock Chisholm, and Canadian expertise and skills were lent to the Food and Agricultural Organization, established to increase the world's food supply. The International Civil Aviation Organization[2] had its headquarters in Montreal and Canadian advisors, equipment and money was channelled through the United Nations all over the world to aid in development.

In the political arena, Canada's significant role was very early noted with the election of Lester Pearson[3] to president of the General Assembly of the United Nations in 1952 and the repeated re-election of Canada to a seat on the Security Council. The culmination of the Canadian commitment and contribution to the United Nations was the awarding of the Nobel Peace Prize in 1957 to our able External Affairs Minister Pearson, for his innovative call for a Peacekeeping Force from the United Nations to secure peace in the Middle East – the first time in history that such an army was ever deployed!

At home, the situation was ever rosier. The Canadian Gross National Product (GNP)[4] literally doubled during the 1950s (from $18.4 billion to $36.8 billion). It was during these years that more than four million babies were born; more than three and-one-half million cars were bought; more than one million new homes were built and more than one and one-half million immigrants embraced Canada as their new homeland. Canada was the second wealthiest nation in the world (next only to the United States). The country's wealth was being augmented by millions of dollars pouring into the economy because of England's war debts and more millions being poured in by American investors, anxious to develop Canada's rich resources of minerals, fuels and forests. It was estimated that in 1950 alone, American investment put $40 (one week's wages) into the pockets of every man, woman and child living in Canada![5]

And with so much of the wealth, so much of the attention was being directed to a new phenomenon on the social scene – the "baby boomers." The birth rate soared after World War II and much of the consumer society was preoccupied with reaching the young people growing up in Canada. Television, of course, created a revolution in the way Canadians lived. The CBC-TV was established in Toronto and Montreal in 1952 and within two years was broadcasting from Halifax to Vancouver. The American channels swarmed Canadian viewers with "Davy Crocket" and we responded with "Radisson," a series which premiered in February 1957. Despite a flurry of press conferences and ambitious marketing schemes, the series failed to draw any significant audience and mercifully was cancelled within a few months. "Howdy Doody" was met by "Uncle Chichamus," a popular puppet show, which ran for years. Canada sought to affirm her identity but soon fell to the seductive lure of the American image. "Our Miss Brooks," Sid Caesar, Jackie Gleason, Joe Friday, Dennis Day, Lucy Ricardo and Matt Dillon – they were as much a part of the Canadian home and family as the American one. Canadians had their own Cliff MacKay, Alex Barris, Juliette, and, of course, "Hockey Night in Canada," but still they remained a comfortable consumer of the broader North American experience.

Music was changing too. As the baby boomers became teenagers in the late 1950s, "Rock and Roll" burst onto the scene, presided over by the king – Elvis "The Pelvis" Presley. Again, Canada had Paul Anka proclaiming his love for "Diana" and Jack Scott singing of his "true love," but for the most part audiences were content to tune into "American Bandstand" every day at 4:00 p.m. and identify with the American teens and the American idols.

The fifties decade was in its final year – 1959 – and Canada was comfortable in her position. Probably the three biggest stories that year were the opening of the St. Lawrence Seaway – a demonstration of our bright industrial future; the death of Maurice Duplessis[6] – an event that would rock Quebec and the rest of Canada with the ensuing Quiet Revolution;[7] and the appointment of Georges Vanier[8] as the first French-Canadian Governor General in 200 years. But for Steven Truscott, none of these events could match the horror of June 9, 1959, and the terrifying days afterwards that would shatter his life and plunge him into a nightmare that would engulf him for the rest of his teenage years and beyond.

It was a hot, sweltering June day that beckoned the children of Clinton, Ontario, to an early taste of the summer days of freedom. There was an exam coming up at school, but tonight was a night for swimming in the river, hunting turtles, playing baseball, going to Brownie meetings, riding your bike or just hanging out with your buddies. For two of the children, Lynne Harper and Steven Truscott, the day would change or destroy their lives irrevocably!

Lynne was young, 12 years old, very bright and very determined, but certainly not as mature as many of her classmates. Steven was two years older, very popular with adults and peers and even younger children (since he always treated them with respect and never teased or made fun of others) regarded as the school athlete and a natural leader in most activities. When Lynne asked him for a ride to the highway sometime after 7:00 p.m. (Steven estimates it was about 7:30 or so) that evening, they would take what Julian Sher called " a ride into history."9 They chatted easily along the way – two young people without any cares in the world. Lynne talked about seeing some ponies up the road, Steven waved to a couple of buddies who were swimming and they soon reached her destination – the highway. Steven dropped her off and headed back towards the bridge over the swimming area. When he glanced back at Lynne, he saw her getting into a Chevy with some type of yellow plate or sticker on it. He stopped at the bridge on the way back and a couple of the boys saw him – this time without Lynne. Steven was in no hurry, because he did not have to be home until 8:30, when he promised his mom that he would be available to babysit his younger brother and sister. Riding around at a leisurely pace, he eventually wound up at the schoolyard where a group of older kids (including his brother) were hanging out. He talked to several of the kids, joked around a bit with his brother Ken and after about 15 minutes (at 8:15), he started back home to take care of his babysitting duties. Steven had always been a responsible boy.

When he got home at 8:25, his mom went over a few last-minute reminders with him and then his parents left him to look after the two younger children. For Steven, it was the end of a fairly aimless, fairly average, fairly pleasant day.

Shortly after the news of the murder became public, Harold Graham, an OPP officer from Toronto, arrived in Clinton to take charge of the case that was horrifying the people of Ontario. The public demanded a speedy resolution. The headline "$10,000.00 DEAD OR ALIVE"[10] was emblazoned in bold print across the top of the *Toronto Telegram* – represented the revulsion that swept across the province. Ten times higher than the normal reward, this was to be payment for information leading only to the arrest, not the conviction. The ominous option, "Dead or Alive," dragged out from the days of the Wild West was flung into the faces of staid conservative Ontarians. Such blatant responses demonstrated the depth of public fear mingled with disgust at this act of a sex fiend. Lynne Harper had been raped and strangled and left in the bushes to decompose by a monster who roamed free.

Within two days, Harold Graham "cracked the case." Picked up without his parent's knowledge, taken to an interrogation room and aggressively questioned for hours into the night, 14-year-old Steven steadfastly maintained his innocence and never deviated from the first story he gave to the police. But Graham was certain he was looking into the eyes of a killer and booked him for murder. Now he had to polish up his case to ensure a conviction.

It is hard for anyone to examine what happened, considering what is known today, without concluding that there was no solid case against Steven. At best, a circumstantial scenario could have been developed to point the finger of suspicion at him. But if one were going to build up circumstantial cases, there were far many more circumstances that pointed away from Steven. Forensic evidence could place the death much later than Dr. Peniston insisted fell into a framework from 7:15 to 7:45 p.m. (indeed, Dr. Peniston later admitted he erred in giving such precise timelines). A strong case could be advanced in favour of Steven's innocence: his normal behavioural appearance; the lack of blood on his person or clothing; the lack of scratches despite the bulletin prepared by police, warning that the suspect had scratches on his face or body; the corroboration of his story by several independent witnesses; the changing testimony of the two key children who testified against Steven Truscott..., the list can go on and has been dealt with extensively not once, but on three different occasions by three different authors.[11] All of these mitigating factors seemed to pale in the face of three strong realities of 1959: a public demanding immediate justice (or revenge); an unthinking faith in both our legal system and our authorities (if he's arrested, there's got to be a damn good reason for it); and the failure of an innocent person to admit he was wrong or show any remorse.

The irony is that Steven had been brought up to respect his elders and to trust people like the police. He was also told to keep his emotions bottled inside – don't show fear or pain ("I seldom show my feelings.")[12] Had he appeared more like the frightened child that he was, he possibly would not have been treated like the sociopathic killer that he was assumed to be. But what do you say to a teenager who is convinced that the "good guys always win" and whose parents' lawyer assures him all the way along that what is happening is going to "unhappen" – it'll all turn out OK. Happy endings were not just the television message; they were the Canadian story.

Steven's life dramatically shifted. The Truscott family had always been unusually close-knit. As a result of moving from air force base to air force base and having often to adapt to new surroundings and forsake new friendships, the family looked inward for warmth, support and growth. Now, Steven was torn from his mother and father and brothers and sister. Home, now a 6X5 foot cell in a nineteenth-century prison in Goderich, Ontario, seemed more suited to a Charles Dickens novel than modern-day Canada. Outings were no longer family rides or solitary trips to the Bayfield River where it flows into Lake Huron, they were the drive from prison to courtroom (a "dingy room that was as familiar as the lobby of the local movie house.")[13] In that courtroom, Steven sat, knowing he was innocent but facing a jury that "knew" he was guilty. The quotes given by several of the jurors are a sad indictment on the effectiveness of the presumption of innocence in our courtrooms in 1959:

> I had no doubt from the beginning, but I did not form any conclusions until the end...

> I knew by the third day no one was going to prove that
> young monster innocent. If we'd a had to stay there all
> winter to convict that fiend, I'd a stayed...
> The way he sat through the trail showed he was capa-
> ble of anything...
> He never shed a tear...
> I knew the boy was guilty right from the start...
> When I looked hard at him, he stared right back, didn't
> even have the decency to drop his eyes...[14]

The jury was honest and sincere, but they focused on the victim as a child and the accused as a monster – a monster who was sitting in the same room as them. It only took two-and-one-half hours to determine his guilt, most of that time spent listening to Judge Ferguson's instructions. What followed is harrowing for any fourteen-year-old to have to hear and chilling for any civilized people to have to acknowledge:

> Steven Murray Truscott...the sentence of this court
> upon you is that you be taken from here to the place
> from whence you came and there be kept in close con-
> finement until Tuesday, the 8th day of December, 1959,
> and upon that day and date you be taken to the place
> of execution, and that you there be hanged by the
> neck until you are dead, and may the Lord have mercy
> on your soul. Remove the prisoner.[15]

Steven stopped believing. He believed his lawyer when he told him the charges would be dropped. He believed his lawyer when he told him that he would be tried in juvenile court. He believed his lawyer when he said the crown had no case. He believed his lawyer when he said the jury would find him not guilty. He no longer believed Frank Donnelly when he told him he wasn't really going to be hanged. Steven may not have cried in public, he may not have shown fear, but a terrified, lonely boy cried in his prison bunk that night and many nights after. One morning, he was actually awakened by the hammering of a carpenter building his scaffold – or so he thought. It was actually a home being built across the street from the jail, but Steven didn't know that. A fourteen-year-old lay in his cold, stark cell from the end of September until November 20, expecting to die. Even on November 20, he did not get a reprieve, but a postponement of his death penalty until February 16, 1960.

The death penalty was commuted, of course. Canada in 1960 was far too civilized, far too humane to hang a fourteen-year-old. He would only be told that he would be in prison for life. Life in 1959 meant at least 25 years (and could mean one's lifetime) and he would be kept dangling on another kind of rope until it was believed that he had suffered enough. So in January 1960, as Steven turned 15, he shifted from hell to purgatory. He no longer faced death; instead, he faced waking up every single day behind bars, away from sunshine and totally devoid of hope. To make certain that Steven understood what awaited him, his guards at Goderich manacled him in chains, securely handcuffed his wrists and pushed him into a car that would take him to Collins Bay Penitentiary in Kingston. Stopping en route, Steven endured the humiliation of shuffling into a restaurant in chains and relying on a sympathetic waitress to cut up his food for him while disbelieving staring eyes gaped at him from all around the room. Arriving that night at Kingston (he had to spend one night in penitentiary before being transferred to a reformatory until he was 18), his knees were shaking from fear and uncertainty. "I was so terrorized and pumped. You're in a state of shock...still expecting someone to come to your rescue."[16]

But there would be no rescue. After a night in the prison infirmary (to protect him from other prisoners), Steven was transferred once again in handcuffs and manacles – to Guelph Reformatory for Delinquents. When other 15-year-olds were entering high schools across Canada, moving into the swinging sixties, going to pep rallies and football games, skating parties and dances, Steven was forming new friendships with people who came from remarkably different backgrounds. He was coming to the realization that this was not some terrible mistake; he would not be set free, there would be no happy ending. Friends and believers would visit him but there was an estrangement. Their lives went on, while his had stopped and there were not as many things to talk about as there had been before. His family was still a virtual lifeline, with regular and cherished visits despite the long distances involved in travelling (his parents bought a trailer in Guelph so the visits from Ottawa would not be so onerous), but more and more, his new friends were people like Mike McGuin – a tough kid who had spent 17 years in various institutions between the ages of six and twenty-five. Lessons consisted not of Latin and Algebra when he turned 18, but of how to avoid the "muscle groups" who could own you and pass you around for a package of cigarettes.

In prison, there were some remnants from his former life. Steven was still an athlete and enthusiastically took part in basketball, baseball, hockey – whatever outlets were provided. Unlike the other team members, Steven could not leave the grounds because he was a federal prisoner "on loan." These restrictions could dampen his enthusiasm, but not his involvement. Similarly, Steven had been well-liked and respected in Clinton and this popularity continued in prison. A leader in his section (of about ten other teenagers), he always successfully urged his team to victory on inspection day – an accomplishment rewarded by radio privileges or free chocolate bars. Steven also gained the support and sympathy of the adult staff who interacted with him. They genuinely liked the lad, and this was reinforced by a growing conviction on the part of many that he did not deserve to have been found guilty. Invariably, in his relationships with others, people became increasingly aware that he was a victim of a miscarriage of justice. From warden to guard to kitchen staff to inmate, more and more people questioned whether he should ever have been put behind bars.

This experience continued when he was transferred to adult penitentiary in Kingston just after his eighteenth birthday. Looking after the tools and machinery in the kitchen, the Farm Annex and the Staff Training School, Steven was a busy inmate, who also found time to get up at 6:00 a.m. every morning to get the prison radio station set up. Every day, Steven went on the air with music and patter. After breakfast, he would tune his stations to outside stations so the inmates could listen to music and news from the other world, while he went about his

The notorious Kingston Penitentiary became both home and school for Steven Truscott after his eighteenth birthday. *Courtesy of the Archives of Ontario, F 1075-H 2672.*

full-time job. On Friday nights, he was the prison's radio disk jockey, broadcasting the latest requests for Elvis Presley or Johnny Cash. Steven kept busy – he even found the time to put together a tractor from various scavenged items that is still being used – but as he himself said, "I could never really become a part of prison life because I was not like the other men. I was not a criminal. ...I became a loner."[17]

The loneliness was compounded by new restrictions now that Steven was in a federal penitentiary – his parents were given the choice of a one-hour visit each month or two half-hour visits each month. Steven eagerly awaited these visits.

There was one set of visits Steven would never eagerly await. Ironically, the one group in the institutions that did not warm to Steven, did not believe his innocence and did not trust or help him, was the group most expected to be of assistance – the endless parade of psychiatrists and psychologists. The dilemma for Steven was their insistence that he admit his guilt as a first step towards recovery. How do you admit guilt when you are not guilty? So Steven was subjected to a barrage of visits, analyses, tests and drugs. Throughout, his story remained the same story told by a nervous fourteen-year-old when first questioned by the police. As Steven himself says, "There was no test that I wasn't willing to go through. I applied for DNA; it sure wasn't because I thought I was guilty. I did truth serum tests in the penitentiary, LSD tests, I went through all that.... Nothing came out to indicate that I was guilty. And it's always me having to prove that I didn't do it. What they did was wrong. And that's all I want them to do: say they were wrong."[18]

And so a paroled Steven Truscott[19] – an individual remarkably free of bitterness – permits a note of bitterness to creep into his voice at the memory of his treatment. In the year 2001, Steven Truscott decided to come out of the cloak of anonymity in one last effort to clear his name – not so much for himself, as for his loved ones.

He is still in a type of purgatory today, albeit a purgatory closer to heaven than to hell. Just as the spectre of death was replaced by the finality of waking every morning in prison, so too, the iron bars that confronted him every day have been replaced by emotional bars that still restrict and punish. He is very happily married to a woman who started off as a supporter of a 14-year-old and became his wife, his lover, his best friend and his most ardent advocate. He has been blessed with a lovely daughter and two sons that any father would be proud of. They know he is innocent of the heinous crime committed on that sultry evening of June 9, 1959. So do his many friends and neighbours who have lived with Steven for three decades and watched his gentle, patient and loving approach to the events and people he faces. His family, led by his mother Doris, has never wavered in its determination to have the truth ring out. Many of his childhood friends and former teachers want to see justice, so long denied, finally granted. Writers who have entered the fray as impartial witnesses are now staunch allies in Steven's fight for his name and reputation.

Yet every morning that Marlene wakes up beside her husband, she is also waking up beside a convicted killer. Every day that his children talk to him, they are talking to a convicted rapist and murderer. When Steven Truscott holds his grandchild in his arms, the baby is looking into the eyes of a man called a "monster" by the newspapers of yesterday. His neighbours, his friends now know him as Steven Truscott, but he can never use the name legally because of the conditions of his parole. Truscott family gatherings will still be confronted with the anomaly of two brothers using different surnames. And the final tragedy in a story overflowing with tragedies – is that despite the latest Federal Report by former Quebec judge, Fred Kaufman, that "a miscarriage of justice likely occurred,"[20] there will always breathe an uncertainty regarding his innocence.

CHAPTER SIXTEEN

Marilyn Bell: Swimming for the Glory of Canada

*J*f the sad saga of Steven Truscott represents night falling on our last innocent decade, then surely the sun shone brightest in these years on an evening in early September of 1954. For that was when Marilyn Bell touched the shoreline of Toronto and completed her miraculous swim "for the glory of Canada."

Marilyn was born in Toronto on October 19, 1937, the first child for Sydney and Grace Bell. He was an accounting clerk for Dominion Stores and received promotions that saw the family move to North Bay in 1939 and then Halifax for the war years. When the war ended, the Bells (with a younger sister for Marilyn born in 1944) moved back to Toronto and the quiet, bright, young girl started attending St. Mary's Convent School. She was an honour student at school, but her parents were searching for an activity that would help her develop other interests. Ultimately, Marilyn, as an anxious nine-year-old, ended up at Alex Duff's Dolphinette Swimming Club. Despite her very slight build, she seemed more suited for long distance swimming than for sprints and soon developed a strong, steady crawl stroke used for longer swims. At the age of ten, she was easily covering one-mile distances and it was then that her father made a fateful decision for her – he entered her in the junior girl's one-mile race at the Canadian National Exhibition in the summer of 1948.

The Exhibition, often called the "Grand Old Lady" by the lake, was as much an institution in Canada as it was in Toronto. The first fair was held as far back as 1846 in Toronto, and by the 1880s, the Exhibition grounds held 23 permanent buildings and a grandstand with seating for 5,000 people. When the Chicago World's Fair of 1893 unleashed a new phenomenon to fair grounds everywhere – the midway – a new trend emerged. The CNE buildings were now joined by ferris wheel rides, sideshows and carnies huckstering games of chance. The modern exhibition was born. The "Roaring Twenties," also known as the "Golden Age of Sports," saw a heightened public interest in competitions among athletes. The auto races and bicycle races helped to satisfy the public craving, as did the sculling and rowing events. But again, it was in Chicago in 1926 that the most famous event of the exhibition was born.

The American chewing gum magnate, William Wrigley Junior, offered a staggering prize of $25,000 to any person who could complete the swim from California to Santa Catalina Island, 20 miles out in the Pacific Ocean. More than 100 of the world's most famous and most successful long-distance swimmers hastened to Los Angeles to seek their gold and glory. A quiet unknown 17-year-old from Toronto, who had ridden from his hometown to Arkansas on his friend's motorcycle, was among them. When the motorcycle broke down, the boys hitched a ride with a young couple and arrived, unheralded, in the City of Angels. After a few weeks of training the young man slicked himself down with grease and silently entered the waters with the rest of the contestants. The race was on! Miraculously, George Young[1] was the only contestant to successfully finish. Fighting off high tides, rough waves, cold water and clinging kelp, George even swam side by side with a curious shark. Finally, George did what none of the other more famous contestants were able to do. A little under 16 hours after the start of the race, George touched shore and a new Canadian hero was born.

Naturally, Canada had to respond to it's hometown hero's accomplishment and on January 16, 1927, the CNE announced that in conjunction with the William Wrigley Company of Canada, it would be presenting a

An early photo-
graph showing
eager participants
in one of the
Canadian National
Exhibition's first
Marathon
Swimming Races,
circa 1930.
*Courtesy of the
Archives of Ontario,
RG 2-71, COT-112.*

Marathon Swim at that year's fair. A long and lucrative marriage between the Canadian National Exhibition and marathon swimming competitions had begun. A record attendance was set that year (an increase of almost 300,000) and although the home crowd was disappointed when George Young had to be pulled, exhausted, from the bone-chilling waters after 5 1/2 miles, they were thrilled and delighted with this brand new event.

When Marilyn's father entered his daughter in the 1948 race, he was introducing her to a different type of competition. She was used to swimming long distances, but not in open, chilly water with high waves. Marilyn finished ninth in the race, but was grateful to receive the praise of an older swimmer, Winnie Roach Leuszler.[2] She was a member of Gus Ryder's Lakeshore Swimming Club, which dominated both the exhibition swimming races and the entire world of marathon swimming. Her words of encouragement to Marilyn lifted her spirits and influenced her into joining this new club in order to gain more training and experience in open water swimming. From that time on, Marilyn came under the tutelage of Gus Ryder, who recognized that marathon swimming was not a race but an endurance test where the heart of the competitor was more important than her physical condition. And in Marilyn, he met a girl who had tremendous heart and spirit.

Success came quickly and steadily to Marilyn. The following year at the Ex she finished a strong 6th, then the next year a very close 2nd. In 1951, the 13-year-old decided to enter the senior women's swim as well as the junior girls. Bad weather pushed both events into the same day, yet Marilyn still succeeded in finishing a strong 2nd in the senior swim and winning the junior. The following year, she turned professional and finished 4th in the three mile marathon for a prize of $300.00. The next year, 1953, saw her finish 3rd and win $500.00. Her improvement was steady and consistent and she was looking forward to 1954 as her breakthrough year to first place.

It was then that the CNE completely changed the rules of the marathon events. In February of 1954, officials from the Ex announced that there would be no marathon competition as there had been for the past several years. Replacing the shorter open water race would be a 30-mile challenge to the entire lake, open to men and women alike.

Then, in April, the officials announced another change of plans. Now there would be no contestants invited, save one. The world-famous Florence Chadwick,[3] 34 years old and conqueror of the English Channel, the Dardenelles, the Straits of Gibraltar and the Catalina Channel would be invited from the United States to challenge Lake Ontario. She would be given an exclusive contract with the CNE. If successful, she would receive $10,000.00; if she failed, nothing. There would also be a support event of a thirty-two mile relay open to any teams of four who wanted to compete. The CNE felt that this back-up plan would provide an alternative entertainment, should Florence Chadwick be unsuccessful. But for the main event, no one else need take part.

The reaction was immediate and vocal. Resentment at the arbitrary announcement mingled with humiliated national pride at being excluded by an American. Gus Ryder told the press he was "surprised and angry"[4] while Marilyn, usually demure and quiet, said she was "burned up."[5] It seemed so unfair to slam the door just when you were about to enter. Nevertheless, the officials were unbending. A contract is a contract and what difference did it make in any case? No one had ever conquered Lake Ontario and the only person with even a remote chance of doing so was Florence Chadwick. Why clutter the lake with needless contestants who would be pulled from the water after just a few hours and divert attention from the real story – Flo versus Lake Ontario?

Thus, Florence Chadwick arrived in Toronto in a flurry of publicity and a contract that gave her the exclusive right to decide when she would enter the lake from Youngstown, New York (it could be anytime in a five-day period, depending on her determination of weather and water conditions). She was also met by the steely resolve of two young Canadian girls. Marilyn Bell and Winnie Roach Leuszler (the same swimmer who had praised Marilyn in her first Lake Ontario swim) announced that they would enter the waters after Florence Chadwick and challenge the American. While Chadwick would be swimming for $10,000.00, the two young women would be swimming for "the glory of Canada."

All of the advantages lay with the American. In addition to her experience and past success, she controlled the playing board. She could rest and mentally prepare herself for the event for which only she knew the timing. Rumours floating from her camp ("the race is tonight"; "no, she'll enter the water tomorrow afternoon") meant the Canadian girls had no chance to rest relax or properly prepare for the start. Finally, at 11:00 p.m. on Wednesday, September 8, Florence Chadwick entered the chilly waters. Exactly 60 seconds later, she was joined in the water by her Canadian counterparts. The Exhibition officials declared that they would not stand in opposition to the Canadian challenge, but there would be no prize or assistance for them from the Ex.

The first shock for Marilyn was the total darkness that engulfed her. She had never swum at night before and she could not even see Flo or Winnie. She would later learn that Winnie lost her guide boat in the dark and had to turn back, leaving Marilyn the lone Canadian competitor.

Next came the lamprey eels. Gus and the other swimmers had warned her about them, but she still felt a jolt of fear when one of them latched on to her bathing suit. Keeping her stroke as steady as possible, she grabbed the slimy thing, pulled it off her body and flung the writhing creature into the darkness. This was the first of many eels that would plague her during her gruelling ordeal.

She continued her stroke through the darkened waters. She had passed Florence Chadwick three hours after her start (it was part of her strategy to surprise and attempt to discourage her competitor), but she had no idea where she was at this stage of the swim. She was not aware yet that the American was beset by water sickness and had violent stomach contractions and vomiting all through the night. In the very early hours of the next day, swimming only on pride, with all thoughts of $10,000 long forgotten, an exhausted Chadwick was pulled from the waters. Marilyn was now alone in the cold forbidden lake.

Marilyn too was feeling the agony of the ordeal. She started tiring five hours into the swim since she had been without sleep by that time for over 18 hours. Her stomach pains had spread to her arms and her legs and her entire body ached from weariness. Was it worth going on? Gus Ryder reminded her of all the crippled kids that Marilyn coached at the Lakeshore Club. They were counting on her and Marilyn couldn't let them down. Inspired, she found new energy and churned forward through the waves. But the waves were powerful. Riding the crests of 12-foot waves, Marilyn rode through the trough and struggled on. She had started at 55 strokes per minutes in order to pass Florence Chadwick, but she was still maintaining a remarkable pace of 50 strokes per minute!

Then about 4 o'clock in the afternoon, Marilyn couldn't go on. Her diet of pablum and corn syrup could no longer help her. Exhortations about the crippled kids counting on her were of no avail. Her swimming was erratic, her head was bobbing and she finally ground to a halt. Crying now, she knew she couldn't go on. Her parents in a nearby boat and her coach in the guide boat sensed her despair. Who could blame the 16-year-old for giving up after so many weary hours in the water? She had already done what others had failed to do and no one would think less of her if she came out. But then her good friend, Joan Cooke, stripped down to her underwear and dove in beside her. Marilyn was revitalized! Joan swam beside her until Marilyn once again firmed her iron resolve. Now, Marilyn was the only person in the lake, but now she would stay in until she had conquered it.

Meanwhile, on shore, interest had swelled. Torontonians scrambled to the rooftop of the Royal York Hotel to scan the horizon with binoculars in search of the tiny figure in the water. Thousands upon thousands of people gathered at the shoreline, anxiously praying for her success. Searchlights were now cutting across the sky and flares were being sent up every 30 seconds to help guide the remarkable teenager. She had been the focus of national attention and it seemed that all of Canada stopped what it was doing to watch the riveting drama unfold in the

Swimmer Marilyn Bell is shown with her coach Gus Ryder and Toronto Mayor Nathan Phillips, 1954. At the time, Marilyn was so popular that she could have supplanted the mayor, who was known as "Uncle Nate, the Mayor of all the People." *Courtesy of the Archives of Ontario, C221-0-0-30.*

cold, choppy waters. Donations and gifts started pouring in and the CNE announced that $10,000 awaited her if she were successful.

But Marilyn knew nothing of this. All she knew was that she had to complete the painful journey she had started. Darkness had again fallen, but Marilyn swam on, inch by agonizing inch. Finally at 8:15 p.m., almost 21 hours after her start, she touched ground at the Exhibition, and national hysteria ensued. Honour upon honour was bestowed on the national heroine. A ticker tape parade, an official civic welcome at City Hall, a parade through the Exhibition grounds, more than $60,000.00 worth of prizes and gifts in addition to the $10,000.00 cheque from the CNE – nothing was too much for the sixteen-year-old who had captured Canadian adulation and Canadian hearts. Television and radio appearances, as well as an offer for a movie contract followed. She appeared in both *Time* and *Life* magazines and was flown to New York to appear on Ed Sullivan's "Toast of the Town." She was headline news across the continent. So great was her acclaim that the next summer she was a headline performer at the same exhibition, which did not want her the year before. All she had to do was dive into a special clear tank measuring 12 x 60 feet and swim a few strokes. This was met with wild enthusiasm from an adoring audience in the grandstand. They were applauding not just a seventeen-year-old who was now a celebrity, but more importantly, a sixteen-year-old who had taken the challenge for no other motive than the "glory of Canada" and in conquering Lake Ontario, also conquered a nation.

CHAPTER SEVENTEEN

Wayne Gretzky: The Great One

H ockey is our passion. Canadians are a people renowned for our diffidence, our quiet self-effacing manner, our courtesy and our lack of excessive emotion. Taking considerable pride in our bland self-image, Canadians constantly compare themselves favourably to their more volatile neighbours south of the border. While Americans are viewed as brash, crass and assertive, Canadians see themselves as quiet, law-abiding, orderly people. Americans exalt July 4, embracing it with an evangelical fervour and an almost orgy of patriotism. Three days earlier, Canadians self-consciously attempt to generate some enthusiasm for our national birthday (is it Dominion Day or Canada Day?). Great American presidents such as the Roosevelts, Lincoln and John Kennedy are renowned for their stirring oratory and their ability to inspire a nation. Our prime ministers are measured by their political longevity and ability to smoothly avert crises. The American West is defined by the gunslingers on both sides of the law – from Billy the Kid to Wyatt Earp, while our west is defined by that staid and stolid symbol of law and order – the Mounties. We say self-control and responsibility; they say freedom and liberty. Restraint seems to be our defining trait.

Yet, hockey is our passion. It is both our national dream and our national obsession. Ironically, the cultural icon that is our national sport draws from Canadians those very qualities that are the antitheses of our national character. Hundreds of thousands of Canadians play the game and millions more watch it. In 1972, our world stopped in September, while national attention focused on a showdown in Moscow. Classes were cancelled and students crowded into gymnasia to watch the action on tiny television sets. Office and factory work shut down as people sat riveted to radios, listening to Foster Hewitt call the play by play. Shoppers clustered around the appliance departments of Eaton's and Simpson's to share in the communal experience of the Canada-Soviet Summit Series.

Similarly, generation after generation of youngsters were glued to their radios (and later, to their televisions) for *Hockey Night In Canada*. Foster Hewitt began broadcasting for the *Toronto Star* from Mutual Street Arena (now demolished) in downtown Toronto in 1923. Within ten years, the CBC was broadcasting coast-to-coast, starting with a Toronto Maple Leafs-Detroit Red Wings game. In 1952, the transition was made to television, and for the past 50 years, Canadians have continually thrust *Hockey Night In Canada* to the top of the ratings in our country – the only exception would be the NHL lockout for the 2004-2005 season. The Canadian Hockey Association (CHA), responsible for amateur hockey in Canada, estimated that there are more than 3,000 arenas, offering 1.5 million games and two million practices every year. More than half a million players are registered with CHA and over four-and-a-half million Canadians are involved as coaches, players, officials and volunteers. These numbers do not include the millions of parents watching the games or the millions of children involved in pick-up games on the streets, on the rivers and ponds and on our countless rinks dotting our landscape. Yes, hockey is, indeed, our passion.

Wayne Gretzky, simply stated, is the greatest player ever to pursue our national dream. But, regrettably, as a child, he also suffered from the fallout of hockey being such an obsession. However, before reaching his twentieth birthday, he placed his personal stamp on our national sport. And he did it with a flair and an elegance that may never ever be matched.

Wayne Douglas Gretzky came into the world on January 26, 1961. It seems appropriate that on the night that he was born, Gordie Howe scored a goal that resulted in a two-two tie in a game between Detroit Red Wings and Chicago Black Hawks. Gordie Howe was considered by most to be the greatest player in the history of the NHL and was to play an important role in the childhood of the "Great One."

And what a childhood it was. Wayne was the eldest child of Walter and Phyllis Gretzky (he would be followed by Kim in 1963, Keith in 1967, Glen in 1969 and Brent in 1972) and lived a life that seemed to be lifted from the idyllic pages of an old *Dick and Jane* reader. His hometown, Brantford, a quiet community of about 60,000 people, was renowned as the home of Alexander Graham Bell while he was working on his invention, the telephone. About a 75-minute drive from Toronto, it offered the relaxed and friendly pace of a small town yet was close to the big city amenities. Even more important than Brantford was a 25-acre farm, a short 20-minute ride from home, in the hamlet of Canning in Oxford County. Tony and Mary Gretzky, Wayne's grandparents, lived here and it was always a second home for the growing Gretzky clan. With the Nith River flowing through it, the market garden farm had cucumbers, potatoes and corn as well as a yard full of chickens that had to be fed (this quickly became Wayne's main job on the farm). For Wayne, it was the best of all worlds.

The farm represented a paradise for the youngster who would eagerly drive out with his family after supper, on weekends and during summers. Throughout the summertime there was swimming, rafting and fishing on the river, while the winters meant skating for hours, then coming to the warm kitchen to have a hot chocolate and get ready for *Hockey Night In Canada*. As a two-year-old, Wayne was already either on skates for hours during the day or in the evenings in the living room, shooting tennis balls past the bruised knees of the first goalie to be beaten by a Gretzky shot – his beloved grandmother, Mary. It was a

Wayne Gretzky's hockey prowess caused people to forget that he excelled in all sports. This is Wayne (centre with the ball) beside other members of his Championship High School Midget Basketball Team. *Courtesy of Heather Pantrey.*

warm family; it was a close family; it was a supportive family. For the shy, blond child, it made him "the happiest kid in Canada."[1] As his father said, "if there was a better way of growing up I don't know what it would be."[2] While pursuing the carefree loves of his childhood, Wayne was also gaining strong moral and spiritual foundations from his family. The main lessons that Walter and Phyllis wanted to impart to their children were simple, yet powerful: always finish what you start; respect others and never feel that you are a better person than someone else just because you are able to do something better; share willingly what you are fortunate enough to have; and be proud always of yourself and your family. These values of commitment, responsibility, generosity and a healthy humility mixed with pride would provide the focus that would guide Wayne through his life.

A gifted athlete, the young Wayne was actively involved in baseball, basketball, lacrosse, hockey, track and field and cross-country. He loved all sports, was talented in virtually all of them, and excelled, in particular, in baseball and hockey. Brantford offered leagues and teams for all these endeavours and Wayne was an enthusiastic participant.

Increasingly, his life was revolving around sports. From his toddler years on skates, Wayne quickly developed a passion for hockey. On his grandparents' farm, he would spend seven to eight hours every day, skating on the river before he was old enough to go to school. By the time Wayne reached kindergarten age, his father was faced with two dilemmas that he had to resolve. The first of these dilemmas was that Wayne seemingly lived to be on the ice. He would drag his willing father to the parks and skating rinks all winter long when he wasn't at his grandparents' farm. Walter would sit for hours, freezing, while his son never seemed to satisfy his insatiable obsession with skating. All Wayne wanted to do in winters was to be on ice. He calls it his "serious addiction to hockey" and Walter was paying the price for feeding this addiction. To solve the first of his dilemmas, the "Wally Coliseum" was born. The Gretzky backyard was frozen – all of it, all winter long – and a neighbourhood skating rink was created behind the house on Varadi Street. For the rest of his childhood, Wayne would have his own private rink to play on (usually with kids much older but not more skilled than him) and this is where he would put in thousands of hours of practice and play – while Walter was now able to watch from the snug, warm comfort of his kitchen.

The second dilemma was that Wayne was just so talented. By the time he was six, he was a seasoned veteran of four years of skating, each year representing thousands of hours of free skating, practising and drills. Wayne wanted to play in a league, but the youngest division was for ten and under. To solve the second dilemma, Walter took his shy, slight six-year-old son to tryout camp against bigger and more experienced ten-year-olds. The smallest hockey sweater engulfed the youngster and hung down to his knees. To give his son a little mobility and freedom, Walter tucked the right side of the sweater into his hockey pants and the famous Gretzky trademark, that would stay with him his entire career, was born. Wayne so impressed the coaches that he made the division as a six-year-old, certainly the youngest player ever to play in the Brantford League. Some eyebrows were raised among the other parents who wondered at the wisdom of sending such a young child out on the ice against boys who were so much bigger. But Wayne had already absorbed the first crucial lesson taught to him by Walter and Phyllis. He had started the season; he would finish the season. Commitment was big in the Gretzky household and even a boy as small as Wayne could embrace that wholeheartedly. So the season was brought to completion. Statistically, it would be Wayne's worst season. He finished with one goal, prompting some of the parents to shake their heads and murmur that he didn't belong in a league with the big boys. But for Wayne, the important thing was that he did finish what he had started. And he showed himself and his teammates that he belonged on the ice with them. He was proud of that year and he had earned the right to be proud.

The next year, one year older but still dwarfed by most of his teammates, Wayne was back. And the beginning of a legend started. His goal production went from one to twenty-seven for the season and he won his first ever award – the Wally Bauer Trophy as the most improved Novice All-Star. It wasn't Wayne's intentions, but his successful season that quieted the voices of the few parents who had whispered that he didn't belong in the league. Little did they – or Wayne – realize that he was on the cusp of three incredible years that would change his life forever. In 1969/70, the eight-year-old stood the league on its head by scoring 104 goals. Along with his 63 assists, he dominated the statistics. This had to be a fluke season. Surely he would not be able to match those numbers ever again. He didn't match them as a nine-year-old, he destroyed them. One hundred and ninety-six goals; one hundred and twenty assist; these types of numbers had never been achieved before. What could he possibly do for an encore in his final year as a "10 and under"? Not one, not two, but three – 378 goals – a number so powerful, it defied logic. His runner-up in the goal-scoring race was about 240 goals behind him. This time, Wayne didn't just shatter the record, he sent into the stratosphere!

With the success came two companions that would dog Wayne for the rest of his childhood. Publicity and controversy started following him from rink to rink. Newspapers had first started to notice him when the quiet six-year-old broke into the league. Now at the age of ten, he was signing autographs. John Iaboni featured him in an article in the *Toronto Telegram* on October 28, 1971. Arenas in towns and cities across Ontario would publicize his participation in up-coming games. He was helping to fill 16,000 seat arenas, granting interviews to national magazines as well as local reporters and had earned a brand new nickname – "The Great Gretzky." Rocket Richard[3] stunned the hockey world in 1944 when he scored 50 goals in 50 games. Wayne would score 50 goals over a weekend in a tournament at Hespeler, Ontario. Yet hockey was not Wayne's only sport. When his remarkable season ended, he pursued two of his other loves. He was captain of the lacrosse team that won the city championship and racked up 158 goals and 66 assists in 31 games. He also played shortstop and pitcher for the Beaver League Baseball Team that ultimately became the Canadian national champions that summer. It should have been the happiest of times for the local phenom from Brantford.

But controversy and criticism tarnished his accomplishments. Wayne had always been a team player. He was taught from the time he first laced on skates that an assist was just as important as a goal. He was not a one-man team; he was part of a group of boys who skated and worked together for a common goal. He was the best player on the team, but it was a team and Wayne never placed himself above others. Respect for others and the notion that you weren't a better person than someone else just because you could do something better were values that Wayne had been taught and had embraced at an early age. So he never had any difficulty with his teammates. They were his friends and his fans. There was no jealousy when Wayne played both forward and defence; when he was double-shifted late in close games; when he skated out for both the power play and the penalty-killing. He was the number one player and the coach knew this, Wayne knew this, his teammates knew this and his

Eleven-year-old Wayne meets his idol Gordie Howe at a Great Man of Sports dinner held at the Kiwanis Club in Brantford, May 4, 1972. *Courtesy of* The Expositor *(Brantford)*.

opponents knew this. There was no jealousy or backbiting in the dressing room or on the ice.

But in the arena seats, it was a different story. Most of the parents could sit back and enjoy watching their children play – win or lose. But for a small minority, hockey, the obsession, spilled into the children's arena. Resentment stirred as Wayne went on the ice while Johnny sat on the bench. Parents would criticize Walter or Phyllis outside the arena for letting Wayne play so much. Some parents would show up at game time with stopwatches to record – to the second – how much ice time Wayne was getting. A few parents let their obsession overwhelm their common sense and common decency. People would openly boo the small boy as he skated onto the ice. He was not Wayne Gretzky, the ten-year-old child; he was Wayne Gretzky, the sporting phenomenon. After games some parents would even stomp into the dressing room, not to console their sons, but to berate Wayne for scoring too many goals. Professional athletes might be able to handle unfair criticism (although that is questionable), but no ten-year-old should be expected to endure it. As his coach, and uncle, said, "All the kids would like to be

Wayne. But parents? There are a lot of parents who despise him. That's a rough word to use, but honest too."[4]

Even at his happiest moments, Wayne would feel the hot glare of publicity. Later that year at the Brantford Sports Banquet, the shy eleven-year-old got to meet his hero, Gordie Howe. Wayne was at the banquet because of his remarkable season. He never expected to have to speak, but suddenly the M.C. called him to the microphone to say a few words. The small child at the adult banquet was terrified. He approached the microphone but was completely tongue-tied. He couldn't even utter a syllable. All he could do was gaze at all those adults who were waiting for him. At that point, his lifetime idol, Gordie Howe, came up, put his arm around his shoulder and said "Anybody who's had the kind of season this boy has had doesn't need to talk."[5] The situation was saved for Wayne and he could return to his seat. Wayne learned two things from Gordie Howe that night. The first – that lesson in dignity and graciousness – would stay with him forever. The second was a practical tip for Wayne on the ice. Gordie told him to always work on his backhand shot because goalies were a bit weaker on those saves. It is interesting that Wayne's first goals scored in Junior B hockey, Junior A hockey, the WHA and the NHL all came on backhand shots.

His final three years in Brantford hockey would be more of the same. For Wayne, it felt like "The world's shortest childhood."[6] He had to hire an agent; he was profiled on *Hockey Night In Canada* as well as in newspaper and magazines across Canada; he now travelled all across the country to participate in tournaments, won more trophies and awards and honed his hockey skills while entering his teenage years. Meanwhile, the verbal and emotional abuse continued and intensified. Parents turned what should have been a triumph into a hell. The climax occurred on February 2, 1975, a week after Wayne's fourteenth birthday. It happened in the most famous symbol of hockey in all of Canada – Maple Leaf Gardens.[7] It was Brantford Day at the Gardens – a day with different Brantford teams of various age levels playing against one another. It was Brantford kids playing; it was Brantford people in the seats and the town's most famous resident since Alexander Graham Bell was skating out onto the ice of Maple Leaf Gardens for the first time in his life. And he was booed. The people of his hometown shouted at him and booed him simply because he was the best player their town – or any town – had ever produced. It was at this point, that Wayne was determined he had to leave his hometown. The pressure was simply too much.

The solution lay 70 miles down along the highway to Toronto, home of the Metropolitan Toronto Hockey League (MTHL), today known as the Greater Toronto Hockey League, the largest minor hockey association in the world. To get there, Wayne would have to overcome three hurdles – convince his parents, secure a release from the Brantford League and gain permission to play in Toronto. The first of these hurdles would be the most difficult. Persuading his mom and dad that his grade 8 education at Greenbriar Public School would ready him for the experience of living away from his family in the big city would be a tough sell. Walter and Phyllis were adamant that their eldest child was too young to endure the isolation and culture shock of life away from his family. But Wayne was equally determined that he couldn't stay in Brantford and his parents had taught him to stay with something once his mind was made up. Finally, Wayne addressed his father's greatest concern – drugs. Wayne said that this was what his father was afraid of – that Wayne would enter high school in an environment that permitted experimentation with drugs. Then, he took his biggest risk. He told his dad to give him twenty dollars, to name any illegal drug and Wayne would be back in 30 minutes with it. Walter caved in. If drugs were in Brantford, there was no point in not trusting his son in Toronto. Wayne could go.[8] What Walter didn't realize was that Wayne didn't have a clue whether or not there were drugs available in Brantford. It was not a part of his world. Had his father given him the twenty dollars, Wayne would have returned home with Baskin-Robbins ice cream or some other treat for the family.

That left two more hurdles. Getting a release from Brantford in

1975 was not a problem and securing permission to play in the MTHL for the Nats Major Bantam team seemed to be "a piece of cake." On June 19, 1975, a court order provided legal documentation stipulating that Walter and Phyllis were granting parental authority to Bill Cornish (manager of the Bantam Team) and his wife Rheta, as legal guardians of their son. Wayne would live with his coach in Toronto and be the responsibility of Bill and Rheta as he entered his high school years. It was a high price to pay, but he could talk to his family every day by phone and go home on weekends, and at least he could play hockey in Toronto – that is, until the Ontario Minor Hockey Association stepped in. In September, three months after the legal guardianship papers had been approved and just as the season was about to start, they decided to turn down Wayne's transfer request. The legal manoeuvering began.

The Gretzkys and another set of parents hired Alan Eagleson's firm to pursue the matter on behalf of their two sons. An appeal was made to the Ontario Hockey Association, but they sent it back to the OMHA. In the courts, the lawyer sought an injunction against the OMHA decision, but the Ontario Supreme Court denied the injunction, until all possible alternative legal avenues had been explored. Just when it appeared that the Gretzkys had hit a brick wall, Bill Cornish came up with an ingenious solution. If Wayne couldn't play in the MTHL, what about Junior B hockey? These were 20-year-olds and beyond the jurisdiction of the OMHA. Rather, Junior B was under the direction of the OHA, which was willing to accept the young player. So Wayne Gretzky, a 14-year-old, weighing 135 pounds, was going to be playing against 20-year-olds weighing over 200 pounds. The OMHA tried one last time to block Wayne by suspending him, but the OHA (which had always honoured suspensions in the past) ignored this petty and vindictive move by the flailing executive, and Wayne was free to play.

The rest of the Wayne Gretzky story is so well known it scarcely needs rehashing. Two years at Junior B, then drafted into Junior A at the tender age of 16. One year at Junior A, then signing a million-dollar contract with Nelson Skalbania and the fledgling World Hockey Association. One year in the WHA and then he joined the National Hockey League at the age of 18 with the Edmonton Oilers. Every step along the way, critics said he could not survive at that level. With every step he proved them wrong: Rookie of the Year in Junior B; Rookie of the Year in Junior A, Rookie of the year in the WHA, outstanding Rookie in his first year in the National Hockey League. He shattered the rookie scoring record in his one year in Junior A. At the age of nineteen, he became the youngest player ever to score 50 goals in the NHL. In his very first season at the highest level of professional hockey in the world – the NHL – he tied for the scoring title, won the Hart Trophy as the most valuable player in league and the Lady Byng as the most gentlemanly player in the league. The year before, in the WHA, he had participated in his first ever three-game match against the Soviet hockey players and helped his team to three consecutive victories. All of this was accomplished before he reached his twentieth birthday. Perhaps the culmination came on January 28, 1979, two days after his eighteenth birthday when Peter Pocklington[9] flew his entire family to Edmonton and Wayne signed a new contract that would commit #99 to the Edmonton Oilers for 20 years – until 1999. Changing fortunes led Pocklington to trade Wayne to the Los Angeles Kings in 1988. The year 1996 found Wayne playing for the St. Louis Blues and later for the New York Rangers.

Wayne retired in 1999, after changing the game of hockey forever. Like another child prodigy, Mozart, he excelled as a child and exceeded his genius as an adult. When he left the NHL – to spend more time with his family – he had played on four Stanley Cup teams and three Canada Cup teams. He had won the NHL Scoring Crown ten times and the Hart Trophy nine times. He held 61 league records, including 40 regular season records, 15 playoff records and six All-Star records. He is the only player to score 100 goals in one season (87 regular and 13 playoff goals in 1983-84) and he straddles like a colossus over all the offensive categories. He is the greatest. And in his latest tribute to the game he loves so much, he organized the Canadian team that brought home the

Olympic Gold Medal for hockey for the first time in 50 years at the 2002 Olympic Games.

Today, the Gretzky legacy continues as Wayne enters a new chapter in his life as coach of the Phoenix Coyotes, a team of which he is part owner. Based on his golden touch to date, Phoenix fans are anxiously awaiting their first Stanley Cup.

CHAPTER EIGHTEEN

Terry Fox: A Marathon of Hope

On July 28, 1958, Rolland (Rolly) and Betty Fox welcomed a little brother for Fred. Terrance Stanley would be named after uncles on both sides of the family and become a part of a growing household of three boys (Darrell was born two years later) and one girl (Judith would complete the Fox family in 1965). Terry could not have chosen better circumstances for a happy childhood had he tried. Betty and Rolly were a team. She was straightforward, always protective of her husband and children as the main focus of homelife. He was quiet, generous and devoted to Betty and the kids. Although Betty became the spokesperson for the family, it would be a mistake to assume that they were not equals in the marriage and the child-rearing. Both were vital in their respective roles. Both would instill values into Terry and his siblings that would lead to the remarkable saga that would mark Terry's life.

"Normal" is the word repeated over and over in describing Terry as a child. There was no hint of greatness, no outstanding traits that foretold a future that would captivate a country of 24 million. One of Betty's favourite recollections of Terry's character is an anecdote from the time he was six months old. As a baby, Terry loved to play with

Family was a vital component of Terry's life and value system. Shown here are (from left to right) Darrell, Fred, and Terry with Judith in the foreground. *Courtesy of Darrell Fox and the Terry Fox Foundation.*

blocks and toy soldiers. When he was just learning to sit up, Terry would stack his blocks and little plastic men. As they fell to the floor, he would methodically pick them up and stack them again. They would fall again and Terry would restack. He'd get angry and he'd throw them, but would always return to the stacking until they finally stood the way he wanted. His mom and dad realized that their second-born was stubborn and determined long before he could even walk.[1]

Other incidents in his childhood demonstrated the young man that he was becoming. The family loved rough-housing. Rolly would be on the floor wrestling with young Fred and Terry, and Terry would never give up. He kept coming back to the fray – searching for that final blow to win the mock battle. It was the same in family discussions. To an outsider, these discussions might appear to be shouting matches. Terry was always determined to win his point, and in childhood that was often accomplished by yelling louder than his opponent.

And sports – Terry loved sports. Entering adolescence, Terry was slight for his age. He stretched to reach five feet in grade eight and was only five feet six inches in grade ten. Yet this didn't deter him from participating. His parents had taught him to work for whatever he wanted and to always finish what he started. These values, along with good manners and respect for others, were engrained in Terry. It was no surprise that in grade eight, the diminutive boy was the nineteenth player on a nineteen-boy basketball team. His total court time accumulated to about one minute for the season and he was on the team only because the coach never cut anyone who showed up for the practices. It was also no surprise that Terry persuaded his best friend, Doug Alward, to spend hours playing one-on-one basketball during the summer. Doug was also of slight build, but a much better player than Terry. Sometimes, they would be joined by Doug's older brother Jack – a gifted athlete. In the fall of grade nine, Terry joined three other boys to form an early morning practice session every day before school. Rolly and Betty did not approve of Terry's disruptive schedule, so he lay in bed as late as possible, then leaped up, gulped down breakfast and ran to school in pitch darkness to make the practice. In grade nine, he was one of the twelve best who shared court time and in grade ten, he was the 5'6" starting guard. Grade twelve also saw Terry and Doug share the "Athlete of the Year" award, with Terry excelling in basketball, soccer and rugby.

He was a skilled athlete, but his success was the result not of natural ability, but of determination, drive and discipline. The young man entering Simon Fraser University was remarkably competitive, but also eager to please, all the while imposing high standards on himself and his peers. It was natural that one of his first acts at school was to approach the basketball coach and express his interest in trying out for the school team. Even though Simon Fraser was a school brimming with outstanding athletes, Terry's toughness, dedication and relentless work ethic propelled him to a spot on the junior varsity basketball team. He seemed to be comfortably headed towards his future – that of a high school phys-ed teacher and coach. Life was good.

Terry had driven across the bridge many times, perhaps too many times. That might explain his inattentiveness as he drove his 1968 Cortina over the familiar route on November 12, 1976. A fateful moment of inattention from a usually focused person resulted in Terry rear-ending a half-ton pickup truck. Although his car was a write-off which would never be driven again, Terry emerged relatively

Terry Fox, the athlete, proudly displays one of his many trophies (this one for basketball) in the family home. *Courtesy of Darrell Fox and the Terry Fox Foundation.*

unscathed. Except for a sore knee (maybe from hitting the dashboard), Terry was unharmed. He hopped a bus to make it to basketball practice, chagrined by his lapse of attention but determined to carry on as usual.

The knee continued to bother him through December and January. Unfortunately, it was basketball season and Terry would just have to play through the pain. It was hurting, but athletes didn't let small aggravations stop them. There would be plenty of time to have it heal or have it looked at when the season ended. Terry would go to the university walk-in clinic in February to take care of it.

They examined Terry and gave him some pills (he did not realize that they were just painkillers). Sure enough, the pain went away, but returned the next month with even greater intensity. His knee was swollen and throbbing and Terry knew something serious was wrong. He had no idea how serious. On March 4 a further test confirmed what the specialist suspected – osteogenic sarcoma or cancer of the connective and supportive bone tissues. Terry, ever courteous, thanked the healthcare workers for running the tests, then faced a life-altering (and ultimately life-destroying) crisis. Remarkably, the courageous, heroic character of Terry was already manifesting itself. The doctor told him that only two years previous the chances of survival were only 15%, but more recent research had improved his odds to almost 50%. Instead of focusing on the spectre of death, Terry started thinking of the value of research. Instead of falling into a natural torpor of self-pity, Terry immediately started plotting his recovery. He would lose a leg the next day, but he would never lose hope. That night, his former high school coach brought him an article from *Runner's World* about Dick Traum, an amputee who competed in the New York City Marathon. A dream was born. There was no despair for Terry on March 9 when he lost his leg to cancer. Rather, there was a determination to conquer his formidable enemy.

But to conquer such a ruthless killer would require incredible strength. It is ironic that the young man who emerged with only one leg was in fact a much stronger person, combining heroic elements of confidence, drive, compassion and selflessness that would prepare him for his mission. Placed in a paediatric ward with younger patients, Terry felt an intuitive empathy and served as a positive role model for the children. Sure, he had suffered a setback, but Terry was a survivor and a fighter and he knew that nothing could hold him back. Even while undergoing chemotherapy, Terry enthusiastically responded to Rick Hansen's[2] offer to try out for the Canadian national wheelchair basketball team. He was weakened from his treatment and he had to retrain his brain to adapt to this brand new approach (where legs are no longer the key part of the game), but he worked his way into becoming a vital cog on the team. Yet even this was but a prelude for his more ambitious plans.

Starting in January of 1979, Terry devoted himself to a new regimen of weights and running. "I ran a quarter of a mile for the very first time…Most of it was falling down and picking myself up…but I ran."[3] And he ran. Through blisters, bruises, shin splints, raw sores and constant pounding on both his good leg and his stump, Terry worked and worked until he perfected the most effective running style for himself. By the summer, he was running ten miles a day and by Labour Day he was ready to enter his first competitive race – the Prince George to Boston, British Columbia, seventeen-mile marathon. Terry finished last in the run, but as his brother Darrell said, "It doesn't matter where you finish – it's only that you finish."[4] Terry may have been the last person to cross the line, but the broad beaming smile on his face and the exuberant cheering of all the other participants who stayed behind to witness this exercise in courage told everyone that Terry was a winner! Terry now could share his secret dream with others – he was going to run across Canada starting the next spring. On one good leg, he would run 200 consecutive marathon races (one every day for over half a year) without taking any days off to rest between runs. This seemed an impossible quest when one considers that healthy world-class marathon runners with two legs must take a recuperation period of three to seven days after completing a marathon. Terry's rest period would consist of one night's sleep and he would run 200 marathons in 200 days. Yet no one who knew Terry doubted him. His best friend Doug Alward knew he would do it; his parents knew he would do it (although they would have done anything they could to stop him from his dangerous mission); Terry knew he would do it.

Moreover, this run could not be about Terry Fox. His mission was not an ego trip, it was a selfless act for others. The purpose of the run was not self-aggrandizement and publicity, but to raise 24 million dollars for cancer research – one dollar for every single Canadian. The goal was not to run over 5,300 miles through rain, cold, steep hills and intimidating transport trailers, but to inspire a nation to dedicate itself to fighting a deadly scourge. In his letter to the Canadian Cancer Society, soliciting their support, Terry emphasized that the goal was not personal, but altruistic. He also recognized the tremendous odds that faced him. But as he said, "I believe in miracles. I have to."[5]

Once the Canadian Cancer Society agreed to support Terry, his next task was to persuade Ford to donate a van, Imperial Oil to donate gasoline and Adidas to donate running shoes. There would be no corporate sponsors, no logos – this was to be a personal and selfless act that would profit only cancer research. Nevertheless, certain funds were needed to secure air passage, food and supplies.

This Terry secured, then faced his final hurdle. His parents were naturally worried about his safety, but they knew they couldn't stop him. A doctor could accomplish what no one else was able to do. If a heart specialist felt that the run was too dangerous, Terry's dream would be in shambles. Unfortunately for Terry, he had an enlarged left ventricle in his heart which was of considerable concern to the examining specialist. This was not your normal enlarged athlete's heart, and he was reluctant to give final approval. In the face of Terry's athletic fitness and steadfast determination, he finally agreed. Yet he warned Terry that should he experience shortness of breath or blurred vision, he must stop immediately. Thus, Terry was given the go-ahead while privately harbouring a potentially deadly secret – he had already experienced all of the warning symptoms that his doctor had tagged during his training for the run. Terry would not only undertake his Marathon of Hope on one leg, he would undertake it with what a heart specialist would consider a diseased heart!

Virtually all Canadians are familiar with the highlights of Terry's spring and summer of 1980. The marathon began on April 12, 1980, when Terry dipped his toe in the Atlantic Ocean at St. John's, Newfoundland. He also collected some water to put in the Pacific Ocean upon the completion of his journey. Accompanied by his best friend, Doug Alward, and joined by a representative of the Canadian Cancer Society, Bill Vigas, and later by his younger brother Darrell (who was given permission to write his high school final exams early and skip his commencement), Terry started his remarkable run. Sometimes, the rain was stinging; sometimes the cold was raw and the wind biting; sometimes transport trucks shook the ground and drove him off the road. Sometimes people would line up and cheer and press donations into the collection box; sometimes there would be no one and nothing but darkness and emptiness on the road ahead. Yet Terry ran on. Through Newfoundland, through Nova Scotia (where a near fatal accident almost took Terry's life and resulted in a transport truck smashing into a CBC camera vehicle), through New Brunswick and into Quebec, Terry forged ahead. There were arguments between Terry and Doug, and Betty and Rolly flew in from British Columbia to help sort things out. Crises were resolved because Terry knew it was not a solitary run, but a team effort. Indeed, every child who thrust a coin into the collection box was an integral part of the Marathon of Hope. For Terry, Doug, Bill, Darrell and every additional contributor were just as important as he was to the ultimate victory over cancer. Terry was the catalyst, but he could never accomplish his mission alone.

In some ways, Quebec was the low point of his run. Weary from not only the run, but the constant demands of attending receptions and fundraisers when he should have been resting, Terry was faced with a new quandary in Quebec. Few people knew of him or his mission. There were few requests for him to speak at receptions. The crowds on the highway were sparse and silent. The transport trucks continued to be a problem and now the Quebec Provincial Police were telling him to get off the highway and run on the backroads. Terry fell in love with the beauty of the landscape, the charm of the small towns and the vibrant history of the province, but he was discouraged by his inability to make this a truly Canadian endeavour.

If Quebec was the ebbtide, coming into Ontario represented the turn of the tide. Publicity from the *Toronto Star* and the CBC, among other media outlets, heralded a hero's arrival in the province. The Ontario Provincial Police announced that they would provide Terry with an escort throughout the province, so his concentration could be focused on his running rather than on avoiding the transport trailers whizzing by him. It was in Ontario that his place in people's hearts was assured. Meeting both Governor General Edward Schreyer and the Prime Minister of Canada, Pierre Trudeau, receiving a standing ovation when he kicked the ceremonial opening kickoff of a football game in Ottawa and having thousands of people line the streets to cheer him on, bolstered Terry on his very first day in the province and steeled his resolve. Running more than 700 miles out of his way to raise funds around the Golden Horseshoe, Terry experienced the thrill of another standing ovation at a Blue Jays game and the rare opportunity for him to meet his hockey idols Darryl Sittler[6] and Bobby Orr.[7] A civic reception at Toronto's City Hall saw 10,000 people packed into the square to meet this great Canadian hero. One day in Toronto saw Terry raise

$100,000 for cancer research. And his marathon continued. Through Gravenhurst on his birthday – hearing the crowds sing "Happy Birthday" to him as he ran; through Bala, then Parry Sound and on up to Sudbury. A joyful reunion occurred with ten-year-old Greg Scott who, like Terry, suffered from bone cancer, and who had developed a special relationship with his hero. Greg bicycled beside Terry outside Thunder Bay and played in the water with the gang near Lake Superior – these were carefree moments in a magic summer. Yet the summer and the magic were coming to an end. Terry knew something was wrong. His hacking cough could no longer be shrugged off as the remnants of the flu. The pulsating pain that knifed through his body was not a runner's stitch. On September 1, 1980, Terry ran the last mile of his Marathon of Hope. He was afraid that he might be suffering from a heart attack, and asked if a doctor could come to his room. The doctor came and Terry was taken to the hospital. X-rays at the hospital had an ominous message – it was probably cancer in the lungs. Someone who had just run a marathon a day for 143 days would be too weak to brush a fly from his face two days later. A remarkable athlete saw his Marathon curtailed. Less than ten months later, on June 28, 1981, death would claim our valiant hero. At 5:30 in the morning, Terry's favourite time of day during his run – when the day was cool and the terrain was calm – he quietly succumbed to the long-time foe that he had so courageously fought.

It is important to remember that Terry was an athlete. He didn't walk or hop across the nation; he ran across it and ran across it on one leg and with a damaged heart. His good foot went through eight running shoes worn to frayed bald soles, while his artificial leg crossed Canada on one shoe. All the strength was from his left leg. Darryl Sittler recognized it. "I've been around athletes a long time and I've never seen any with his courage and stamina."[8] and Doug Alward,[9] now one of Canada's top marathon runners in his age category, recognized it. "As the years go by, I realize that I witnessed one of the most incredible athletic events ever."[10] Canadian sports writers and editors all across Canada recognized it when they endorsed him as the overwhelming favourite in winning the Lou Marsh Award as the outstanding Canadian athlete of 1980. The Canadian Sports Hall of Fame recognized it when they inducted him in 1981 and TSN recognized it in December of 1990 when it announced that Terry Fox had beaten out such notables as Wayne Gretzky and Michael Jordan as the Athlete of the Decade. Yes, Terry was an athlete.

But more importantly, Terry was a hero when Canada cried out for one. The year of his Marathon was a troubling time period for our country. We were in the throes of a constitutional crisis that saw virtually all of the provinces aligned against the federal government. The political situation was marked by a weary Liberal government that was in office in Ottawa not by affirmation, but rather by rejection of the weak alternatives. Our economy seemed drifting and damaged by recession and uncertainty, while the social fabric of Canada was being ripped in different directions as a result of opposing voices on such issues as women's rights, aboriginal rights and multiculturalism. We were a nation in turmoil and Terry Fox was the restorative antidote to our poisoned psyche.

Terry Fox was a hero unlike any other past hero in Canadian history. There are three categories of heroes – the personal, the national and the universal. What made Terry unique was that he filled all three categories.

A personal hero is someone to whom the individual feels a direct and real emotional bond. It may be a mother, a neighbour or a stranger, but something occurs that makes that person an integral part of your own dreams and aspirations. You cheer when your hero succeeds and shed tears when your hero stumbles. Terry connected with people on a personal basis. There may have been hundreds of people along the roadside, but this was not a crowd. Rather it was hundreds of individuals, each of whom had a direct connection to the courageous young man who had captured each of their hearts. It was not the swelling thunder of a crowd that greeted Terry, but the individual exhortation of "Way to go, Terry" and "God bless you Terry" repeated over and over by each person. Terry became a part of our lives and we all lost this important part when Terry died. Our grief was personal and profound.

Yet Terry was also a national hero. He answered the call of a nation suffering from malaise and lifted our spirits and our pride. He not only inspired Canadians, he exemplified the values and ideals that represented the best of Canada. Like John A. Macdonald, Terry had a national dream. His Marathon of Hope, like Canada's great enterprise of a national railway, would cross this vast land and unite a people from sea unto sea. Terry embodied the key elements of our national identity. He was selfless, remarkably courageous under fire, compassionate and proud to be a Canadian. As Pierre Trudeau[11] so eloquently eulogized Terry Fox in the House of Commons: "It occurs very rarely in the life of a nation that the courageous spirit of one person unites all people in the celebration of his life and in the mourning of his death."[12] Our grateful nation has recognized its debt to Terry in a variety of ways. Schools, community centres and countless streets and buildings proudly bear his name. The Canadian Press named him the Canadian of the Year in both 1980 and 1981. A mountain in the Rockies and a stretch of our Trans-Canada Highway have been named after him. He is the only Canadian placed on a national stamp prior to the obligatory ten years wait following his death, the youngest member ever of the Order of Canada, and the only person other than the reigning king or queen to appear on a Canadian coin. Terry is our hero.

Yet Terry is also a universal hero. His run was in Canada, but he belongs to the world. Like Martin Luther King[13] or Mother Teresa,[14] Terry is a universal hero. He is one of those rare individuals whose message and sense of purpose, whose accomplishments and whose legacy are so profound that he changed the direction of history. The Marathon of Hope was not about Terry Fox. It was about fighting and defeating a debilitating enemy of mankind. Terry emphasized this when he stated that "If I don't make it, the Marathon of Hope will continue."[15] Terry lost his first skirmish with cancer when he lost his leg to osteogemic sarcoma. He lost his battle when the cancer of the bone spread into his lungs and struck him down after he had completed more than 3000 miles of his run. But Terry will win the war. His goal was to raise 24 million dollars for cancer research. He lived to see that accomplishment met.

A CTV telethon held shortly after Terry's run had ended raised over $10 million. The Marathon of Hope has spread from Canada to over fifty other countries and has raised almost $400 million in the twenty-five years since that miraculous summer. Isadore Sharp, Chairman and CEO of Four Seasons Hotels and Resorts, had lost his son to cancer. When Terry faltered, Sharp picked up the flag and initiated the annual Terry Fox Run which will continue until cancer is beaten. In his original letter to the Canadian Cancer Society asking for its support of his run, Terry said "Somewhere the hurting must stop."[16]

When it does, the war will be over.

NOTES

CHAPTER 1: DOMAGAYA AND TAIGNOAGNY:
IROQUOIS HEROES AND VICTIMS

1.   For more information, see Diamond Jenness, *The Indians of Canada*. Ottawa: National Museum of Canada, 1963. (Sixth edition)

2.   Marriage had the same spiritual and physical significance for the people of the Iroquois nations as it does for contemporary readers. The ceremonies, however, vary considerably from culture to culture and from era to era. For the Iroquois of the 16th century, after a formal courtship, a couple would come to an understanding that the male could move into the female's family longhouse as her husband. This custom is significant because it is further evidence of the equality of sexes that existed prior to the advent of missionaries and the Christian patriarchal concepts.

3.   For more information on Iroquois customs and rituals, see W.D. Lighthall, *Hochelagas and Mohawks: A Link in Iroquois History* (Ottawa: Royal Society of Canada Transactions, Series 2, Volume 1899, Section II, 1933) 191-211, in the Toronto Reference Library (TRL), Baldwin Room, FILM R 8889. See also Fraser Symington, *The First Canadians* (Toronto: Natural Science of Canada Ltd., 1978) 37-49.

4.   With reference to both the factual Hiawatha and the mythical Dekhanahwideh, it is significant that the Mohawk had a primary role in the founding of the Confederacy in the mid-fifteenth century. Both accounts are consistent with the Mohawk ascendancy in the Confederacy.

The Tuscarora First Nation joined the other five nations in the Confederacy in 1713 to form the League of Six Nations. Today the Six Nations Reserve is located along the Grand River near Brantford, Ontario.

5.   By "wars," the author means formal conflicts declared for economic, territorial, religious or military gains as experienced on the European continent at this time. Some non-Native historians have imposed the Eurocentric definition of "war" on Native Peoples, while virtually all Native historians reject this interpretation. This author accepts the Native analysis based on the First People's value system which has been documented by such ethnologists as Daniel Garrison Brinton of the University of Pennsylvania and Pierre Martin, renowned French author of *Le Montagnais: langue algonquienne du Québec* (Paris: Peeters, 1991), who established the Native rejection of economic and territorial acquisition. After the arrival of the Europeans, the broader concept of war was introduced to North America. For more information on this concept, see Alan D. McMillan, *Native Peoples and Cultures of Canada: An Anthropological Overview* (second edition) (Vancouver: Douglas & McIntyre, 1995).

6.   There was no formal name for the practice of incorporating the roles of "torturer" and "tortured" into the Iroquois persona. Rather, it was a grasping of expectations that evolved into a distinct understanding of what was to occur. The torture itself, when experienced, was perceived as a ritual or ceremony.

7.   Diamond Jenness, *The Indians of Canada*, Chapter IX, "Social and Political Organizations," 118-132.

8.   E.N. Williams, *Penguin Dictionary of English and European History* (London: Allen Lane, 1980).

9.   The Renaissance refers to the time period in European history from roughly 1350 to 1550, when the continent was radically transformed. The literal meaning is rebirth and it refers to the renewed interest in the Classical period of Greek and Roman Ancient History and a revolution in the writing, art, architecture and philosophy of Europeans. Its central thrust was humanism. Humanism is the underlying philosophy behind the Renaissance. Based on the Latin term *humaniora*, it is the study of humanity. This study emphasizes the liberal arts such as history, writing, languages and philosophy over the more technical studies of mathematics and sciences. There is also a renewed interest in the classics – both as a study in itself and as a method of learning.

10.   This reference to Francis I of France and the killing of 3,000 people at Provence refers to the notorious acts of persecution and barbarity perpetrated, between Roman Catholics and Protestant Huguenots in France during the sixteenth century between the two Christian sects. The period culminated in the St. Bartholomew's Massacre of 1572 and resulted in the Edict of Nantes in 1598, granting tolerance and freedoms to the minority Huguenots.

11.   Scurvy was a common disease during the age of the voyages of discovery in the fifteenth and sixteenth centuries. In his journals, Cartier referred to it as a "pestilence." Caused by a lack of Vitamin C, sailors on long trips were particularly vulnerable because of the absence of fresh fruits and vegetables. The disease starts with swollen limbs and quickly spreads to the torso and neck. Teeth become rotted and fall out and victims gradually weaken and die.

12.   For more information on Cartier's attitude and observations, see Jacques Cartier, *The Voyages of Jacques Cartier* (translated by H.P. Biggar and edited by Ramsey Cook) (Toronto: University of Toronto Press, 1993).

CHAPTER 2: ÉTIENNE BRÛLÉ: FIRST COUREUR DE BOIS

1.   The primary reason for the alliance between the Huron First Nation and the French was an accident of geography. When Champlain arrived in what is present-day Quebec City, the Iroquois site of Cartier's day (established seventy years earlier) had been abandoned and the Huron were now the middlemen controlling the

region and the trade with the Europeans, largely furs but also tobacco from Southern Ontario and sea shells from the American South. They were accustomed to trading with other Europeans during the summers, and thus formed a natural partnership with Champlain and the French.

2.   Thomas Joseph Campbell, *Pioneer Laymen of North America*, Volume I (New York: America Press, 1915) 96-99.

3.   Olga Jurgens, "Étienne Brûlé," in *Dictionary of Canadian Biography*, Volume I (Toronto: University of Toronto Press, 1966) 130-33.

4.   The Récollets were a religious order, founded in France in the late 16th century, members of the reformed branch of the Franciscan Observants. They sent missionary priests to New France.

5.   St. Jean de Brébeuf (1593-1649) lived among the Hurons and completed a Huron language grammar and dictionary begun by Father Sagard. Brébeuf was captured by invading Iroquois in 1649, tortured and killed. He was canonized in 1930.

6.   To the English, Captain David Kirke was the first governor of Newfoundland and a heroic sailor in the British Royal Navy. To the French, he was an adventurer and a pirate. His controversial career ended when he was recalled to England for withholding taxes for personal gain. He subsequently died in prison.

7.   The Huron were actually an Iroquoian people. Although the two groups were enemies, they were of the same linguistic group – Iroquoian – and shared many of the cultural patterns of the nations of the Confederacy. Some people mistakenly place the Huron in the Algonkian linguistic group because of their close relationship with many Algonkian nations. For more information on the Huron First Nation, see R. Bruce Morrison and C. Roderick Wilson, *Native Peoples: The Canadian Experience*, 2nd ed. (Toronto: McClelland & Stewart, 1995).

8.   Harold Horwood and Edward Butts, *Pirates and Outlaws of Canada, 1610-1932* (Toronto: Doubleday Canada, 1984) 50.

CHAPTER 3: MADELEINE JARRET: HEROINE OF VERCHÈRES

1.   Louis XIV, King of France, was the most powerful ruler of his day. His reign lasted from 1638 to 1715. So absolute was his authority that he is still remembered for the phrase, "L'état, c'est moi," or "I am the state."

2.   Many of these stories were recorded for posterity by the French governors and intendants of New France, as well as in religious records, notably the Jesuit Relations.

3.   Georges-Emile Diguere, "Isaac Jocques," in *Dictionary of Canadian Biography*, Volume I (Toronto: University of Toronto Press, 1966), 387-390.

4.   Pierre Esprit Radisson was the person who brought the fantastic economic opportunities available from harvesting the fur in Canada, to the attention of the London merchants who were to become the financial backers of the Hudson's Bay Company.

5.   Lachine, optimistically but mistakenly, was named "China" by the French who thought, at the time, that they had located a passage to the Far East. Lachine is located up river from Quebec City on the St. Lawrence River.

6.   Sir William Phips was the British Commander of the New England forces, which had arrived from Boston on behalf of England. Phips had already captured Port Royal of Acadia (Annapolis, Nova Scotia, as it is known today).

7.   Louis de Baude, Comte de Frontenac, was born in France in 1622 and died while serving as governor of New France in Quebec City in 1698. In this role, Frontenac oversaw the expansion of the colony through the establishment of forts and trading posts extending all the way to the Mississippi River. He was interested in the profit produced by the fur trade and, as a result, often waged war against the Iroquois. His inability to deal effectively with the Native Peoples may have led to his recall had he not died in office.

8.   In 1716, the Governor of New France wanted a written record of what was common knowledge in the settlement. For that reason, he asked Madeleine de Verchères to submit a sworn written testimony of the events that transpired during the siege by the Iroquois. Madeleine had written a letter to the Contesse de Mauripas telling of the attack on Verchères, which had been verified by Intendent Champigny. Her report, prepared for the governor (Marquis de Beauharnois) and dated 1716, was published by the Archives of Canada on the 200th anniversary of the end of Frontenac's term of office. A translated version of this document is in the Library and Archives Canada and may be read on the Web site, www.canadahistory.com/sections/documents/bravery_of_madeleine_de_verche res.htm, accessed December 13, 2005. It is the basis of works on Madeleine de Verchères and is the main source of the information provided in the book.

9.   Ibid, from Madeleine's report, 1716.

10.   For more information on the attack on Fort Duquesne, see Arthur G. Doughty, *A Daughter of New France: Being a Story of the Life and Times of Magdelaine de Verchères, 1665-1692* (Ottawa: Mortimer Press, 1916).

CHAPTER 4: JOHN TANNER: OJIBWA ODYSSEY

1.   This is in reference to the book by Morley Torgrov, *A Good Place to Come From* (Toronto: Lester and Orpen, 1974).

2.   While living in Sault Ste. Marie, where he moved to in 1828, John Tanner recounted his story to Doctor Edwin James, who compiled an account of the story

and had it published in 1830. Information on the life and experiences of John Tanner was taken from Edwin James (ed.), *A Narrative of the Captivity and Adventures of John Tanner.* Baldwin and Cradock, 1830, located in the Toronto Reference Library (TRL).

3.   John Tanner as quoted in Edwin James, *A Narrative of the Captivity and Adventures of John Tanner (U.S. Interpreter at the Saut de Ste. Marie): During Thirty Years Residence Among the Indians of North America* (Minneapolis, MN: Ross and Haines Inc., 1956) 12 (a reprint of John Tanner's *Narratives,* with a new Introduction.)

4.   The Ottaways or Odaways were part of the Ojibwa First Nation. They lived in the northern reaches of Ontario between Sault Ste. Marie and Sudbury and were one of the First Nations people who accepted women as chiefs in an administrative rather than military capacity. For more information on the Ottaways, see Diamond Jenness, *The Indians of Canada* (Ottawa: National Museum of Canada, 1963).

5.   John Tanner as quoted in Edwin James, *A Narrative of the Captivity and Adventures of John Tanner,* 26.

6.   For more information on Native feasts, see Fraser Symington, *The Canadian Indians: The Illustrated History of the Great Tribes of Canada* (Toronto: McClelland & Stewart, 1969). See also R. Bruce Morrison and C. Roderick Wilson (eds.), *Native Peoples: The Canadian Experience,* 2nd edition (Toronto: McClelland & Stewart, 1995).

7.   William W. Warren, *History of the Ojibway Nation* (Minneapolis, MN: Ross & Haines, 1957) 68-71.

8.   Ibid, 68-82. See also Doctor Edwin James, *A Narrative of the Captivity and Adventures of John Tanner,* 101-111.

9.   Edwin James, *A Narrative of the Captivity and Adventures of John Tanner,* "Introduction," 101-111.

10.   Lord Selkirk, Thomas Douglas, 5th Earl of Selkirk, was born in Scotland in 1771. He resettled eight hundred Scottish Highlanders to Prince Edward Island in 1803, established a second settlement in Upper Canada in 1804 at Baldoon (today's Wallaceburg) and launched a similar project in 1811 when he purchased a large tract of land from the Hudson's Bay Company (in the Red River Region of present-day Manitoba). His settlement clashed with the North West Trading Company and with Native Peoples and Métis people in the region. The settlement lasted until 1818. For more information, see Lucille Campey, *The Silver Chief: Lord Selkirk and the Scottish Pioneers of Belfast, Baldoon and Red River* (Toronto: Natural Heritage Books, 2003).

CHAPTER 5: BILLY GREEN: HERO OF STONEY CREEK

1.   Sir Isaac Brock, born in Guernsey Island, England, in 1769, first arrived in British North America in 1809 with his military regiment. Francis Gore was the Lieutenant Governor of Upper Canada at the time. When Gore's term expired in

1811, Brock succeeded him as provisional administrator for Upper Canada. From that point on, he worked vigorously to prepare the colony for a possible invasion by the United States. When war was declared in 1812, Brock was in charge of the defense of the colony. Eight years after his heroic death at Queenston Heights in 1812, government officials moved his body to the summit of the hill he had attempted to capture. A massive column was erected as a monument to mark his final resting place. This monument, completed in 1824, was blown up in 1840 by a disgruntled veteran of the 1837 rebellion; it was replaced by the present one in 1856, the result of public contributions.

2.   United Empire Loyalist is the name given to the American colonists who supported the British cause during the American Revolution (although in the United States, they are referred to as traitors). In total, close to 100,000 of these refugees left the colonies during the years 1776 to 1784, including Native Americans, free Blacks, fugitive slaves and white settlers. Of the approximately 40,000 who chose British North American colonies as their new home, about 30,000 settled in Nova Scotia, leading to the creation of the Colony of New Brunswick. About 10,000 settled in Quebec, leading to the creation of the Colony of Upper Canada (Ontario) by the Constitutional Act of 1791. The reasons for the Loyalists departure from their homeland varied widely from financial hardship and persecution to matters of conscience and a determination to remain British subjects.

3.   For more information on Simcoe's appeal for American settlers and the granting of land to the Americans in 1792, see S.R. Mealing, "John Graves Simcoe" in *The Canadian Encyclopedia*, Volume III (Edmonton: Hurtig Publishers, 1985) 1699-1700.

4.   Born in 1743, Thomas Jefferson was one of the most brilliant individuals to occupy the office of the President of the United States. An intellectual, he was a leading proponent of the principles of the Enlightenment, as so eloquently articulated in his Declaration of Independence. An academic, he not only taught law, but founded the University of Virginia. He served as president of the American Philosophical Society and was fluent in English, French, Italian, Greek, Spanish and Latin. He was an architect who designed the plans for his mansion at Monticello as well as all the buildings of the University of Virginia. Finally, he was a farmer who developed scientific techniques that are still used on farms today. The only odious blot on an otherwise sterling character was his ownership of slaves.

As the third President, he negotiated with Napoleon of France and secured the Louisiana Purchase which more than doubled the size of the nation. As president just prior to the War of 1812 (1801 to 1809), he left office secure in the knowledge that his successor and close follower, James Madison, would continue his foreign and domestic policies. Jefferson died on the most significant date on the American calendar – Independence Day, July 4, 1826.

5.   "A mere matter of marching" is a quote taken from Jefferson's letter to

Congress on the eve of the outbreak of war. Because it is a pithy and literate summary of American expectations, it is used by both American and Canadian historians writing about the War of 1812.

6.   Until recently, the story of the role of Black United Empire Loyalists in Upper Canada, some of them fugitive slaves, has been overlooked in the historical accounts of the War of 1812. For more information, see Peter Meyler and David Meyler, *A Stolen Life: Searching for Richard Pierpoint* (Toronto: Natural Heritage Books, 1999).

7.   The Americans attacked Queenston Heights on the Niagara River in October of 1812. Brock, fresh from two victories at Forts Michilimackinac and Detroit, was hastily bringing his troops to Queenston Heights to engage the enemy. In the meantime, 80 Mohawk warriors, led by Joseph Brant's "adopted son," Major John Norton, (Teyoninhokarawen, born circa 1760 to a Cherokee father and a Scottish mother) valiantly held off the Americans who outnumbered them fifteen to one. When Brock and his army of about 1000 arrived, he led the assault up the heights. Brock was killed, but his troops were successful. Nine hundred and twenty-five American soldiers were captured, two American armies were destroyed and, significantly Canada held possession of the key strategic point. For more information on John Norton, see Barbara Martindale, *Caledonia: Along the Grand River* (Toronto: Natural Heritage Books, 1995) 17-22. See also *The Journal of Major John Norton, 1816* (edited by Carl F. Klinck and James J. Talman) (Toronto: The Champlain Society, 1970), and "Major John Norton" in *Canada: A People's History.*

8.   William Henry Harrison was born in 1773 and became the ninth American president in 1840. He was well-known as an Indian fighter in his capacity of governor of Indian Territory from 1801 to 1812. He defeated Tecumseh's brother, the Prophet, at the Battle of Tippecanoe (1811) in the Ohio Valley in present-day Indiana, and proceeded to drive the Shawnees out of their own land and destroy their settlements. For this, he was acclaimed a hero by the Americans. When the War of 1812 broke out, Harrison was appointed as general, in charge of the North Western Army, which was to attack British North America. Later in the war, he defeated and killed Tecumseh at the Battle of Moraviantown (near present-day London) on the Thames River. Elected president, he gave the longest inaugural speech on record in March of 1841. The most notable comment was that he would not run for re-election. This was prophetic, as he contracted pneumonia and died one month later.

9.   Born in England in 1764, John Vincent joined the British army in 1781. He was appointed to the rank of colonel when he came to British North America in 1802. The next year, he was assigned to Upper Canada and in 1813, appointed general, replacing Roger Schaeffe who had taken over from the slain Brock. Vincent had a strong disdain for the colonial militia whom he regarded as disloyal and untrustworthy, and was reluctant to accord them any credit in the war effort. At the outset of the Battle of Stoney Creek, Vincent fell of his horse, got lost in the woods and

wandered into the battle scene after it was over. When the war ended, he returned to England and spent his remaining years as lieutenant governor of Dunbarton Castle in Scotland. He died in 1848.

John Harvey, born in 1778, was appointed lieutenant colonel and deputy adjutant to General Vincent upon arriving in Upper Canada in 1812. He was a brilliant strategist who not only led the British forces to victory at Stoney Creek, but also fought at Crysler's Farm, Oswego, Lundy's Lane and Fort Erie. After the war, he became lieutenant governor of Prince Edward Island (1836), New Brunswick (1837), Newfoundland (1841) and Nova Scotia (1846). No other individual has ever served as lieutenant governor for four colonies in British North America. He died in 1852 while still serving in Nova Scotia.

10.   For more information on Billy's activities that day, see Mabel W. Thompson, "Billy Green, the Scout" in *Ontario History*, Volume XLIV, October 1952.

11.   Billy Green recounted his story, which was supported by several eyewitnesses at the battle, to a government official, S.D. Slater. Slater recorded the account in his diary over the winter of 1818-1819, often paraphrasing quotes from Billy Green. Later, Billy told his grandson, John W. Green the same story and his grandson also recorded it. Both accounts are virtually identical and have been cited in newspaper and historical accounts of the battle. The narrative form of Billy's story is available on the official Web site for the government museum Battlefield House, www.battlefieldhouse.ca, accessed in June 2004.

12.   For the complete story, see *The Diary of S.D. Slater*, Hamilton, ON: Wentworth Historical Society, Volume V, 1908 in the Hamilton Public Library, Special Collection Department, Archives File: Slater, S.D. See also *Hamilton Spectator*, March 12, 1938, and Web site: www.battlefieldhouse.ca. It might be mentioned that the official report sent by Colonel Harvey makes no mention of Billy Green. This is not unusual, since it was customary for the British to ignore the role of the colonials in their transcripts. However, the historical accuracy of Billy's account is supported by several pieces of compelling evidence. The official British record also neglects to mention the absence of their own general from the action. People at the battle site confirm Billy's story as did an American leader who wrote to the *Baltimore Whig* newspaper two days after the battle and acknowledged the role of Billy (although not by name) and blamed the loss on his "treachery." Finally, the government of Upper Canada (and later the government of Canada) have formally recognized Billy's contributions with an historical plaque as a part of the official record. Annually in June, re-enactors create a simulated battle at Stoney Creek. As well, there is a locally subscribed plaque on the site which states, "In memory of Billy Green 'the Scout' who led British troops in a surprise night attack winning the decisive battle of Stoney Creek. Born February 1794, died March 15, 1877."

13.   S.D. Slater, *The Diary of S.D. Slater*.

14. Ibid.

15. The American forces had successfully burned the capitol of Upper Canada, York, and secured full possession of the Niagara Peninsula, outnumbering the British regular and militia forces by a margin of three to one. It is little wonder that the British command was forced to consider the feasibility of pulling back to Kingston to regroup.

16. The family of Dr. James Gage lived in a farmhouse in Stoney Creek that became the headquarters for the American forces. After the battle it was used as a hospital for the wounded from both armies. Doctor Gage and Billy Green worked side by side in the temporary hospital. Today, the former home is a museum, Battlefield House, which commemorates the battle and the participants – including Billy Green.

CHAPTER 6: OSBORNE ANDERSON: SURVIVOR OF HARPER'S FERRY

1. This is the same Captain David Kirke discussed in Chapter 2: Étienne Brûlé. See Chapter 2, Note 6.

2. Olivier LeJeune was born in Africa, possibly Madagascar, but was captured by slave traders during a raid on his village. He arrived in New France in 1628 and was subsequently sold to a French Canadian merchant. Ultimately, he was baptized in 1633 (taking the name of the priest who baptized him, Father Paul LeJeune). He died at the age of 32 in 1654. For more information see Daniel G. Hill, *The Freedom-Seekers: Blacks in Early Canada*, 2nd edition (Toronto: Stoddart, 1992) 3.

3. For more slavery in Upper Canada and Blacks in early Toronto, see Adrienne Shadd, Afua Cooper and Karolyn Smardz Frost, *The Underground Railroad: Next Stop, Toronto!*, 2nd edition. (Toronto: Natural Heritage Books, 2005).

4. For a description of life as a slave and of the escape to Canada (in this case, ultimately to Owen Sound, Ontario), see Peter Meyler (ed.), *Broken Shackles: Old Man Henson From Slavery to Freedom* (Toronto: Natural Heritage Books, 2001).

5. For more information, see Herbert Aptheker (ed.), *A Documentary History of the Negro People in the United States*, Volume 1 (New York: Carol Publishing Group, 1951) and Henry Steele Commager, *Documents of American History*, Volume I to 1898 (ninth edition) (Englewood Cliff, NJ: Prentice-Hall, Inc., 1973). See also Peter Meyler and David Meyler, *A Stolen Life: Searching for Richard Pierpoint* (Toronto: Natural Heritage Books, 1999).

6. Daniel G. Hill, *The Freedom-Seekers*, 21, 23, 214.

7. The Underground Railroad was in operation from roughly 1840 to 1861. A metaphor for escape to Canada, it was a series of safe houses and people who assisted slaves in their flight to freedom. The route connected fugitives from the Southern slave states to the Northern free states, and ultimately over the border into Canada.

8.   The Compromise of 1850 is the name given to five separate statutes passed by the U.S. Congress in the fall session of 1850. Henry Clay was architect of the compromise, which was intended to resolve the dispute over slavery, but it broke down within four years. According to the five statutes, California would be admitted to the Union as a free state, New Mexico and Utah would become territories with no mention of free or slave status, Washington DC would be closed to slave trading and transport and, finally, the Fugitive Slave Act would take effect. This last statute was the most controversial because it stated that any Black could be deemed a fugitive slave if a claimant filled out an affidavit stating title to ownership of him or her. Moreover, magistrates would be given $10 for every returned slave, but only $5 if they released the Black person, obviously encouraging the magistrates to side with the slave owners. The practical effect of this meant that free Blacks living in the free Northern states were no longer safe. Canada became the destination for freedom.

9.   Secession was the culmination of the argument between States' Rights advocates and federalists. States rights asserted that the United States was a creation of the various states and that, consequently, any state could withdraw from the Union at will. Federalists asserted the supremacy of the Union over the states and said that no state had the right to unilaterally withdraw from the Union. The Southern states that were anxious to preserve slavery forcefully advanced their argument against the more populous North. Led by South Carolina, these states withdrew from the Union after the election of Abraham Lincoln who was hostile to the expansion of slavery.

10.   Mary Shadd was born a free Black in Wilmington, Delaware, in 1823. Since it was illegal for a Black to receive an education in Delaware, her parents sent her to a Quaker school in Pennsylvania. After the passage of the Fugitive Slave Act, the Shadd family moved to Upper Canada. Mary taught school for two years in Windsor, then moved to Chatham where she became the first female publisher and editor of a newspaper in North America, the *Provincial Freeman*. Shadd was an ardent advocate of abolition, integration and women's rights. When Abraham Lincoln proclaimed the Emancipation Proclamation, freeing slaves, she returned to the United States in 1863 and acted as a recruiting officer during the Civil War. When the war ended, Shadd remained in Washington DC and became the second Black woman to graduate from law school in North America. She practised law until her death in 1893. For more information see Rosemary Sadlier, *Mary Ann Shadd: Publisher, Editor, Teacher, Lawyer, Suffragette* (Toronto: Umbrella Press, 1995).

11.   Reverend William King, born in Ireland in 1812, received his Divinity degree from the University of Glasgow in 1846 and was sent to Canada West as a Presbyterian minister. Having emigrated to the United States in 1833 and married there into a slave-owning family. he was very familiar with the horrors of slavery. Working within the Black community, he developed a zeal for social reform and a desire to establish a Black community for the new immigrants from the United

States. He realized his dream on November 28, 1849, when he opened the Elgin Settlement in Upper Canada. Ironically, the settlement was made up of 15 slaves that his American father-in-law had left him and whom King had emancipated. He later established the much larger Buxton Settlement, consisting of a post office, a school and church, fertile farmland and 320 people. This thriving community was the only self-supporting Black community in all of North America. For more information, see Victor Ullman, *Look to the North Star: A Life of William King* (Boston: Beacon Press, 1969) (Canadian edition, Toronto: Umbrella Press, 1994.)

12.   Josiah Henson was the model for the title character in Harriet Beecher Stowe's *Uncle Tom's Cabin*. Born a slave in Maryland in 1789, Henson arrived in Upper Canada as a fugitive slave in 1830. He founded the Dresden Settlement near his home for Black fugitives arriving across the Windsor/Detroit border. He remained active in fundraising for his settlement until it closed in 1868. Josiah Henson wrote his autobiography in 1881, two years prior to his death. Josiah Henson, *An Autobiography of the Reverend Josiah Henson* (Reading, MA: Addison-Wesley Publishing Company, 1969).

13.   Henry Walton Bibb was a publisher and editor who founded *The Voice of the Fugitive* newspaper. Born in Kentucky in 1815 of a slave mother and slave-owning father, Bibb escaped in 1842 and came to the Windsor area of Upper Canada. His newspaper was important for chronicling accounts of fugitive slaves' lives in America and Canada. Unfortunately, he quarreled with Mary Shadd and was tainted with the charge of helping to defraud the people he was supposed to be helping. His autobiography, *Narrative of the Life and Adventures of Henry Bibb: An American Slave*, was published in 1849. He died in 1854. A commemorative plaque recognizing Henry Bibb's contributions was erected in Windsor, Ontario, in October 2005.

14.   George Brown was born in Scotland in 1818. After his arrival in Upper Canada in 1837, he quickly became involved in publishing and politics. His Toronto newspaper *The Globe* was a voice for reform in politics. Promoting such issues as abolition of slavery, separation of church and state, westward expansion and representation by population, he soon became leader of the Reform Party (Clear Grits) in Canada West (formerly Upper Canada). In 1864, he put aside his political and personal animosity towards John A. Macdonald to propose the Great Coalition which led to Canadian Confederation in 1867. George Brown was a key representative at all the conferences and is regarded as one of the most important fathers of Confederation. He died a premature death in 1880, when a disgruntled former employee of *The Globe* shot Brown in his office. Infection set in and he died shortly after. George Brown House on Beverley Street in Toronto is operated by the Ontario Heritage Foundation.

15.   The abolitionist claims were calculated by a combination of census statistics, claims for loss of property by slave owners, newspaper and anecdotal accounts and a desire for propaganda that inflated the actual numbers.

16.   Information on spirituals (often referred to as freedom songs) comes from anecdotal evidence collected by William Troy and compiled in his book, *Hairbreadth Escapes from Slavery to Freedom* (Manchester, UK: W. Bremner Publisher, 1861). See also Ken Alexander and Avis Glaze, *Towards Freedom: The African-Canadian Experience* (Toronto: Umbrella Press, 1996). The following sources provide for a more detailed study of slave music: John Wesley, *American Negro Songs* (Mineola, NY: Dover Publications, 1998); Geoffrey Ward and Ken Burns, *Jazz: A History of America's Music* (New York: Alfred A. Knopf, 2000); Lawrence Cohn, *Nothing But the Blues* (New York: Abberville Press, 1993).

17.   Dr. Alexander Milton Ross was a noted natural scientist who was born in Belleville in 1832 and settled in Toronto in 1865. While in Toronto, he published a number of books on flora and fauna as well as two important biographies, recounting his experiences as a reformer. In his books on natural science, he tended to inflate his credentials, although he was elected to the British Association for the Advancement of Science. However, in his recollection of his abolitionist activity, his role was well-documented and corroborated by such notables as William Seward, President Lincoln's secretary of state. Recently, however, some of his claims are being questioned by academic researchers studying the Underground Railroad. For more information, see *Dictionary of Canadian Biography*, Volume 12 (1891 to 1900), (Toronto: University of Toronto Press, 1990).

18.   For more on John Brown, see Jean Libby (ed.), *John Brown Mysteries* (Missoula, MT: Pictorial Histories Publishing Company, 1999).

19.   Frederick Douglass was born a slave in Maryland in 1818. His father was the plantation owner and his mother a household slave. He escaped from slavery, disguised as a sailor in 1838 and settled in New Bedford, Massachusetts. He was a brilliant speaker, social reformer and writer who was able to combine radical activism with pragmatic cooperation with authorities to effect change. He was one of the most important of the abolitionists in the North prior to and during the Civil War. He continued speaking and writing about the necessity of change until his death in 1895.

20.   Frederick Douglass as quoted in Ward, Geoffrey, with Ken Burns and Ric Burns, *The Civil War: An Illustrated History* (New York: Alfred A. Knopf, 1990) 4.

21.   Osborne Anderson as quoted in Jim Bearden and Linda Jean Butler, *Shadd: The Life and Times of Mary Shadd Cary* (Toronto: NC Press, 1977) 197.

22.   Ibid, 201.

23.   Ibid.

24.   This was John Brown's last written statement prior to his execution. The final sentence read, "I, John Brown, am quite certain that the crimes of this guilty land will never be purged away but with blood." His letter was released to the public and became a rallying cry for abolitionists in the press, pulpit and platform and

remains a popular statement in American history texts. See Stephen B. Oates, *To Purge This Land With Blood: A Biography of John Brown*, 2nd edition (Amherst, MA: University of Massachusetts Press, 1984) 351. The original letter resides at the Chicago Historical Society (John Brown Papers), Chicago, Illinois.

25.   For more details on the death of Osborne Anderson, see Ken Alexander and Avis Glaze, *Towards Freedom: The African-Canadian Experience* (Toronto: Umbrella Press, 1996).

CHAPTER 7: ANNA SWAN: NOVA SCOTIA'S GIANTESS

1.   The term "ballerinas of the sea" was an expression employed by sailors in the late nineteenth century to describe the grace of the schooners on the water. See William Stephenson, *Dawn of the Nation, 1860-1870* (Toronto: Natural Science of Canada, 1977). The term "bluenose" was first used by the famed novelist, Thomas Chandler Haliburton of Nova Scotia in the 1830s. Originally used to describe residents of Nova Scotia, it was later applied to products of the province. The most famous "Bluenose" is the schooner that is immortalized on the Canadian dime.

2.   For more information, see Phyllis R. Blakely, *Nova Scotia's Two Remarkable Giants* (Windsor, NS: Lancelot Press, 1970).

3.   Ibid, 9.

4.   The Civil War was the bloodiest conflict ever fought on this continent. The central issues of the abolition of slavery and the preservation of the Union were closely connected, leading to the outbreak of the conflict which lasted from 1861 to 1865. The northern states (Union) were fighting to preserve the union and, later, to abolish slavery. The southern states (Confederacy) were fighting for the right to withdraw from the United States and form a new nation which would be based on the institution of slavery. The war ended with the surrender of General Robert E. Lee of the Confederate States of America to General Ulysses S. Grant of the United States of America and the triumph of the union and abolition of slavery.

5.   Tom Thumb was born Charles Sherwood Stratton in 1838 in Bridgeport, Connecticut. Perfectly proportioned, he grew to a height of about one metre (three feet, four inches) and was a famous entertainer in the employ of P.T. Barnum. In 1863, he married Lavinia Warren who was a bit shorter than himself. He died in 1883.

6.   P.T. Barnum as quoted in Barnum, P. T. and Waldo R. Browne, *Barnum's Own Story* (New York: Dover Publications Ltd., 1961) 331.

7.   For more information on Barnum's American Museum, see Barnum and Browne, *Barnum's Own Story*.

8.   James Buchanan was President of the United States from 1856 to 1860.

9.   Jefferson Davis (1808-1889) was a former United States senator and cabinet minister (Secretary of War under Franklin Pierce from 1853 to 1857) who was chosen by the Provisional Confederate Congress for the states that seceded from the Union as their President. He served in this capacity for the duration of the Civil War and was arrested for treason but never brought to trial. He died in 1889.

10.   For more information, see Irving Wallace, *The Fabulous Showman: The Life and Times of P.T. Barnum* (New York: Knopf, 1959).

11.   Ibid.

12.   For more information, see Phyllis R. Blakely, "Anna Hainings Swan (Bates)" in *Dictionary of Canadian Biography*, Volume XI (1881-1890) (Toronto: University of Toronto Press, 1982) 865-66.

CHAPTER 8: FRED BAGLEY: YOUNGEST MOUNTIE

1.   James Fenimore Cooper, born in 1789, was one of the most notable of the nineteenth-century American writers. His book, *The Last of the Mohicans*, published in 1926, is his most famous work that chronicled the American frontier at the turn of the nineteenth century. Cooper died in 1851.

2.   The Battle of the Little Bighorn was fought on June 25-26, 1876. Colonel George Armstrong Custer, supporting illegal white encroachment on sacred Native land in the Black Hills of Montana, disregarded orders and marched his army at full speed to the Sioux and Cheyenne camp. He ordered his tired force to attack the campsite, not realizing his 225 men were outnumbered by about 4,000 to 5,000 Native warriors, who were defending a camp of some 12,000 to 15,000 peoples. Custer's forces were surrounded and completely destroyed, but the response in the United States was an even stronger determination to exterminate the Native Peoples.

3.   Crowfoot was the famed leader of the Blackfoot First Nation after 1865. Born a Blood around the year 1830, Crowfoot was adopted by the Blackfoot and quickly demonstrated his courage in battle. As a leader, Crowfoot was farsighted and realistic. He understood that his people had no option but to arrive at an accommodation with the numerically superior whites. Recognizing the role of the Roman Catholic Church in providing support and the role of the North West Mounted Police in driving out the whisky traders, Crowfoot persuaded his people to sign Treaty 7, which ceded the West to the Canadian government. His reward was betrayal and disillusionment with the broken promises and cruel reservation life that followed. Nevertheless, he remained a voice of peace until his death in 1890.

Poundmaker, adopted son of Crowfoot, was leader of the Cree around Battleford, North-West Territories (now Saskatchewan) during the second Riel Rebellion of 1885. Although Poundmaker consistently opposed violence and prevented his warriors from harming an army that came to arrest them, he was held responsible for damage inflicted on the village of Battleford by his followers during the Rebellion. Sentenced to three years in jail, he was released in one year due to the rapid deterioration of his health while behind bars. He died two weeks later (1886) while visiting his father Crowfoot on a reserve.

4.   Ogden Tanner, *The Canadians* (Alexandria, VA: Time-Life Books, Inc., 1977) 152.

5.   Mark Starowicz, *Canada: A People's History*, Volume 10: "The Taking of the West," CBC/Radio-Canada, 2001.

6.   The first contingent of 150 of the NWMP recruits, led by Inspector James Walsh, left Toronto by train to Collingwood, sailed on the steamer *Cumberland* to Prince Arthur's Landing (now part of Thunder Bay) and then travelled overland via the Dawson Road to Fort Garry. Fred Bagley's contingent was the second group to leave Toronto. Together they represent "The Long March," although they marched separately.

7.   Fred Bagley, "The '74 Mounties: The Great March Across the Plains," (unpublished manuscript, 1938, Glenbow Archives, Calgary, Alberta) 3.

8.   Ibid, 11.

9.   For more information, see Ogden Tanner, *The Canadians*, 160-61.

10. For more information regarding the Frank James encounter, see David Cruise and Alison Griffiths, *The Great Adventure: How the Mounties Conquered the West* (Toronto: Penguin, 1997).

11. Fred Bagley's Diary (1874-1884), excerpt dated June 20, 1874, Glenbow Archives, Calgary, Alberta, M-44.

12. James Macleod, born in Scotland in 1836, moved to Canada West (Ontario) as a child. Joining the 1870 expedition against Louis Riel, Macleod subsequently joined the North West Mounted Police and was appointed assistant commissioner under Colonel George Arthur French. He was responsible for suppressing the whisky trade and acted as a key negotiator in Treaty 7. He resigned from the Mounted Police in 1880 and served as magistrate and Supreme Court Justice for the North-West Territories until his death in 1894.

13. Born in Canada West (Ontario) in 1849, Sir Samuel Steele was attracted to martial life early in life. Joining the militia as a teenager, he fought against the Fenian raiders from the United States in 1866 and, four years later, fought against the Métis at the Red River Rebellion. He was a Sergeant Major in the North West Mounted Police and promoted to Superintendent in 1885. Steele was the main source of law and order in the Yukon during the Klondike Gold Rush (1898) and fought in the Boer War as division leader from 1899 to 1902. When the First World War broke out, Steele led the second Canadian Division overseas and was retired on July 15, 1918. He fell victim to the influenza epidemic of 1918 and died the

following year, just after his 70th birthday. Today's historic Fort Steele in British Columbia is named after him.

14.   Jerry Potts was born in 1840 of a Scottish fur-trader father and Blood Indian mother. A fierce warrior, he acquired 16 scalps while fighting in Native wars. Joining the North West Mounted Police as a scout in 1874, Potts served in that capacity until his death in 1896. The Mounties accorded him a full military burial with a three-gun salute at his funeral.

15.   Information on the powwow is taken from Fred Bagley's Diary, which is available from the Glenbow Archives in Calgary. The archives will provide a copy of the original to a public library for patron perusal.

16.   Fred Bagley, "The '74 Mounties: The Great March Across the Plains," 54-55.

17.   James Walsh was born in Canada West (Ontario) in 1843 and served as an Inspector in the North West Mounted Police from 1873 to 1883. He forged a close personal friendship with Sitting Bull and was largely responsible for the harmonious relationship between the Sioux and the Canadian government after Sitting Bull arrived in Canada following Little Big Horn. Walsh left the North West Mounted Police in 1883 to found Dominion Coke, Coal and Transportation in Winnipeg, but rejoined the force as Commissioner of the Yukon Territory in 1897. He died in 1905.

18.   T. Morris Longstreth, *The Scarlet Force: The Making of the Mounted Police* (Toronto: Macmillan of Canada, 1974) 79.

CHAPTER 9: GEORGE GREEN: A HOME CHILD IN ONTARIO

1.   The Industrial Revolution was the process by which England was transformed from a rural, cottage industry type of society to a more urban and machine-driven society. The growth of industrial technology occurred from approximately 1760 to 1840. By the late nineteenth century, England was the undisputed industrial power in the world. The benefits of the Industrial Revolution – from mass production and greater productivity to increased wealth and more consumer goods – are undeniable. However, the costs in terms of pollution, slums and the exploitation and impoverishment of children, women and the people of the lower economic classes are also undeniable.

2.   Jack the Ripper is the sobriquet of one of the most notorious serial killers in the annals of crime. From August to November of 1888, he took the lives of at least seven prostitutes in the Whitechapel area of London. (Whitechapel was in the east end of the city on the Thames River and was noted for its poverty, prostitution and immigrant population.) He was a focus of fascination because of the brutal mutilation of the bodies, the public taunts that he issued through letters to the press and the inability of the police to identify the fiend. Today, more than 100 books have been written speculating on the identity of the Ripper, but it remains one of history's unsolved mysteries.

3.   William Booth was born in England in 1829 and founded the Salvation Army in 1878. He believed that eternal damnation was the fate of those people not converted to Christianity and he had a social conscience with respect to the neglected victims of the Industrial Revolution. As a result, he established a church mission, later called the Salvation Army, in Whitechapel, the most downtrodden section of London. An activist, he worked for the provision of shelters, retraining for immigrants and prostitutes, assistance for alcoholics and other denizens of the slums and for overall social reform. He died, a general in his Army, in 1912.

4.   Social Gospel refers to the reform movement that was popular in Protestant denominations of Christianity in the late nineteenth century in both England and North America. The central premise of this movement was that Christians have a responsibility to confront and try to overcome social evils and injustices such as alcoholism, child labour and prostitution. The belief existed that the Christian should be active in his or her community in alleviating these conditions. This is a contrast to the notion of individual responsibility for sins and contemplation over action to overcome them.

5.   Evangelicalism refers to the notion popular in the late nineteenth century that the Christian Church has a responsibility to go into communities that need Christian assistance and work with the people. It is connected to the Social Gospel Movement and is based on the premise that Christianity is an active rather than contemplative religion and the need to move into the community to preach and convert people.

6.   For more information on young immigrants and "home children" see Marjorie Kohli, *The Golden Bridge: Young Immigrants to Canada, 1833-1939* (Toronto: Natural Heritage Books, 2003).

7.   For more information on the procedures of the Barnardo program, see June Rose, *For the Sake of the Children: Inside Dr. Barnardo's 120 Years of Caring for Children* (Toronto: Hodder and Stoughton, 1987).

8.   Norfolk County is located in southwestern Ontario on Lake Erie, between Windsor and Fort Erie. See Joy Parr, "George Everitt Green" in *Dictionary of Canadian Biography*, Volume XII (Toronto: University of Toronto Press, 1990) 387-88.

9.   For more information, see Ken Bagnell, *The Little Immigrants: The Orphans Who Came to Canada* (Toronto: Macmillan of Canada, 1980).

10.   *Owen Sound Times*, November 21, 1895

11.   For more information on the conditions at the Finlay farm, the testimony of the trial of Helen Finlay is covered in the *Owen Sound Times*, November 14, 19, 21 and 28, 1895. The trial testimony is also available on microfilm at the Ontario Archives and a number of public libraries.

12.   *Owen Sound Times*, November 14, 1895.

13.   Ibid, November 21, 1895.

14.   *Toronto Evening Star*, November 1895.

15.   Lucy Maud Montgomery, *Anne of Green Gables* (London, Ontario: Gatefold Books Ltd., 1980) 7.

16.   For an account of a young Scottish girl sent to a farm in Oxford County, see Mary Pettit, *Mary Janeway: The Legacy of a Home Child* (Toronto: Natural Heritage Books, 2000).

CHAPTER 10: ALAN MCLEOD: FIRST WORLD WAR AIR ACE

1.   For more information on Canada's preparedness for war, see John Sweetenham, *Canada and the First World War* (Toronto: Ryerson Press, 1969).

2.   Sam Hughes was Prime Minister Robert Borden's Minister of Militia after the outbreak of the First World War. He successfully raised, trained, equipped and sent overseas more than 30,000 Canadian soldiers within two months of the start of the war. However, by 1916, his image was tarnished considerably because of wartime profiteering by his friends at the expense of the quality of equipment provided to our troops. Borden sought and secured his resignation in 1916.

3.   Clifford Sifton (1861 to 1929) was the Minister of the Interior under Sir Wilfrid Laurier. He was the minister responsible for bringing in 3,000,000 immigrants to the Canadian West and helping to create two new provinces – Alberta and Saskatchewan in 1905. However, he broke with Laurier because of his (Sifton's) opposition to extending rights to French Canadians in the new provinces. During the First World War, he was regarded as the leader of the Western Liberals and agreed to accept Robert Borden's proposal to unite and form a Unionist government. He led a number of Liberals into the coalition and helped secure a victory for the Unionist Party in the 1917 election.

4.   Henri Bourassa, grandson of Louis-Joseph Papineau, was born in 1868. He became a Liberal Member of Parliament under Wilfrid Laurier and was Laurier's most trusted advisor in Quebec. However, he opposed Laurier's willingness to be involved in the Boer War and broke with him on the issue of Canadian support for British imperialism. After the break in 1901, Bourassa became spokesperson for French-Canadian nationalism, founding *Le Devoir* newspaper in 1910 and becoming leader of the Ligue Nationaliste, a federal political party in Quebec. Bourassa supported the war effort in 1914, seeing it as an opportunity for Canada's two official races to cooperate. However, he opposed compulsory enlistment (conscription) and was an outspoken critic of the Unionist government.

5.   Wilfrid Laurier was Prime Minister of Canada from 1896 to 1911. Born in 1841, he is regarded as one of Canada's greatest Prime Ministers and was consistently struggling to bridge the gap between the French Canadians and the English

Canadians. As Laurier said, "In English Canada, I am branded as a French Canadian; in Quebec, I am branded as an English Canadian. I am neither; I am a Canadian." When the First World War broke out in 1914, Laurier was Leader of the Opposition and pledged his full support for Canadian participation in the war effort. However, he always insisted that the contribution should be in the form of money, supplies and volunteers. When Prime Minister Borden asked him to join the Unionist Party as co-leader, Laurier refused. The purpose of the Unionist coalition was to introduce conscription and Laurier could not agree to that without a plebiscite. As a result, the Liberal Party split and a large number of English-speaking Liberals joined the Union Party. Borden won the election and Laurier continued as Leader of a smaller Opposition until his death in 1919.

6.   Rudyard Kipling, born in England in 1865, was one of Britain's most successful and popular writers at the turn of the twentieth century. He won the Nobel Prize for Literature in 1907 as a result of such works as *The Jungle Book*, *Just So Stories* and *Kim* in children's literature and *Captains Courageous* and *Puck of Pook's Hill* for adult readers. His adult books emphasized the glorification of British imperialism, while his children's stories took the reader to exotic locales. Kipling died in 1936.

7.   Mary Pickford, "America's Sweetheart," was born Gladys Smith in Toronto, Ontario, in the year 1893. As a child, she appeared on Canadian and American stages and made her film debut in 1909. She became a fan favourite, usually playing a sentimental teenager in the silent movies. With the advent of the "talkies," Pickford changed her image and won an Academy Award for her first talking picture, *Coquette*, in 1929. Retiring as an actress, but continuing as a producer, she was an influential figure in Hollywood into the 1940s. She died in 1979. Today, a plaque is located on the corner of Elm Street and University Avenue on the site of her birth – the present-day location of the Hospital for Sick Children.

8.   The First World War broke out on August 1, 1914, and continued until November 11, 1918. The original protagonists were the Allies (the British Empire, France and Russia along with some other countries) against the Central Powers (Germany and the Austro-Hungarian Empire). The war quickly became a world war, with fighting taking place in Europe, Africa and Asia. It was also the first war to be fought on land, sea and air, and the first war in which the civilian population was mobilized for a total effort on the Home Front. It ushered the world into the twentieth century and a new and much more horrifying type of warfare.

9.   Wilbur and Orville Wright were the two American brothers who made human flight possible. In 1900, they experimented with glider planes in Kitty Hawk, North Carolina, because the United States Weather Bureau identified this area as one of the breeziest locations in America By 1903, the brothers had attached a motor to their gliders and Orville was successful in flying 120 feet, while Wilbur flew 852 feet. The beginning of flight had occurred. Within five years, the United States Army

purchased the first plane from the Wright brothers, beginning the concept of the airplane as a military weapon. Orville Wright lived from 1867 to 1912, while Wilbur lived from 1871 to 1948.

10.   Billy Bishop, born in Owen Sound, Ontario in 1894, was Canada's most successful pilot in the First World War. He is recorded as having a total of 72 "hits" or enemy kills, including five on one day – June 19, 1918. Only two other pilots in the entire war had more hits. He was also the first Canadian airman to win the Victoria Cross for exceptional bravery. During the Second World War, Bishop was honorary Air Marshal of the Royal Canadian Air Force. He died in 1956. See *The Canadian Encyclopedia*, Volume I (Edmonton: Hurtig Publishers, 1985) 187.

11.   Raymond Collishaw was born in Nanaimo, British Columbia, in 1893 and died in Vancouver in 1976. His sixty victories in the air during the First World War placed him second to Billy Bishop among Canadians and fifth among all pilots. When the war ended, he remained in England to fight against the communists in the Russian Civil War of 1919. Later, in World War II, he served as Commander of the Royal Air Force in Egypt, but was relieved of his duties in 1941. He retired with the rank of Vice-Marshal in 1943.

12.   The Bolshevik Revolution was the second of two revolutions in Russia n 1917. The first revolution overthrew the regime Czar Alexander Romanov and established a provisional democracy under Alexander Kerensky. However, Kerensky insisted on Russia continuing in the war and the government never secured a strong foundation of support. The Bolsheviks, under Vladimir Lenin, seized power in late 1917 and established a communist government. Although fighting continued between the Reds (Communists) and the Whites (their opponents) until 1919, the Communist regime was in power and negotiated for peace with Germany. Consequently, the Soviet Union, as it then began to call itself, withdrew from the war in March of 1918.

13.   Manfred von Richtofen, known as the Red Baron, was the most famous pilot of the First World War. Born to a military, aristocratic family, von Richtofen joined the German Army in 1912. He became a combat pilot in 1916 and was the commander of Fighter Group 1 – the famous "Flying Circus." Von Richtofen shot down 80 enemy aircraft before being shot down and killed by a Canadian pilot, Roy Brown, on April 21, 1918. So respected was von Richtofen that the Allies stopped fighting on the day of his funeral and gave him a military gun salute.

14.   As mentioned above, von Richtofen was shot down on April 21, 1918. A second theory circulated is that Australian infantrymen shot him down from the ground. Although there is no definitive answer, many military historians accept Roy Brown from Carleton Place, Ontario, as the individual responsible for the end of the Red Baron.

15.   For more of the text found in McLeod's letter, see Edmund Cosgrove, *Canada's Fighting Pilots* (Toronto: Clark, Irwin, 1966).

16.   "No Man's Land" is the name given to the space between the enemy trenches on the Western Front. The two opposing sides dug into their trenches and settled down for a prolonged war. The fortifications including land mines and barbed wire made attack very difficult. Compounding this difficulty was the use of poison gas, machine guns, grenades and bombs which made any advance virtually impossible. If soldiers attempted to attack, they had to advance into "No Man's Land" where casualties were enormous.

17.   For more information on the terror that gripped Canada during the Spanish Flu epidemic, see the television series, *Canada: A People's History*, Volume 12, "Ordeal by Fire, 1915 to 1929."

CHAPTER 11: ARMAND BOMBARDIER: INVENTOR OF THE SNOWMOBILE

1.   Henry Ford, born in Dearborn, Michigan, in 1863. While still in his 30s, he formed the Ford Motor Company and, in 1908, introduced the Model T Ford. His innovation in the fledgling automobile industry was the introduction of the assembly line and mass production. This enabled unskilled labourers to put together the product piecemeal instead of requiring a skilled worker to make the product from scratch. The result was more automobiles produced at a lower cost, enabling him to establish a price of only $500.00 for a new car. This, in turn, ushered in the age of the automobile which transformed the economy, the society and the lifestyle of people around the world.

2.   Wilfrid "Wop" May was born in Manitoba in 1896. During the First World War, he became part of the famed Canadian branch of the Royal Air Force. He was actually being pursued by von Richtofen, when the Red Baron was shot down and killed in 1918. After the war, May gained additional prestige as a bush pilot who flew people and supplies into the frontier lands of northwestern Canada during the mining boom of the 1920s. May died in 1952.

3.   Robert Samuel McLaughlin was one of the automotive pioneers in Canada. Born in 1871, he worked with his father in the carriage business in Tyrone, Ontario, before opening his own shop in Oshawa in partnership with his father and brother. McLaughlin began manufacturing Buick and Chevrolet automobiles for the American owner of Buick Motors (William Durrant). Durrant was bought out by General Motors and Sam McLaughlin became president of General Motors of Canada. Oshawa became one of the most important automobile factories in the world during the 1920s and McLaughlin became famous for his business acumen and philanthropic endeavours. He died in 1972, five years after becoming a member of the Order of Canada.

4.   Reginald Aubrey Fessenden was born in Milton, Ontario, in 1866. He worked for both Thomas Edison and George Westinghouse in the United States, but set up his

own company in 1902. He was the creator of a number of inventions and innovations, including the development of AM radio broadcasting. Fessenden died in 1932.

5.   Edward Samuel Rogers was born in Toronto in 1900. He had an early interest in the new invention, the radio, and, as a thirteen-year-old, won a prize for building a radio. In 1925, he developed the alternating current radio tube which permitted people to listen to the radio without having to wear bulky headphones. This made it possible for the radio to become a popular source of entertainment in homes throughout the world. Rogers died in 1939, but his son Ted Rogers continues his legacy as head of Rogers Telecommunications Limited.

6.   Doctor Frederick Banting and Charles Best were the co-discoverers of insulin in 1921. Banting was born in 1891 and died in 1941. Charles Best, a student at University of Toronto, was born in 1899. He was working with his professor, Doctor Banting on a summer project when the two of them came up with the life-saving discovery. Banting received the Nobel Prize for the discovery of insulin in 1923, which he shared with another co-worker, but not with Best. Although Best did not get the Nobel Prize, Doctor Banting publicly praised his vital role and insisted on sharing the prize money equally with Best. Best died in 1978.

7.   The Conscription Crisis of 1917 occurred when the Prime Minister of Canada, Robert Borden, felt obliged to break his earlier pledge of a completely voluntary army to fight overseas. Believing that compulsory military service was necessary, he waged an election campaign on the pledge to introduce conscription (the name given to this mandatory sign-up). He won the election, but the results demonstrated the split in the nation, with French Canadians, labour and farmers opposing Borden and generally urban English Canadians and businessmen supporting him. Conscription was introduced in 1917, leading to riots in Quebec and the need to exempt farm labourers.

8.   See Mason Wade, *The French Canadians, 1760-1967*, Volume II 1911-1967. (Toronto: Macmillan, 1968).

9.   For more information on the young Armand, see Carole Precious, *J. Armand Bombardier* (Markham, ON: Fitzhenry and Whiteside, 1984).

10.   Voltaire is the pen name for François-Marie Arouet who lived in France from 1694 to 1778. He was one of the greatest writers and philosophers of his day whose work promoted a passion for justice and a call for the universal rights of humankind. He believed in religion and the existence of a God, but he was critical of religious intolerance and Church corruption. His writings are regarded as an important foundation for the French Revolution and the overthrow of the *Ancien Regime*.

11.   Speech by Armand Bombardier, June 10, 1952 as quoted in Carole Precious, *J. Armand Bombardier*, 50.

12.   Ibid, 205.

13. For more information, see Roger Lacasse, *Joseph-Armand Bombardier: An Inventor's Dream Come True* (Montreal: Libre Expression, 1988).

14. Armand Bombardier's will and testament as quoted in Carole Precious, *J. Armand Bombardier*, 200-201.

CHAPTER 12: TOY JIN "JEAN" WONG: SPIRIT OF THE DRAGON

1. John A. Macdonald, born in Scotland in 1815, was Canada's first prime minister and the main force in creating a nation from four colonies (Confederation of Canada). He served as prime minister from 1867 to 1873 and from 1878 until his death in 1891. His concern was to consolidate the nation and expand it from sea to sea. His role in initiating the construction of the Canadian Pacific Railway is regarded as one of the great accomplishments in Canadian history.

2. Charles Leland (author of the book, *Fusang: The Discovery of America*) as cited in Lee Wai-man, *Portraits of a Challenge: An Illustrated History of the Chinese Canadians* (Toronto: Council of Chinese Canadians in Ontario, 1984) 1-2.

3. Lindalee Tracey, *A Scattering of Seeds: The Creation of Canada* (Toronto: McArthur & Company, 1999) 151-152.

4. Pierre Berton, *The Last Spike* (Toronto: McClelland & Stewart, 1971) 3.

5. Edgar Wickberg (ed.), *From China to Canada: A History of the Chinese Communities in Canada* (2nd printing) (Toronto: McClelland & Stewart, 1988) 21. See also Peter S. Li, *The Chinese in Canada* (Toronto: Oxford University Press, 1988) 17.

6. There are two methods of transcribing Chinese script to English – the Giles-Wade and the Pinyin. For most people the most readily recognizable is the Giles-Wade, but the more current method is the Pinyin. For example, Confucius is the Giles-Wade transliteration of the name of the great Chinese philosopher. In Pinyin, his name is Kongfuzi. Since the proper names of places and people such as Toy Jin Wong are still presented in the Giles-Wade format, the decision was made to stay with that method in this book but recognize the fact that the Pinyin method is replacing this form of transliteration.

7. Peter S. Li, *The Chinese in Canada*, 15. See also Sheyla Burney, *Coming to Gum San: The Story of Chinese Canadians* (Toronto: D.C. Heath Canada for the Multicultural History Society of Ontario, 1995) 13.

8. Pierre Berton, *The Last Spike* (Toronto: McClelland & Stewart, 1971) 204. See also Margaret Wong (producer) and Dora Nipp (Director), *Under the Willow Tree* (Montreal: Produced by Margaret Wong for the National Film Board of Canada, 1997).

9. *Port Moody Gazette* quote from Sheyla Burney, *Coming to Gum San: The Story of Chinese Canadians*, 14.

10. From *Under the Willow Tree* (National Film Board, 1997).

11. Author interview with Arlene Chan (daughter of Jean Lumb), November 2005.

12. Confucianism, a social ethical or philosophical approach to life was initiated by the great Chinese scholar, Confucius, who lived from 551 BC to 479 BC. Confronted with political violence and social upheaval, Confucius responded with a set of teachings that emphasized loyalty to oneself, reciprocity in relationships, righteousness and filial piety. His emphasis on family and the perfectibility of all people was so attractive, that within a century after his death, his teachings were required learning for all Chinese civil servant candidates. This requirement remained in effect until the early years of the twentieth century.

13. Major M.J. Crehan, Vancouver School Trustee, as quoted in Lee Wai-Man, *Portraits of a Challenge: An Illustrated History of the Chinese Canadians*, 248.

14. Edgar Wickberg (ed.), *From China to Canada*, 182.

15. Jean Lumb as quoted in Evelyn Huang with Lawrence Jeffery, *Chinese Canadians Voices From a Community* (Vancouver: Douglas & McIntrye, 1992) 38.

16. Jean Lumb as quoted in Arlene Chan, *Spirit of the Dragon: The Story of Jean Lumb, a Proud Canadian* (Toronto: Umbrella Press, 1997) 30.

CHAPTER 13: THE BABY DERBY: ESCAPING THE GREAT DEPRESSION

1. The "hungry thirties" is a name applied to the time period of the Great Depression that began with a stock market crash in 1929. It was so named because of the widespread hunger and suffering endured during the period. More information on the Great Depression is in Note 6 below.

2. Will and testament of Charles Vance Millar as quoted in Edwin C. Guillet, "The Toronto Maternity Sweepstakes: An Account of the Trials and Other Proceedings Resulting From the Will of Charles Vance Millar" (Famous Canadian Trials, Volume 13, (Toronto: s.n. typewritten, 1944) II, Toronto Reference Library, Baldwin Room, 343.lg77V.13. As a point of interest, the Baldwin Room librarian identified Edwin Guillet as the Pierre Berton of 60 years ago. There are over 148 books by Guillet at the library. He typed up this manuscript and had only five copies made before his death.

3. "Relief lines" refers to the common sight during the Depression of hundreds of people lining up on city streets to secure a meal at a local charity food kitchen. Organizations such as churches and the Salvation Army offered free meals to be distributed to the needy at local centres. Legislation for unemployment insurance would not be enacted until 1935, but was declared unconstitutional and not established until a constitutional amendment of 1941.

4. The area was named after the explorer, John Palliser, who mounted an expedition through the Rocky Mountains and Red River region from 1857 to 1860. He concluded

that there was fertile land surrounding an arid region that was not hospitable to vegetation and farming. The arid region came to be called the Palliser Triangle.

5.   Richard Bedford Bennett (1870-1947) had the misfortune to serve as prime minister of Canada during the worst economic crisis in Canadian history. Born in New Brunswick, Bennett moved to Calgary as a young man and soon became a Conservative politician and Party leader in 1927. He won the 1930 election on the promise to end the depression that had just started in Canada. In office, however, he did little more to deal with the economic crisis than raise tariffs (which reduced trade even further) and provide funds for relief programs. So unpopular was Bennett that Canadians applied his name to symbols of the Depression. "Bennett Buggies" were cars with their motors removed and pulled by horses. Farmers could not afford the cost of gas and car maintenance so this became a popular mode of transportation on the Prairies. Similarly, "Bennettville" was the name applied to the Hobo towns that sprang up along the railway lines on the outskirts of towns. These became the temporary residences of the desperate individuals searching for work across Canada. Bennett lost the election of 1935 and moved to England, where he became a Member of the British House of Lords.

6.   The Great Depression from 1929 to 1939 was the most severe peace time challenge that ever confronted Canada. The stock market crash of October 1929 is recognized as the onset of this economic catastrophe. Although the crash was the event that precipitated the Depression, there were a number of underlying causes that created the crisis. Over production, the availability of easy credit, stock market speculation and an unfair distribution of the wealth are among the causes cited by economists. The Depression was marked by unemployment, a drought on the Prairies that resulted in falling production, a fall in industrial production and world trade and widespread suffering. Aggravating the crisis was the fact that no "safety network" of social legislation (unemployment insurance, workman's compensation and other such safeguards) existed at the time. Consequently, there was little support from the government for the suffering people. It is said that the outbreak of the Second World War and the production of weapons and equipment were the ultimate reason for the Depression ending.

7.   The liquor permit was a certificate that was issued to every adult who wished to purchase alcohol from a government store in Ontario. It was established in the 1920s and abolished after the Second World War.

8.   For more information on relief conditions, see Barry Broadfoot, *Ten Lost Years: Memories of Canadians Who Survived the Depression* (Toronto: McClelland & Stewart, 1973).

9.   For more information on the Maritime economy, see E.R. Forbes, "The Origins of the Maritime Rights Movement," in R. Douglas Francis and Donald B. Smith, *Readings in Canadian History Post-Confederation* (Toronto: Harcourt Brace and Company Ltd., 1998).

10. "Riding the rods" refers to the practice of thousands of young men and women who illegally climbed aboard the box cars of freight trains in a desperate search for employment elsewhere in Canada. If they were not caught and removed, they would travel by rail to other locations. It was a common sight and a symbol of the suffering endured during these years.

11. Adolf Hitler was born in Austria in 1899 and was leader of the National Socialist (Nazi) Party from 1920 until his death in 1945. He became leader of Germany (Chancellor) in 1933 and boasted of a regime that would last one thousand years. His aggressive foreign policy plunged the world into the Second World War and within twelve years, his country lay in ruins and he lay dead. With the liberation of Europe from the Nazi tentacles came the worldwide horror at the crimes perpetrated by the Nazi government against humanity.

12. Benito Mussolini (1893 to 1945) was the founder of Italian fascism and the leader of Italy from 1922 until his imprisonment in 1943. He was a persuasive orator and took the Italian nation into World War II, with visions of establishing a new Roman Empire. The war did not go well for the Italians and the army met with a string of defeats. Hitler and the German soldiers assisted the Italians in Greece and North Africa, but the Italian people were growing weary of war. They overthrew Mussolini and imprisoned him in 1943, but again, Hitler sent in German commandos to rescue him. When he returned to Italy to attempt to set up a new government in 1945, he was captured and killed by the Italian people in Milan, Italy.

13. Joseph Stalin (born Joseph Dzugashvili) changed his name to the Russian word for "steel" when he joined the Bolsheviks in 1903. With the death of Lenin in 1924, Stalin emerged from the power struggle as the new leader of the Soviet Union, a position he held until his death in 1953. His tactics were ruthless, involving forced labour, mass starvation, purges, murders and "gulags" or prison camps. Millions of citizens died during his years in power as a direct result of his actions.

14. Foster Hewitt was the voice of the Toronto Maple Leafs, and the most famous broadcaster in Canada from 1923 on radio until 1972 on television. Born in Toronto in 1902, he was a sportswriter for the *Toronto Daily Star* prior to broadcasting. His famous expression, "He shoots; he scores!" sent chills up and down the spines of enthralled listeners across Canada. Hewitt died in 1985.

15. Francis "King" Clancy was one of the most popular person ever to play hockey for the Toronto Maple Leafs. Purchased from the Ottawa Senators in 1931, he was an all star defenseman for the team during the 1930s. Afterwards, he served as a referee for the NHL and later coach and vice-president for the Toronto Maple Leafs. Born in Ottawa in 1903, Clancy died in Toronto in 1986.

16. Edward William Shore (1902-1985) was one the best defencemen to play in the National Hockey League. He was a stalwart of the Boston Bruins team from 1926 to 1939. He won the Hart Trophy as the most valuable player in the NHL four times and is a member of the Hockey Hall of Fame.

17.   The Kid Line consisted of Joe Primeau at centre, Harvey "Busher" Jackson on left wing and Charlie Conacher on right wing. So named because of the youth of the three players who were all in their early 20s, it was a top scoring combination that led the team to the Stanley Cup. All three members have been inducted into the Hockey Hall of Fame.

18.   The Dionne Quintuplets (Annette, Emilie, Yvonne, Cecile and Marie) were the first quintuplets ever to survive beyond infancy after their birth in 1934. They became the centre of world interest because of their unique circumstances and their beautiful, photogenic faces. Their birth place at Callander, Ontario, just outside of North Bay, was the most popular tourist destination in Canada in the late 1930s with over 3,000,000 million visitors. Hollywood made movies about them, songs were written about them, Dionne dolls were best sellers and they appeared in newspapers and magazines all over the world. Importunely, their later years were marred by death, estrangement from their family and considerable unhappiness. In 1998, the three surviving sisters (Emilie, Yvonne and Cecile) left their reclusive existence to hold a press conference in 1998 in which they asserted that the Ontario government had never paid them their share of the profits promised. Accountants estimated they were owed forty million dollars, but they settled for four million and returned to their private lives. The Dionne Quints Museum in North Bay displays memorabilia of their lives. For more information, see Pierre Berton, *The Dionne Years: A Thirties Melodrama* (Toronto: McClelland & Stewart, 1977).

19.   When his father King George V died, Edward VIII became the next monarch of England and also, King of Canada. However, his formal coronation was not to occur for another six months. In the interim, it was discovered that he was in love with an American divorcee who was not descended from royalty. This created a constitutional crisis in England with some supporting his right to choose whomever he wanted as a wife, and others saying that the King as head of the Church of England could not marry a divorced person. The crisis was resolved when Edward gave up the throne for "the woman I love" – Wallis Simpson.

20.   Grey Owl was the name adopted by an Englishman called Archie Belaney. Living with the Ojibwa People in Northern Ontario, he so admired their values and life style that he passed himself off as a Native person to both the Canadian and international public. His speeches and writings on nature and the environment made him a celebrity in the 1930s. It was not until after his death in 1938 that the public became aware that he was an imposter.

21.   Clark Gable and Carole Lombard were two famous movie actors of the 1930s. Gable won an Academy Award for his lead role in "It Happened One Night" in 1934 and is still remembered as Rhett Butler in "Gone With the Wind." Lombard was a brilliant comedienne who starred in a number of screwball comedies of the 1930s. Their romance and subsequent marriage, which ended with Lombard's tragic death in a plane crash in 1942, was one of the most endearing human interest stories of the decade.

22. Mitch Hepburn as quoted in Edwin Guillet, "The Toronto Maternity Sweepstakes," Chapter IX.

23. For more information on the families involved in the Baby Derby, see Mark Orkin, *The Great Stork Derby* (Don Mills, ON: General Publishing Ltd., 1981), for all finalists came from Orkin.

24. Mark Orkin, *The Great Stork Derby*, 118.

25. Ibid, 152

26. Ibid.

27. Frank Timleck as quoted in Mark Orkin, *The Great Stork Derby*, 320-321.

CHAPTER 14: ERWIN SCHILD: ACCIDENTAL IMMIGRANT

1.   This refers to the tax that was placed on Chinese immigrants wanting to enter Canada. In 1885, the tax was set at $50.00 and, by 1903, it had been increased to $500.00. More about this tax can be found in the Chapter 12 on Toy Jin Wong (Jean Lumb).

2.   This quote became the title of a book by Irving Abella and Harold Troper, *None is Too Many: Canada and the Jews of Europe, 1933-1948* (Toronto: Lester & Orpen Dennys, 1982).

3.   Abella and Troper, *None is Too Many*, v.

4. The term "Accidental Immigrants" comes from the title of a two-part article by Paula Draper, published in the *Canadian Jewish Historical Society Journal*, Volume II, Number 1, Spring 1978 and Volume II, Number 2, Fall 1978.

5.   Anti-Semitism has been a long standing blight on European and North American societies. It was particularly virulent during the hard times of the Great Depression when people were seeking a scapegoat for their troubles. One of the most blatant examples occurred in Toronto, following a baseball game between a Jewish and a Gentile team. Tempers flared and fights broke out directed against Jewish spectators and neighbourhood residents.

6.   Adrian Arcand was a marginal, but despicable, figure in Canadian politics of the 1930s. From his home in Quebec, he founded the National Social Christian Party to protect Roman Catholicism against Communists and other "atheist" groups. It was Canada's strongest official Nazi Party, but gained little inroad into popularity. Arcand was arrested and imprisoned when the Second World War broke out. After his release, he returned to obscurity.

7.   Frederick Blair was the Deputy Minister of Immigration during the 1930s. As such, he was the main architect of Canada's immigration (and deportation) policies during these years. Blair's blatant anti-Semitism was evident in his statements and his policies. From 1933 until 1945, Canada admitted 5,000 Jewish refugees

while United States admitted 240,000 and Great Britain admitted 85,000.

8.   For more information on Prime Minister Mackenzie King's relationship with Adolf Hitler, see H. Blair Neatby, *William Lyon Mackenzie King: A Political Biography, Volume III: 1932-1939: The Prism of Unity* (Toronto: University of Toronto Press, 1976). See also Brian Nolan, *King's War: Mackenzie King and the Politics of War 1939-1945* (Toronto: Random House, 1988, 15).

9.   Nick Brune, *Defining Canada: History, Identity, and Culture* (Toronto: McGraw-Hill Ryerson, 2003) 428.

10.   Erwin Schild's interview with author, February 1989.

11.   Concentration camps were first set up by England to deal with the Boers of South Africa during the Boer War (1899-1902). After securing power in Germany in 1933, Hitler commenced setting up these prison camps to deal with his enemies – Jews, Communists, socialists, homosexuals, gypsies, Christian opponents and others. Prisoners had to wear identification badges such as the pink star for homosexuals and the Star of David for Jews. The first camps were located in Germany, but after Hitler advanced into Eastern Europe, he set up camps in that area. By then, his concentration was on his "final solution" to the Jewish question and since extermination was the goal, the camps were located closest to where the majority of Jews resided. Ultimately, 12,000,000 people perished in these camps, including 6,000,000 Jews. Dachau, in Germany, was not officially a death camp, but the reality was that by 1945, all the concentration camps were in the process of destroying the prisoners.

12.   Erwin Schild's interview with author, February 1989. Evidently earlier conditions at Dachau were more lenient.

13.   *Globe and Mail*, November 21, 1938, 1.

14.   Winston Churchill was born at Blenheim Palace in England in 1874, a direct descendant of the first Duke of Marlborough, the founder of family's fortune and greatest soldier of the late 17th and early 18th centuries, and who traded his sister's honour (she became James II's mistress) for the title.

Churchill served as a Liberal cabinet minister before, during and after the First World War (1908 to 1929). Becoming increasingly conservative, he changed allegiance to his political party from Liberal to Conservative. During the 1930s, he was outside the government but was the most vocal of the voices of concern regarding the potential menace of Germany under Hitler. When war broke out, he was brought into the government once again and became prime minister in 1940. His accomplishments as war time leader and his stirring speeches in defense of democracy are justifiably world-renowned. In 1945, he was voted out of office but was re-elected in 1951 and served until his retirement in 1955. Churchill died in 1965.

15.   The Geneva Conventions were a series of international treaties negotiated in the first half of the twentieth century. The 1929 convention established a specific set of guidelines for the safeguard of the rights of Prisoners of War. These guidelines protected them from mistreatment, but made no mention of interned "enemy aliens" who were regarded as a domestic, rather than international concern. Geneva was the site of the signings because of the long-standing neutrality of Switzerland.

16.   Erwin Schild's interview with author, February 1989.

17.   Hassidic Jews refers to the devout Orthodox Jews who were concerned with the influences upon Judaism in the early eighteenth century. They were formed in 1848 as a formal rejection of the Westernization that was occurring, and are distinguished by their distinctive black clothing and hairstyles.

18.   Erwin Schild's interview with author, February 1989.

19.   Ibid.

CHAPTER 15: STEVEN TRUSCOTT: A STRUGGLE FOR JUSTICE

1.   The United Nations was the creation of the wartime allies against Hitler. These leaders (particularly the leaders of United States, England and Canada) were determined that future wars should be avoided through the process of international cooperation. At the charter meeting in San Francisco in the spring of 1945, principles and rules were established and New York City was agreed upon as the headquarters for the world organization. The United Nations continues to be an effective advocate of a better world with its promotion of peace, respect for human rights and social development of poorer nations.

2.   Formed in 1947, the International Civil Aviation Association was set up to promote air transportation safety. It continues to play a vital role in this objective today.

3.   Lester Bowles Pearson (1897 to 1972) was one of Canada's most notable statesmen and prime ministers. He was Canadian Ambassador to the United Nations from its inception and was regarded as one of the most respected diplomat in the organization. He became minister of External Affairs in 1948 but continued to play an influential role in the world organization. His innovative peacekeeping proposal for resolving the crisis in the Middle East resulted in his winning the Nobel Peace Prize in 1957. He became prime minister of Canada in 1963, with a minority Liberal government. He was re-elected in 1965, but again with a minority. Pearson resigned in 1968 and was replaced by Pierre Trudeau. While prime minister, he saw Canada secure its own flag, oversaw the establishment of a national healthcare program and unified the Armed Forces.

4.   Gross National Product (GNP) means the monetary value of all the goods and services produced in a country during the given year. It is regarded as one of the most accurate means of determining the wealth of a nation.

5.   For more information on the measurement of wealth in Canada during the 1950s, see Alexander Ross, *The Booming Fifties, 1950-1960*. (Toronto: Natural Science of Canada, 1977).

6.   Maurice Duplessis was born in Quebec in 1890 and died in office as premier of Quebec in 1959. As leader of the Conservative Party in Quebec, he persuaded nationalists and unhappy Liberals to join him in forming a new party – the Union Nationale – in 1933. This party won the election of 1935 and Duplessis became premier. As leader of the French-Canadian province, he was a controversial figure. Promoting French-Canadian survival, he fought with the Prime Minister William Lyon Mackenzie King over provincial rights following his return to office in 1944 (he had been defeated in the 1939 election). He fought against labour unions, reformers and opponents of his arbitrary rule but enjoyed the support of businessmen and the Roman Catholic Church. During his years in office, he was determined to preserve the French-Canadian society in the face of modernization. His death is one of the main reasons for the Quiet Revolution that followed in 1960.

7.   The Quiet Revolution refers to the years that Jean Lesage served as premier of Quebec (1960 to 1966). It was a period of rapid change and modernization as Quebec moved more forcefully into the twentieth century. Reforms occurred in industrialization, in education, in politics and in society. Under the slogan "*Maîtres chez nous*" or "Masters of our own house," Quebec gained a renewed pride in her identity and insisted on powers from the federal government that would secure the changes desired. The issues that continue to challenge French Canadians and English Canadians with respect to Quebec's role in Canada stem from the Quiet Revolution.

8.   Georges Vanier was the first French-Canadian Governor General since the days of New France (1760). Born in Quebec in 1888, Vanier was a hero in the First World War and an individual respected in both English Canada and French Canada. He was installed as Governor General in 1959 and served until 1967, the year of his death.

9.   Julian Sher, *Until You Are Dead: Steven Truscott's Long Ride Into History* (Toronto: Knopf, 2001).

10.   *Toronto Telegram*, June 12, 1958.

11.   The books are Isabel LeBourdais, *The Trial of Steven Truscott* (Toronto: McClelland & Stewart, 1966); Bill Trent with Steven Truscott, *Who Killed Lynne Harper?* (Toronto: Optimum Publishing Company, 1979); and Julian Sher, *Until You are Dead: Steven Truscott's Long Ride Into History* (Toronto: Knopf, 2001).

12.   Bill Trent with Steven Truscott, *Who Killed Lynne Harper?*, 88-89.

13.   Ibid, 91.

14.   Isobel Le Bourdais, *The Trial of Steven Truscott*, 220.

15. Mr. Justice Ferguson as quoted in Isobel Le Bourdais, *The Trial of Steven Truscott*, 208.

16. Julian Sher, *Until You Are Dead*, 342.

17. Bill Trent with Steven Truscott, *Who Killed Lynne Harper?*, 97.

18. Julian Sher, *Until You Are Dead*, 554.

19. In 1969, Steven Truscott was granted parole ten years after entering prison because of his exemplary behaviour while serving his sentence. One condition of his parole was that he was to take on a new identity and not use the name "Truscott."

20. *Toronto Star*, November 29, 2005, A4.

CHAPTER 16: MARILYN BELL: SWIMMING FOR THE GLORY OF CANADA

1. George Young was born in Scotland in 1910 and moved to Canada as a two-year-old. He was an accomplished swimmer as a young boy, and won five national titles while still an amateur. He seemed to come from nowhere to capture the prize and the celebrity status following his conquest of the Santa Catalina to California Race. He continued swimming competitively for a number of years, but nothing matched his accomplishment of 1926. After three failed attempts to swim Lake Ontario, he acknowledged defeat. He died in Niagara Falls in 1972.

2. Born in 1926, Winnie Roach Leuszler was the first Canadian to swim the English Channel in 1951. She was greeted with a ticker-tape parade in her hometown of Toronto and was one of the most famous of our marathon swimmers of the 1950s. Leuszler was virtually the only long distance swimmer who swam competitive races while she was pregnant. Her professional debut occurred two months after her first child and she was to have five children while during her years of competition. She died in 2004.

3. Florence Chadwick was born in the United States in 1918. She was an American long distance swimmer who became the first woman to swim the English Channel both ways. She also swam the Straits of Gibraltar, the Dardenelles and the Bosporus Sea. Her swim from Catalina Island to California was completed in less than fourteen hours, the fastest time ever recorded.

4. A.W. "Bill" Leveridge, *Fair Sport: The History of Sport at the Canadian National Exhibition, 1879-1977 Inclusive* (Toronto: Canadian National Exhibition and M.S. Printers, 1978) 29.

5. Ibid, 29.

CHAPTER 17: WAYNE GRETZKY: THE GREAT ONE

1. Wayne Gretzky with Rick Reilly, *Gretzky: An Autobiography* (Toronto: HarperCollins, 1990) 8.

2.   Walter Gretzky as quoted in Walter Gretzky and Jim Taylor, *Gretzky: From the Back Yard Rink to the Stanley Cup.* (Toronto: McClelland & Stewart, 1984) 47.

3.   Joseph-Henri Maurice Richard – the "Rocket" – was the greatest player to ever skate out of Quebec into the National Hockey League (NHL). Born in 1921, he started his NHL career in 1942 at the age of twenty-one. In 1944-45, he set a new record with an amazing fifty goals in fifty games. His fiery temperament, exciting style and determination to win, made him a folk hero in the Province of Quebec. Authors wrote stories of him (most notably, Roch Carrier's *The Hockey Sweater*) and when he was suspended in 1955, for hitting another player with his stick then attacking the linesman who tried to intervene, a riot broke out in Montreal – the worst sports riot in Canadian history. At the time of his retirement in 1960, he had accumulated 544 goals, a record at that time. When the Rocket died in the year 2000, there was a public outpouring of grief that was unparalleled in Canadian sports.

4.   Bob Hocken, as quoted in Walter Gretzky and Jim Taylor, *Gretzky*, 81.

5.   Gordie Howe at the Brantford Sports Banquet, 1972 as reported by Andrew Podnieks, *The Great One: The Life and Times of Wayne Gretzky* (Toronto: Doubleday Canada, 1999) 10.

6.   Wayne Gretzky with Rick Reilly, *Gretzky: An Autobiography*, 23.

7.   Maple Leaf Gardens – "The House that (Conn) Smythe Built" – was one of the most famous hockey shrines in North America. Conn Smythe purchased the Toronto St. Patricks and renamed them the Toronto Maple Leafs in 1927. His next objective was to build an appropriate arena for his team. Unfortunately, he started construction during the Great Depression and was unable to secure financing. His innovative solution was to offer shares to the construction workers, while still retaining majority ownership. As a result, the Maple Leaf Gardens opened in time for the 1931 hockey season. For more than sixty years after that, it was not only home to the Leafs, it was the most famous hockey arena in the world. Saturday night broadcasts from the gondola in Maple Leaf Gardens brought the team into the living rooms all across Canada, and made the Leafs Canada's team. The Gardens was also the venue of circuses, of rock stars (including Elvis Presley and the Beatles), of boxing matches (including Muhammad Ali and George Chuvalo) and countless other forms of entertainment. The last Leaf game at the Gardens was played on February 14, 1998. Maple Leaf Gardens is still owned by Toronto Maple Leafs Sports and Entertainment and stands on Carlton Street, just east of Yonge, a reminder of the glory days of NHL hockey and the Toronto Maple Leafs.

8.   This story is recounted by Walter Gretzky and Jim Taylor in *Gretzky*, 100-03, and in Wayne Gretzky with Rick Reilly, *Gretzky: An Autobiography*, 22-25.

9.   Peter Pocklington was born in Canada in 1941. By the early 1970s he had

amassed a considerable amount of money through his Pocklington Financial Corporation in Edmonton. This wealth enabled him to pursue his love of sports and he purchased the Edmonton Oilers Hockey Team, the Edmonton Trappers Baseball Team and the Edmonton Drillers Soccer Team. In addition, he was a world class jet-boat racer and a partner with Paul Newman in Can-Am automobile racing. After accumulating five Stanley Cups in hockey, financial setbacks prompted him to trade Wayne Gretzky to the Los Angeles Kings in 1988 and to sell his interest in his beloved Oilers in 1998. He currently lives in Los Angeles.

CHAPTER 18: TERRY FOX: A MARATHON OF HOPE

1.   Anecdotes on Terry Fox early years are told by Rolly and Betty Fox in Floyd Lansing (director), *Twenty-five Years of Hope: The Legacy of Terry Fox,* Out to Seas Production (Vancouver) for CBC television, 2005, broadcast on CBC Television, September 16, 2005.

2.   Richard Hansen was born in British Columbia in 1957. At the age of fifteen, he was paralyzed from the neck down, the result of a truck accident. He went on to excel in wheelchair athletics in basketball, volleyball, sprints and marathons. He won twelve gold medals in the British Columbia games and a gold, silver and bronze medal in the 1980 Wheelchair Olympics. His famous "Man in Motion" tour covered 40,000 kilometres and raised $20,000,000. He is currently President and CEO of the Man in Motion Foundation.

3.   Terry Fox interview in *Twenty-five Years of Hope: The Legacy of Terry Fox.*

4.   Darrell Fox as quoted in Douglas Coupland, *Terry* (Vancouver: Douglas & McIntyre, 2005), 29.

5.   Terry Fox as quoted in Leslie Scrivener, *Terry Fox: His Story* (revised edition) (Toronto: McClelland & Stewart, 2000), 63.

6.   Darryl Sittler, born in St. Jacob's, Ontario, in 1950 was one of the most popular captains of the Toronto Maple Leafs. He played for the Leafs from 1970 to 1982 and was captain from 1975 to 1981. He scored ten points – still a record – in one game in February of 1976. He currently works in public relations for the Toronto Maple Leafs.

7.   Bobby Orr was born in Parry Sound, Ontario, in 1948 and revolutionized the way hockey was played during his years in the NHL (1966 to 1979). He holds the record for most assists in a single season (102) and most points by a defenseman in a single season (139). His number 4 has been retired by the Boston Bruins, he is a member of the Hockey Hall of Fame.

8.   As quoted by Darryl Sittler in Leslie Scrivener, *Terry Fox: His Story,* 126.

9.   Doug Alward became Terry's friend in grade seven and remained his best

friend for the rest of Terry's life. A natural athlete as a youngster, Doug's presence was essential for the Marathon of Hope. Had he not agreed to accompany Terry, there would have been no Marathon. Today, Alward is one of the top marathoners in his age group, He lives in his hometown near Vancouver, British Columbia.

10.   Doug Alward as quoted in the *Toronto Star*, September 14, 2005.

11.   Pierre Trudeau was the prime minister of Canada from 1968 to 1979 and from 1980 to 1984, the longest serving French-Canadian prime minister in our nation's history. Trudeau is best remembered for patriating our Constitution with an entrenched Charter of Rights and Freedoms.

12.   Pierre Trudeau as quoted in Leslie Scrivener, *Terry Fox: His Story*, 182.

13.   Martin Luther King Jr., born in 1929 and died in 1968. King, like his grandfather and father, became a Baptist preacher. In 1954, he was transferred from his home town of Atlanta to Montgomery, Alabama. There he helped organize the bus boycott to end segregation on public transit. His strategy of peaceful, non-violent protest was a successful method of achieving change. Although he was arrested over 20 times, his efforts led to integration in the south. The high point of his career was the "March on Washington," which attracted 250,000 people and was climaxed by his "I have a Dream" speech. King became the youngest person to win the Nobel Peace Prize when he was awarded it in 1964 at the age of thirty-five. King was assassinated in Memphis, Tennessee, while organizing a protest in 1968.

14.   Mother Teresa, born Agnes Gonxha Bojaxhiu, in Macedonia in 1910 was of Albanian descent. She joined a Roman Catholic religious order in 1928 and took her vows in India in 1931. There she taught high school until 1948. After receiving permission, she opened her own order – the Missionaries of Charity – and worked in the slums of Calcutta. Her order spread all over the world and she was awarded the Nobel Peace Prize for her work. Mother Teresa died in 1997.

15.   Terry Fox in a speech in Scarborough as quoted in Leslie Scrivener, *Terry Fox: His Story*, 123.

16.   Ibid, 183.

BIBLIOGRAPHY

A. GENERAL SOURCES

BOOKS

Bennett, Paul W. and Cornelius J. Jaenen, *Emerging Identities: Selected Problems and Interpretations in Canadian History*. Scarborough, ON: Prentice-Hall Canada, 1986.

Cook, Ramsey, with John C. Ricker and John T. Saywell, *Canada: A Modern Study*. Toronto: Clarke, Irwin, 1963.

Durnford, Hugh (ed.), *Heritage of Canada*. Montreal: Reader's Digest Association (Canada); Ottawa: Canadian Automobile Association, 1978.

Francis, R. Douglas, Richard Jones and Donald B. Smith, *Destinies: Canadian History Since Confederation*. Toronto: Holt, Rinehart and Winston of Canada, 1992.

_____, *Origins: Canadian History to Confederation*. Toronto: Harcourt Brace Canada, 1996.

Fryer, Mary Beacock and Charles Humber (eds.), *Loyal She Remains: A Pictorial History of Ontario*. Toronto: United Empire Loyalists' Association of Canada, 1984.

Hehner, Barbara (ed.), *The Spirit of Canada*. Toronto: Malcolm Lester Books, 1999.

Lunn, Janet and Christopher Moore, *The Story of Canada*. Toronto: Lester Publishing and Key Porter Books, 1992.

TELEVISION

Starowicz, Mark (Producer), *Canada: A People's History*, Volumes 1-16. CBC Radio-Canada, 2001.

B. SOURCES BY CHAPTER

Chapter 1: Domagaya and Taignoagny: Iroquois Heroes and Victims

BOOKS

Cartier, Jacques (Ramsay Cook, ed.) *The Voyages of Jacques Cartier* (translated by H.P. Biggar). Toronto: University of Toronto Press, 1993.

Guizot, M. and Madame Guizot de Witt (translated by Robert Black), *The History of France from Earliest Times to 1848*, Volume 3. New York: Thomas Y. Crowell and Company, 1885.

Knecht, R.J., *Francis I*. Cambridge: Cambridge University Press, 1982.

Jenness, Diamond, *The Indians of Canada*. Ottawa: National Museum of Canada, 1963 (sixth edition).

Spence, Jonathan, *The Question of Hu*. New York: Knopf, 1988.

Trudel, Marcel (translated by Patricia Claxton), *The Beginnings of New France, 1524-1663*. Toronto: McClelland & Stewart, 1973.

Symington, Fraser, *The First Canadians*. Toronto: Natural Science of Canada, 1978.

Williams, E.N. *Penguin Dictionary of English and European History, 1485-1789*. London: Allen Lane, 1980.

MICROFILM WORK

Bailey, Alfred Goldsworthy, *The Significance of the Identity and Disappearance of the Laurentian Iroquois*. Ottawa: The Royal Society of Canada Transactions 1886-1949, Series 3, Volume XXVII (1933), Section II, 97-108.

Lighthall, W.D., *Hochelagas and Mohawks: A Link in Iroquois History*. Ottawa: Royal Society of Canada Transactions 1886-1949, Series 2 (1899), 199-211.

Chapter 2: Étienne Brûlé: First Coureur de Bois

BOOKS

Campbell, Thomas Joseph, *Pioneer Laymen of North America*, Volume 1. New York: America Press, 1915.

Hayes, John F., *Wilderness Mission: The Story of Sainte-Marie-Among-the-Hurons*. Toronto: Ryerson Press, 1969.

Horwood, Harold and Edward Butts, *Pirates and Outlaws of Canada, 1610-1932*. Toronto: Doubleday Canada, 1984.

Jurgens, Olga, "Étienne Brûlé," in *Dictionary of Canadian Biography*, Volume I. Toronto: University of Toronto Press, 1966.

Morrison, R. Bruce and Wilson, C. Roderick, *Native Peoples: The Canadian Experience*, 2nd edition. Toronto: McClelland & Stewart, 1995.

Wade, Mason, *The French Canadians, 1760-1967*, Volume I (1760-1911). Toronto: Macmillan, 1968.

Chapter 3: Madeleine Jarret: Heroine of Verchères

BOOKS

Doughty, Arthur G., *A Daughter of New France: Being a Story of the Life and Times of Magdelaine de Verchères, 1665-1692*. Ottawa: Mortimer Press, 1916.

Raymond, Ethel T., *Madeleine de Verchères*. Toronto: Ryerson Press, 1928.

Trigger, Bruce G., *The Indians and the Heroic Age of New France*, revised edition. Ottawa: Canadian Historical Association, 1989.

Wade, Mason, *The French Canadians, 1760-1967*, Volume I (1760-1911). Toronto: Macmillan, 1968.

WEB SITE

www.canadahistory.com/sections/documents/bravery_of_madeleine_de_verche res.htm, accessed October 15, 2003/December 13, 2005.

Chapter 4: John Tanner: Ojibwa Odyssey

BOOKS

Hilger, Sister M. Inez, *Chippewa Childlife and Its Cultural Background.* Washington, DC: United States Government Printing for Smithsonian Institution, 1951.

James, Edwin (ed.), *A Narrative of the Captivity and Adventures of John Tanner (U.S. Interpreter at the Saut de Ste. Marie): During Thirty Years Residence Among the Indians in the Interior of North America.* Minneapolis, MN: Ross and Haines, 1956.

Leechman, Douglas, *Native Tribes of Canada.* Toronto: W.J. Gage, 1956.

Morrison, R. Bruce and C. Roderick Wilson (eds.), *Native Peoples: The Canadian Experience*, 2nd edition Toronto: McClelland & Stewart, 1995.

Owen, Roger C., James J.F. Deetz and Anthony D. Fisher (eds.), *The North American Indians: A Sourcebook.* New York: Macmillan, 1968.

Symington, Fraser, *The Canadian Indian: The Illustrated History of the Great Tribes of Canada.* Toronto: McClelland & Stewart, 1969.

Warren, William W., *History of the Ojibway Nation.* Minneapolis, MN: Ross & Haines, 1957.

Chapter 5: Billy Green: Hero of Stoney Creek

BOOKS

Ballantyne, Lereine, *The Scout Who Led an Army.* Toronto: Macmillan of Canada, 1963.

Berton, Pierre, *Flames Across the Border, 1813-1814.* Toronto: McClelland & Stewart, 1981.

Hitsman, J. Mackay, *The Incredible War of 1812: A Military History.* Toronto: University of Toronto Press, 1965.

MacKirdy, K.A., J.S. Moir and Y.F. Zoltvany, *Changing Perspectives in Canadian History: Selected Problems.* Toronto: J.M. Dent and Sons (Canada), 1971.

ARTICLES

Fisher, John, "Billy Green," Toronto Reference Library, Baldwin Room, John Fisher Research File MU 4179.

Powell, R. Janet, "Annals of the Forty," Number 5, 1954, a series published by the Grimsby Historical Society. Toronto Reference Library, Baldwin Room, has several.

Slater, S.D., *The Diary of S.D. Slater*. Hamilton, ON: Wentworth Historical Society, Volume V, 1908, in the Hamilton Public Library, Special Collection Department, Archives File: Slater, S.D.

Thompson, Mabel, "Billy Green, the Scout," in *Ontario History*, Volume XLIV, October 1952.

INTERVIEW WITH AUTHOR

Green, Barbara (great-great-granddaughter of Billy Green), May 1989.

WEB SITE

Battlefield House Museum, www.battlefieldhouse.ca, accessed June 5, 2004.

Chapter 6: Osborne Anderson: Survivor of Harper's Ferry

BOOKS

Alexander, Ken and Avis Glaze, *Towards Freedom: The African-Canadian Experience*. Toronto: Umbrella Press, 1996.

Anderson, Osborne P., *A Voice From Harper's Ferry, 1859*. New York: World View Forum, 2000. See also Jean Libby (ed.), *John Brown Mysteries*. Missoula, MO: Pictorial Histories Publishing Company, 1999.

Beardon, Jim and Linda Jean Butler, *Shadd: The Life and Times of Mary Shadd Cary*. Toronto: NC Press, 1977.

Hill, Daniel G., *The Freedom-Seekers: Blacks in Early Canada*, 2nd edition. Toronto: Stoddart, 1992.

Libby, Jean (ed.) *John Brown Mysteries*. Missoula, MT: Pictorial Histories Publishing Company, 1999.

Meyler, Peter and David Meyler, *A Stolen Life: Searching for Richard Pierpoint*. Toronto: Natural Heritage Books, 199.

Oates, Stephen B., *To Purge This Land with Blood: A Biography of John Brown*, 2nd edition. Amherst, MA: University of Massachusetts Press, 1984.

Sadlier, Rosemary, *Mary Ann Shadd: Publisher, Editor, Teacher, Lawyer, Suffragette*. Toronto: Umbrella Press, 1995.

Still, William, *The Underground Railroad*. Chicago: Johnson Publishing Company, 1970 (originally published by Porter and Coates, Philadelphia, 1872).

Ullman, Victor, *Look to the North Star: A Life of William King*. Boston: Beacon Press, 1969. Canadian edition: Toronto: Umbrella Press, 1994.

Ward, Geoffrey, with Ken Burns and Ric Burns, *The Civil War: An Illustrated History*. New York: Knopf, 1990.

DISSERTATION

Farrell, John, *The History of the Negro Community in Chatham Ontario, 1787-1865*. Ottawa: University of Ottawa Press, Ottawa, 1955 (PhD Thesis, University of Ottawa, 1955).

Chapter 7: Anna Swan: Nova Scotia's Giantess

BOOKS

Blakeley, Phyllis R., *Nova Scotia's Two Remarkable Giants*. Windsor, NS: Lancelot Press, 1970.

Barnum, P.T. and Waldo R. Browne, *Barnum's Own Story*. New York: Dover Publications, 1961.

Stephenson, William, *Dawn of the Nation, 1860-1870*. Toronto: Natural Science of Canada, 1977.

Wallace, Irving, *The Fabulous Showman: The Life and Times of P.T. Barnum*. New York: Knopf, 1959.

WEB SITE

www.picturehistory.com/find/p/14977/mcms.html, accessed November 21, 2003.

Chapter 8: Fred Bagley: Youngest Mountie

BOOKS

Cruise, David and Alison Griffiths, *The Great Adventure: How the Mounties Conquered the West*. Toronto: Penguin, 1997.

Longstreth, T. Morris, *The Scarlet Force: The Making of the Mounted Police*. Toronto: Macmillan of Canada, 1974.

Tanner, Ogden, *The Canadians*. Alexandria, VA: Time-Life Books, Inc., 1977.

DIARY

Frederick Augustus Bagley Diary (1873-1884), Glenbow Archives, Calgary, Alberta, M-44.

MANUSCRIPT

Bagley, Frederick Augustus, "The '74 Mounties: The Great March Across the Plains," unpublished manuscript, 1938. Glenbow Archives, Calgary, Alberta, M-43.

WEB SITE

Glenbow Museum: www.glenbow.org, accessed May 14, 2004.

TELEVISION SERIES

Starowicz, Mark (Producer), *Canada: A People's History*, Volume 10: "The Taking of the West," CBC/Radio-Canada, 2001.

Chapter 9: George Green: A Home Child in Ontario

BOOKS

Bagnell, Kenneth, *The Little Immigrants: The Orphans Who Came to Canada*. Toronto: Macmillan of Canada, 1980.

Corbett, Gail H., *Barnardo Children in Canada*. Peterborough: Woodland Publishing, 1981.

Glazebrook, G.P. de T., *Life in Ontario: A Social History*. Toronto: University of Toronto Press, 1971.

Harrison, Phyllis (ed.), *The Home Children: Their Personal Stories*. Winnipeg, MB: Watson & Dwyer, 1979.

Kohli, Marjorie, *The Golden Bridge: Young Immigrants to Canada, 1833-1939*. Toronto: Natural Heritage Books, 2003.

Parr, Joy, *Labouring Children: British Immigrant Apprentices to Canada, 1869-1924*. Montreal: McGill-Queen's University Press, 1980.

Rose, June, *For the Sake of the Children: Inside Dr. Barnardo's 120 Years of Caring for Children*. London: Hodder and Stoughton, 1987.

Splane, Richard B., *Social Welfare in Ontario, 1791-1893: A Study of Public Welfare Administration*. Toronto: University of Toronto Press, 1965.

Wagner, Gillian, *Barnardo*. London, UK: Eyre and Spottiswoode, 1980.

ARTICLES

McIvor, Marilyn. "Growing Up in Mid-Nineteenth Century Rural Ontario," 1976, Library and Archives Canada, MicF.TC-26174.

NEWSPAPERS

The Globe, Editorial, November 1895.

Owen Sound Times, November 14, 1895; November 21, 1895; November 28, 1895; December 19, 1895.

Toronto Evening Star, November 1895.

Toronto News, November 1895.

DISSERTATION

Parr, Gwyneth, "The Home Children." (Unpublished PhD Thesis, Yale University, 1977.)

Chapter 10: Alan McLeod: First World War Air Ace

BOOKS

Bishop, Arthur, *Courage in the Air*, Volume 1. Toronto: McGraw-Hill Ryerson, 1992.

Cosgrove, Edmund, *Canada's Fighting Pilots*. Toronto: Clarke, Irwin, 1966.

Craig, John, *The Years of Agony, 1910-1920*. Toronto: Natural Science of Canada, 1977.

Harris, John Norman, *Knights of the Air: Canada's Aces of World War I*. Toronto: Macmillan, 1958.

Milberry, Larry, *Aviation in Canada*. Toronto: McGraw-Hill Ryerson, 1979.

Morton, Desmond, *Years of Conflict, 1911-1921*. Toronto: Grolier Ltd., 1983.

Shores, Christopher, Norman Franks and Russell Guest, *Above the Trenches: A Complete Record of the Fighter Aces and Units of the British Empire Air Forces 1915-1920*. London, UK: Grub Street, 1996.

Sweetenham, John, *Canada and the First World War*. Toronto: Ryerson Press, 1969.

TELEVISION SERIES

Starowicz, Mark (Producer), *Canada: A People's History*, Volume 12: "Ordeal by Fire, 1915 to 1929," CBC/Radio-Canada, 2001.

Chapter 11: Armand Bombardier: Inventor of the Snowmobile

BOOKS

Bothwell, Robert and J.L. Granatstein, *Our Century: The Canadian Journey in the Twentieth Century*. Toronto: McArthur and Company, 2000.

Brown, Craig (ed.). *The Illustrated History of Canada*. Toronto: Lester Publishing, 1991.

Cook, Ramsey, *Canada and the French-Canadian Question*. Toronto: Macmillan of Canada, 1966.

Lacasse, Roger, *Joseph-Armand Bombardier: An Inventor's Dream Come True*. Montreal: Libre Expression, 1988.

Precious, Carole, *J. Armand Bombardier*. Markham, ON: Fitzhenry and Whiteside, 1984.

Wade, Mason, *The French Canadians, 1760-1967*, Volume II: 1911-1967. Toronto: Macmillan, 1968.

WEB SITES

Canadian Science and Engineering Hall of Fame: http://www.sciencetech.techno-muses.ca/english/about/hallfame/u_i15_e.cfm, accessed April 22, 2002.

http://collections.ic.gc.ca/heirloom_series/volume4/224-227.htm, accessed March 19, 2002.

Chapter 12: Toy Jin "Jean" Wong: Spirit of the Dragon

BOOKS

Berton, Pierre, *The Last Spike: The Great Railway 1881-1885.* Toronto: McClelland & Stewart, 1971.

Burney, Shehla, *Coming to Gum San: The Story of Chinese Canadians.* Toronto: Published by D.C. Heath Canada for the Multicultural History Society of Ontario, 1995.

Chan, Arlene, *Spirit of the Dragon: The Story of Jean Lumb, a Proud Chinese Canadian.* Toronto: Umbrella Press, 1997.

Guo, Jin, *Voices of Chinese Canadian Women.* Toronto: Women's Press, 1993.

Hoe, Ban Seng, *Beyond the Golden Mountain: Chinese Cultural Traditions in Canada.* Hull, QC: Canadian Museum of Civilization, 1989.

Huang, Evelyn, with Lawrence Jeffery, *Chinese Canadians: Voices From a Community.* Vancouver: Douglas & McIntyre, 1992.

Li, Peter S., *The Chinese in Canada.* Toronto: Oxford University Press, 1988.

Tracey, Lindalee, *A Scattering of Seeds: The Creation of Canada.* Toronto: McArthur & Company, 1999.

Wai-man, Lee, *Portraits of a Challenge: An Illustrated History of the Chinese Canadians.* Toronto: Council of Chinese Canadians in Ontario, 1984.

Wickberg, Edgar (ed.), *From China to Canada: A History of the Chinese Communities in Canada,* 2nd printing. Toronto: McClelland & Stewart, 1988.

Yee, Paul, *Struggle and Hope: The Story of Chinese Canadians.* Toronto: Umbrella Press, 1996.

VIDEO PRODUCTIONS

Gavreau, Gil (Director), *Spirit of the Dragon.* Toronto: Convergence Productions Ltd., 2002.

Nipp, Dora (Director), *Under the Willow Tree.* Montreal: Produced by Margaret Wong for the National Film Board of Canada, 1997.

NEWSPAPERS

The Colonist (Victoria, BC), May 3, 1884; September 13, 1907.

The Port Moody Gazette, April 12, 1884.

INTERVIEW WITH AUTHOR

Arlene Chan, November 2005.

Chapter 13: The Baby Derby: Escaping the Great Depression

BOOKS

Berton, Pierre, *The Dionne Years: A Thirties Melodrama.* Toronto: McClelland & Stewart, 1977.

Broadfoot, Barry, *Ten Lost Years, 1929-1939: Memories of Canadians Who Survived the Depression*. Toronto: Doubleday Canada, 1973.

Gray, James H., *The Winter Years*. Toronto: Macmillan of Canada, 1990.

Guillet, Edwin C., *The Toronto Maternity Sweepstakes: An Account of the Trials and Other Proceedings Resulting From the Will of Charles Vance Millar* (Famous Canadian Trials, Volume 13). Toronto: typewritten, 1944.

Orkin, Mark, *The Great Stork Derby*. Don Mills: General Publishing, 1981.

NEWSPAPERS

Toronto Daily Star, January 13, 1933; October 5, 1934; August 24, 1936; April 8, 1937.

Chapter 14: Erwin Schild: Accidental Immigrant

BOOKS

Abella, Irving and Harold Troper, *None is Too Many: Canada and the Jews of Europe, 1933-1948*. Toronto: Lester & Orpen Dennys, 1982.

Brune, Nick, *Defining Canada: History, Identity and Culture*. Toronto: McGraw-Hill Ryerson, 2003.

Koch, Eric, *Deemed Suspect: A Wartime Blunder*. Halifax, NS: Goodread Biographies, 1985.

Neatby, H. Blair, *William Lyon Mackenzie King: A Political Biography, Volume III: 1932-1939: The Prism of Unity*. Toronto: University of Toronto Press, 1976.

ARTICLES

Draper, Paula, "The Accidental Immigrants" (in two parts), in *Canadian Jewish Historical Society Journal*, Spring 1978, Volume II, Number 1, and Fall 1978, Volume II, Number 2.

Schild, Erwin, "A Canadian Footnote to the Holocaust," in *Canadian Jewish Historical Society Journal*, Spring 1980 (Volume IV, Number 1).

_____, "My Exodus from Germany: Reminiscences on a 50th Anniversary" (Erwin Schild's sermon given at the Adath Israel Synagogue, Toronto, January 17, 1989).

_____, "My Father's 100th Birthday" (sermon at Adath Israel Synagogue, Toronto, May 11, 1985).

INTERVIEW WITH THE AUTHOR

Rabbi Erwin Schild, February 1989.

NEWSPAPERS

Globe and Mail, November 15, 1937; November 21, 1938; November 22, 1938; November 4, 1940.

Chapter 15: Steven Truscott: A Struggle for Justice

BOOKS

Lebourdais, Isobel, *The Trial of Steven Truscott*. Toronto: McClelland & Stewart, 1966.

Ross, Alexander, *The Booming Fifties, 1950-1960*. Toronto: Natural Science of Canada, 1977.

Sher, Julian, *Until You Are Dead: Steven Truscott's Long Ride Into History*. Toronto: Knopf Canada, 2001.

Trent, Bill, with Steven Truscott, *Who Killed Lynne Harper?* Toronto: Optimum Publishing Company, 1979.

NEWSPAPERS

Toronto Telegram, June 12, 1959; June 16, 1959; September 30, 1959; October 1, 1959.

Chapter 16: Marilyn Bell: Swimming for the Glory of Canada

BOOKS

Leveridge, A.W. "Bill," *Fair Sport: The History of Sport at the Canadian National Exhibition, 1879-1977 Inclusive*. Toronto: Canadian National Exhibition and M.S. Printers, 1978.

McAllister, Ron, *Swim to Glory: The Story of Marilyn Bell and the Lakeshore Swimming Club*. Toronto: McClelland & Stewart, 1954.

Ross, Alexander, *The Booming Fifties, 1950-1960* (Chapter 3: "The Discovery of the Teenager"). Toronto: Natural Science of Canada, 1977.

Withrow, John (editorial advisor), *Once Upon A Century: 100 Year History of the Ex.* Toronto: J.H. Robinson Publishing, 1978.

NEWSPAPERS

Toronto Daily Star, September 8, 1954; September 9, 1954.

Chapter 17: Wayne Gretzky: The Great One

BOOKS

Dryden, Ken, *The Game: A Thoughtful and Provocative Look at a Life in Hockey*. Toronto: Macmillan of Canada, 1983.

Ferguson, Ted, *Superkid, Wayne Gretzky, 99*. Loughborough, UK: Ladybird Books, 1983.

Gretzky, Walter and Jim Taylor, *Gretzky: From the Back Yard Rink to the Stanley Cup.* Toronto: McClelland & Stewart, 1984.

Gretzky, Wayne, with Rick Reilly. *Gretzky: An Autobiography.* Toronto: HarperCollins, 1990.

Morrison, Scott (ed.), *Wayne Gretzky: The Great Goodbye.* Toronto: Key Porter Books, 1999.

Podnieks, Andrew, *The Great One: The Life and Times of Wayne Gretzky.* Toronto: Doubleday Canada, 1999.

Staff of Beckett Publications, *Wayne Gretzky* (*Beckett Great Sports Heroes* Series). New York: House of Collectibles, 1996.

NEWSPAPERS

Toronto Telegram, October 28, 1971

VIDEO PRODUCTION

Wayne Gretzky: Above and Beyond, Ross Sports Production Inc., Live Home Video. 1990 (copyright: Wayne D. Gretzky).

Chapter 18: Terry Fox: A Marathon of Hope

BOOKS

Coupland, Douglas, *Terry.* Vancouver: Douglas & McIntyre, 2005.

Scrivener, Leslie, *Terry Fox: His Story.* Toronto: McClelland & Stewart, 2000 (revised edition).

VIDEO PRODUCTIONS

Lansing, Floyd (director), *Twenty-five Years of Hope: The Legacy of Terry Fox.* Vancouver: Out to Seas Production for CBC Television, 2005, broadcast on CBC Television, September 16, 2005.

McBrearty, Don (director), *Terry Fox Story.* Toronto: Shaftesbury Film with CTV Television Inc. Production, 2005, broadcast on CTV Television, September 11, 2005.

WEB SITES

www.terryfoxrun.org, accessed September 20, 2005.

NEWSPAPERS

Toronto Star, September 14, 2005, A7; September 16, 2005, A7; September 18, 2005, A9.

INDEX